D0147060

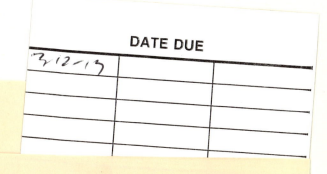

DATE DUE

3-12-19		

MISSION FOR HAMMARSKJOLD

Rajeshwar Dayal

MISSION FOR HAMMARSKJOLD

THE CONGO CRISIS

PRINCETON UNIVERSITY PRESS
PRINCETON, NEW JERSEY

Printed photolitho in Great Britain by
Ebenezer Baylis and Son Ltd
The Trinity Press, Worcester, and London

To my wife
Susheela

My guide, and mine own familiar friend,
We took sweet counsel together; and walked
in the house of God as friends.

after Psalm 55: 13–14

CONTENTS

ILLUSTRATIONS

Acknowledgement

The photographs are all reproduced by the kind permission of the United Nations Organization, except for the portrait of Lumumba which appears by permission of Magnum Photos (Marc Riboud).

ACKNOWLEDGEMENTS

The incitement to write this book I owe principally to the late Ralph Bunche, a dear friend and colleague. Himself a towering pillar of the United Nations, he strongly felt that in the interest of historical accuracy, the story of the United Nations in the Congo should be told by one of its participants. Hence this book which I offer as a tribute to the ideals of the Organization which I have tried to serve in various capacities for almost twenty-five years.

My profound thanks are due to the late U Thant, who, as Secretary-General of the United Nations, permitted me to have access to my official correspondence with his predecessor on matters concerning the Congo. I have relied heavily on this source material in presenting the facts as objectively as possible.

By a strange but appropriate quirk of fortune, the book was written at two great institutions, both named after the statesman who conceived the idea of international peace as a collective responsibility. To the Woodrow Wilson School of Public and International Affairs at Princeton I owe a debt of gratitude for providing me with the facilities for my research and writing. The book was completed at the Woodrow Wilson International Center for Scholars at Washington, D.C., an institution set up as a living memorial to him whose name it carries. The stimulating atmosphere of scholarship and ideas which pervades the Center is ideal for creative work, and I am deeply thankful to Benjamin Read that I had the opportunity to benefit from it. The book could not have been written without access to the material available in the great libraries of Princeton University and of the Congress at Washington, and at the United Nations.

My sincere appreciation is due to all those who have spared their time to help me in my work in a variety of ways. I am most thankful, in particular, to Brian Urquhart and William Cox of the United Nations for discussing with me many aspects of the Congo story and to Robert Payne, Raja Rao, and Arthur Gregor for their very helpful suggestions and encouragement.

My research assistants, Rala Stone at Princeton, and Eric Hoaglund and Hermann Knippenberg at Washington, worked indefatigably in helping me to gather and organize my material. The task of typing fell to Deirdre Randall, Helen Clayton, and Badri Narain Das, all of whom showed great patience and diligence and deserve my sincere thanks.

ABBREVIATIONS

Abako:	Alliance des Ba-Kongo
A.N.C.:	Armée Nationale Congolaise
CRISP:	Centre de Recherche et d'Information Socio-Politiques (Brussels)
Forminière:	Société Forestière et Minière du Congo
GAOR:	*General Assembly Official Records*
M.N.C.:	Mouvement National Congolais
ONUC:	Organisation des Nations Unies au Congo
Otraco:	Organisation des Transports du Congo
SCOR:	*Security Council Official Records*

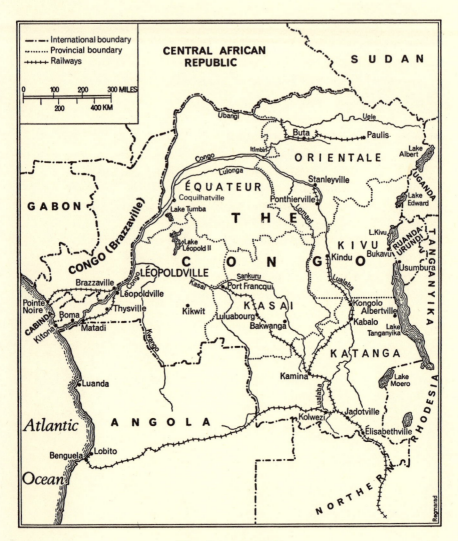

The Congo in 1960

CHAPTER 1

The Opening Chapter

The crisis in the Congo burst upon an unsuspecting world soon after that country's accession to independence on 30 June 1960. Little news of affairs in Belgium's giant colony had been allowed to percolate to the outside world, and whatever came through was rather reassuring. It was generally thought that Belgian rule was beneficent and the Congolese people happy and contented. It was also believed, as Belgian official statements and propagandists tirelessly made out, that Belgium was following an enlightened policy of balanced development, of raising the standards of living and education, of leading the country in an orderly way towards self-government. It was known that the Congo had a very large number of schools and hospitals, modern towns, and highly organized industries. The Congo was a rich country with ample natural resources and immense scope for development. It was, therefore, assumed that all its inhabitants shared in the general prosperity and were content to allow the process of evolution to a higher political status to take its course. Little had been heard of any active or organized opposition to the colonial régime. When the Brussels Round Table Conference took place in January 1960, at which the Congolese received a promise of independence within six months, there was mild surprise at the pace of change, accompanied by admiration for Belgium's benevolence and foresight.

It was only after the coming of independence that the full facts of Belgium's colonial rule came to light, and of the circumstances which had made the precipitate transfer of power inevitable. The Belgians themselves had been deluded by their propaganda into believing that everything was right with the colony. Belgium had failed to see that a policy of gradualism and horizontal development could not sublimate the urge to freedom among the Congolese people, and particularly at a time when the process of decolonization in Africa, as in Asia, was already far advanced. This miscalculation on the part of a nation known for its commercial shrewdness and business acumen was largely responsible for the catastrophic turn of events in the Congo after Independence. For if normal political activity had been allowed, responsible political leaders encouraged, and training imparted in the arts of politics and governance, progress towards independence would have been more orderly and peaceful. Denied any significant role, especially at the upper levels of policy-making and execution, till the eleventh hour, and condemned to a second-class status in their own country, the Congolese harboured resentments which later took extreme and often militant forms against the colonial authority. Even enlightened Belgian opinion had envisaged that progress towards independence would take decades to complete; the actual process had to be telescoped into a matter of months. No wonder, therefore, that the new state, unready and unprepared, began its life amidst so much turmoil and tumult.

When power was hurriedly transferred into Congolese hands, the new Central Government, like that of any other newly independent country, wished to be master in its own house and not to submit to a status of tutelage or subordination to the former metropolitan power. But the Congolese politicians, who were hastily catapulted into positions of leadership, lacked the experience essential for their great responsibilities. They also lacked a trained civil service capable of filling the administrative vacuum, particularly at the higher levels.

The final repository of state power was the army. But the army was riddled with discontent over its emoluments and the fact that it was almost entirely officered by Belgians. When the mutiny broke out within four days of Independence, leading to the wholesale departure of Belgian officials and functionaries, the administration came to the verge of collapse. The Belgian Government, under pressure from its public opinion, intervened militarily for the protection of its citizens. Powerless either to evict the Belgian troops or to provide order and security, the Congolese Government appealed to the United

Nations for help. The world community promptly responded to the call of the infant state and launched a massive operation to bring about the early withdrawal of the Belgian forces and assist the Government in the maintenance of law and order. Combined with these functions, the United Nations undertook an extensive programme to provide the technical services required to keep the country from total collapse and disintegration. In view of the size of the country, the complexity and magnitude of the problems facing it, and the sharp political differences that arose at the United Nations regarding the interpretation and execution of the mandate, the task became the most difficult and complicated peace-keeping enterprise ever undertaken by that organization.

Over fifteen years have elapsed since the United Nations effort in the Congo (now Zaïre) was launched, and many of the principal personalities involved are no more. Hammarskjold, Kasavubu, Lumumba, Tshombe have all gone, and frank appraisals about them and their ideas and actions are now possible. By a curious twist of history the Congo Operation which was so vociferously criticized at the time from different angles and often for contradictory reasons, has now come to be regarded as the United Nations' most successful peace-keeping enterprise.

After four years of effort the United Nations was able to leave the Congo in a much better state than when it first entered. The country was on the road to unification, the widespread outbreak of civil war was averted, the economy was rescued from total collapse, a modicum of peace and order was established, the more blatant forms of foreign intervention were excluded, and the Congolese people were given some training in their new responsibilities.

To some extent the treatment of my subject will be autobiographical, as I was head of the Operation from 8 September 1960 to 27 May 1961—for almost two-thirds of the time that Hammarskjold was responsible as Secretary-General for the work of the United Nations Mission in the Congo. Thus it was that Hammarskjold's and my fortunes became interlinked and our respective roles became complementary. The beginning of the Operation and the end were particularly crucial, although all along its agitated course it demanded sustained effort. I arrived at Léopoldville at a time when the fall of Lumumba took place, followed shortly after by the military *coup* of Colonel Mobutu, with which I had to deal during the full length of my stay. That period was in many ways decisive, for the events that took place then, the decisions taken and the interpretations made both in New York and in Léopold-ville, the attitude of the member states of the United Nations, and international public reactions to the developments, condi-tioned the course of the Operation throughout its troubled life.

When Independence came to the Congo, there was dancing in the streets and celebrations in the provinces. The Belgian flag was hauled down and the pale blue Congolese flag with a yellow star hoisted in its place. The common people waited expectantly for the imagined benefits of Independence. It did not take long for them to realize that their lives had changed very little. The peasants in their fields and the tribesmen in the bush continued as before with their daily toil. The factory or plantation workers, who had expected higher wages, re-mained under the same Belgian masters. The petty officials, denied a rise in status and wages, returned to their accustomed desks. The higher civil servants, who had been clamouring for the more senior jobs reserved for Belgians, found their posi-tions unchanged. Everyone had expected some tangible gains from the long-awaited Independence: a little more money, better living conditions, greater opportunities. But there was a vast gap between promise and fulfilment. Nothing seemed to have changed; the visible tokens of Belgian supremacy were omnipresent. Belgians remained entrenched in government offices, in the army, and in the economic structure of the country.

The only Congolese to benefit were the politicians. At the centre and in the provinces, those whom the Belgians had taught the common people to despise as parasites and trouble-makers moved into the mansions of the colonial rulers and drove about in chauffeured limousines. They were courted by foreign embassies and foreign businessmen. With their new status came a new affluence. The ministers had given them-selves generous salaries and other benefits, their political parties had ample funds, and the more unscrupulous among them were supplementing their resources by other means. Few among them knew how to handle their responsibilities, which they left largely to their Belgian advisers and officials. They were too busy with their political intrigues and with helping themselves to the best houses and automobiles to have time to attend even their offices. They had voted themselves a fivefold increase in their own salaries, raising them to half a million francs a year.

All this was resented by the Congolese people, but even more by the army. The Force Publique was in a surly mood. It had been used by the Belgians during their rule to put down disaffection with a heavy hand, and the politicians, especially Kasavubu and Lumumba, feared that it would be employed by Belgium to stifle the movement for independence. Contacts had been established between the politicians and the under-officers on a wide scale, often on an ethnic basis, and also with the more articulate among the rank and file. The Congolese politicians therefore tried to render the army ineffective to serve what they imagined to be a Belgian purpose, by riddling it with discontent. Two years of propaganda among the troops directed largely against their Belgian officers had begun to have effect. The Belgian officers, for their part, had always derided the Congolese politicians, and they had conveyed their contempt to the troops under their command. On the one hand, the Congolese soldiers had lost their confidence in their Belgian officers, largely as a result of propaganda by the politicians, and on the other, they had had instilled in them contempt and dislike for the politicians.

Trouble started at Camp Léopold on 4 July 1960. Some soldiers were noticed inciting the troops and committing acts of indiscipline. There was grumbling all round, and the Belgian Commandant conveyed his apprehensions to General Janssens, the Belgian Commander-in-Chief, who proceeded to the camp and punished the guilty. The General made a speech rejecting the demands of the soldiers, especially regarding Africanization. He insisted that everything must continue as before and, to emphasize the point, he wrote an equation on the blackboard: 'Before Independence = After Independence'. This was all that was required to trigger off the violence that followed.

The soldiers mutinied and attacked their Belgian officers. The Belgian Embassy advised the departure of European women and children, but appealed to the men to remain at their posts. A number of Congolese ministers valiantly rallied to the protection of the Belgians and tried to reason with the mutinous soldiery. Parliament remained in session and decided to rename the Force Publique the Armée Nationale Congolaise, and to transfer the posts of command to Congolese. Joseph Mobutu, who for six years had been a clerk in the army before he turned to journalism, and had been a junior Minister since Independence, was chosen Chief of Staff.

Meanwhile, in Belgium, public opinion was getting very agitated and the Government's position began hardening as a result. Belgian para-commando reservists were recalled to the colours and the entire fleet of aircraft of the Belgian Sabena airline was commandeered for the transportation of refugees. The Congolese troops offered little resistance to the Belgian troops, generally fleeing in panic before them and disappearing into the bush, although in some places there were brief but bloody encounters. The Belgians fanned out into the countryside, rescuing stranded families and occasionally exacting reprisals. Some 10,000 Belgian troops were involved in the operation at its peak. The interventionist troops suffered very few casualties in action; the Congolese an unknown number.

From the political point of view, the results of Belgian intervention were calamitous. There was a clear violation of the Treaty of Friendship between Belgium and the Congo, according to which Belgian troops could be called in to assist the Congolese Government, but only at its request. Belgium did not even try to invoke the terms of the Treaty to justify her action; it was claimed that under international law a state had the right to intervene in another country for the protection of its nationals. This was a novel and dangerous doctrine based on nineteenth-century concepts of Africa and Asia. Whatever chances remained of Belgo-Congolese cooperation were by now completely shattered. A request to the United Nations by the President of the Congolese Republic, Joseph Kasavubu, and the Prime Minister, Patrice Lumumba, for international military aid was made 'to protect the national territory against the present external [Belgian] aggression which is a threat to

international peace'. The Secretary-General, Dag Hammarskjold, called an urgent meeting of the Security Council to consider the Congolese request. Acting with remarkable speed, the
Council authorized the Secretary-General to provide the military assistance asked for by the young state.

The Security Council adopted a carefully worded resolution
that called upon Belgium to withdraw her troops and directed
the Secretary-General to take the necessary steps, in consultation with the Congolese Government, to provide it with such
military and technical assistance as might be necessary until
the national security forces were able to meet their tasks. It
was a brief and skeletal expression of the Council's consensus
which left the interpretation and implementation largely to
the Secretary-General.[1]

Dr. Ralph Bunche was designated Special Representative
of the Secretary-General[2] and Commander of the U.N. Force
in the Congo. The task was a stupendous one as he had to
organize the whole Operation from practically nothing. He
had to make a rapid assessment of the requirements of international troops and technical assistance, to undertake negotiations with the Belgian military commanders, and to secure
the cooperation and understanding of the Congolese leaders.
Within a couple of days following the adoption of the Security
Council's resolution, the first units of the U.N. Force began to
arrive in Léopoldville. A makeshift international secretariat

[1] Resolution S/4387, adopted by the Security Council on 14 July 1960.
[2] The office of Special Representative had been one of Hammarskjold's characteristic inventions. Peace-keeping missions were initially headed by government
representatives answerable to the Security Council. But in the Congo, since the
Security Council had entrusted the task to the Secretary-General, his representative was answerable to him alone. The Secretary-General's choice of a representative could fall on any of the known and tried senior members of his Secretariat
or on an outsider enjoying his confidence. For politically sensitive missions, particularly those of long duration, Hammarskjold cast his net beyond his immediate
official circle. There was undoubtedly an element of risk in this, since the Secretary-
General would be publicly accountable for the actions of somebody outside
his official family. Balanced against this, however, was the consideration that an
outsider could be more easily replaced than a permanent international official.
But this element was largely hypothetical because of Hammarskjold's deep understanding and sense of personal loyalty.
It was, at best, a difficult and exacting relationship, which in the context of
the Congo required an unusual degree of trust and mutual adjustment. The
system worked because of Hammarskjold's skill in delegating authority and
encouraging initiative. To preserve the autonomous nature of a field operation,
Hammarskjold generally refrained from issuing categorical orders or directives,
preferring a system of joint consultation. Thus a feeling of shared responsibility
was created, essential in a mission so full of imponderables.

was quickly organized and the provisioning and deployment of troops arranged.

Living and working conditions in Léopoldville were wildly chaotic and the heavy burden of responsibility which the Special Representative had to carry was a test of human endurance. But it was even more difficult to retain the confidence and support of the Congolese Government. The Prime Minister, Patrice Lumumba, was initially accommodating, but when Bunche's views of the competence and mandate of the United Nations Force differed from his own, Lumumba refused to have any further dealings with him. Bunche then felt—six weeks after the Operation was launched—that his utility in the Congo had been exhausted. He had, in any case, not come prepared for a long stay, and was anxious to return to New York where he had certain obligations to meet. He therefore asked the Secretary-General to relieve him and hoped that he could leave the Congo by the end of August.

Hammarskjold was thus faced with the urgent problem of finding a successor. It was obvious that the involvement of the United Nations in the Congo would be a protracted affair. The U.N. mission, far from being a purely humanitarian, technical-assistance effort, had become politically complex. Its responsibilities were ostensibly of an advisory and supporting nature, but, in view of the prevailing anarchy, they in fact extended to the heart of the functions of governance.

An international operation requires individuals imbued with an international spirit to carry it out. The Secretary-General's ideas on the attributes of an international civil servant, always precise and demanding, were later spelt out in his famous Oxford address.[1] Hammarskjold insisted that in the final analysis it 'is a question of integrity, and if integrity in the sense of respect for law and respect for truth were to drive him [the international civil servant] into conflict with this or that interest, then that conflict is a sign of his neutrality—then it is in line, not in conflict, with his duties as an international civil servant'. As Hammarskjold put it in a characteristic phrase, an international civil servant should be politically celibate, but not virginal. He should serve in an international spirit,

---

[1] 'The International Civil Servant in Law and in Fact'; lecture by Dag Hammarskjold at Oxford University, 13 May 1961.

with objectivity and dedication, holding himself answerable not only to his superiors and to his oath of office, but in the final resort to the ultimate judge, his own conscience.

When Hammarskjold returned to his Headquarters on 9 August after his first visit to the Congo carrying Bunche's request with him, he discussed the question of a successor with his closest advisers. The result was the following message which he sent to the Prime Minister of India:

9 August 1960

Dear Mr. Nehru,

I am certain that you have followed the phases of the Congo crisis which has engaged us in the first full scale effort of the United Nations to save a country and forestall a war which it might have been very difficult to contain. You therefore will appreciate the strain under which it has put the Secretariat and all our resources, and that we have had to press our possibilities to the utmost limit. So far, this has worked, but, of course, it cannot go on, as the Secretariat is not equipped with such reserves as would permit a drain of the present scope.

If, as I hope, this venture succeeds, we soon reach a stage of consolidation when the key personalities from the Secretariat can, to some extent, take up their regular work again and new men step in, shouldering the immediate responsibility for the Congo operation. We have made some beginnings, one of which is the recruitment of Brigadier-General Rikhye. We are very happy to have him on our senior staff. He has already made an outstanding contribution under difficult conditions. I thank you most warmly for your understanding and kind assistance; I know that the sending of Rikhye from his previous assignment in Assam was a real sacrifice, showing the generosity of your approach and your interest in the success of what we are trying to do.

I have in this context one overriding problem, and that is who should be the head of the whole operation in the Congo. As you know, Dr. Ralph Bunche has had that function until now and he should continue a little while, but he must come back soon to Headquarters where he has to give his time to other matters and where he must take up not only what I delegate of the Congo problem but also the most essential parts of his regular work. I thus must seek a substitute for him, combining great diplomatic tact, real understanding of the problems of a people like the Congolese, the highest intelligence and the highest integrity. You will certainly in no way be surprised—you may even have guessed whom I have in mind. Running over the area of possibilities—and it is much smaller than one would believe, even with the fairly good knowledge we now have of the personalities who may be considered—there is one name that stands out, and that is Rajeshwar Dayal.

Once before, you have kindly permitted us to use him in another crucial assignment, where he performed his exacting duties with all the skill of which he is capable. I have hesitated to come back to you requesting him to be made free once again, but he is so obviously the right choice that I feel I have to do it. I would not say that, for the present, it would be necessary to make an arrangement for more than half a year, as we do not know much about how this whole venture will develop in the long run under the pressure of rather chaotic circumstances. But as a matter of course, I would be happier the longer we could keep him, if the Congo problem remains with us as I personally think it will.

I know that it is not easy for you to take him away from his present important assignment, but in the wide terms of international coopera-tion and collective security his assignment in Léopoldville would be such as to justify the sacrifice.

Of course, I have not approached him before contacting you, but I do hope that he will be able to help me. He should, preferably, come to Léopoldville before Dr. Bunche leaves, that is, if possible, already in August. I hope therefore that you will be able to give this appeal your early attention so that, if you would not find it possible to agree to my proposal, I would have some time to explore such other possibilities as there may be.

Thanking you in advance for your kind attention to my problem, I remain, Mr. Prime Minister, with warm and respectful regards,

Most sincerely,
Dag Hammarskjold

On 12 August I received a telegram from New Delhi when I was on an official visit to Dacca, capital of the then eastern province of Pakistan, where I was serving as India's High Commissioner. Nehru had designated me to that post two years earlier, but when I had come home on leave in June 1958 from my former post as India's Ambassador to Yugoslavia, I had also then had an urgent summons from Hammarskjold to serve, in his phrase, as one of the three 'experienced and im-partial personalities' on the U.N. Observation Group in the Lebanon. That assignment, which Hammarskjold thought would be of six weeks' duration, actually lasted six months. But it was perhaps the neatest and most successful United Nations enterprise in the field of peace-keeping.

One of Nehru's firm foreign policy principles was to extend ungrudging support to the United Nations in peace-keeping whenever his help was sought. He saw in the Congo Operation an opportunity to demonstrate, in a very practical way, India's concern for the welfare and stability of a young African country. Having fought against colonialism all his life, a struggle which did not cease with India's Independence, he wished to help a sister state which was threatened with disintegration at birth. Besides, romantic as in some ways he was, Nehru was struck by the idea of an Indian—a product of the Foreign Service that he had created—being chosen to head the biggest and most challenging enterprise to be undertaken by the world Organization.

I realized that it was futile to argue with Nehru about Hammarskjold's letter and reconciled myself to what so clearly appeared to be inevitable. Nehru assured me that my post in Pakistan would be kept vacant during my absence. He then sat down to write a telegram to Hammarskjold which he showed me. I had only one comment to make. I asked him to add that my services 'would be available for six months or so', remembering my experience in the Lebanon. Nehru smiled, adding, 'I see what you mean: you don't want to spend the rest of your life in the Congo!'

While I was busy with preparations for departure, I tried to acquaint myself with the United Nations activities in the Congo. But the U.N. documents and reports hardly provided an inkling of the complexities of the situation, or of the nature of my responsibilities. That I was to get, and in ample measure, on reaching New York on the last day of August.

Certain impressions of those hectic days in New York stand out vividly in my mind. I was both surprised and impressed by the amount of time the Secretary-General was devoting to the Congo problem in the midst of his other heavy duties. Hammarskjold carried about him an aura of supreme confidence, the immensity of his responsibilities seeming only to exhilarate him. He told me that the task of the United Nations in the Congo was unique in the experience of the Organization both in regard to its character and magnitude. A new course in international cooperation was being charted that would expand the frontiers of the Organization's responsibilities and functions and greatly stimulate its future growth. He was particularly elated at the fact that, for the first time, every specialized agency of the United Nations was participating in an Operation under the leadership of the parent body.

Hammarskjold had developed a highly personal style of dealing with his vast responsibilities. He had gathered around him on the thirty-eighth floor of the United Nations Building a close group of confidants with whom a sort of informal conference was constantly in progress. There would be daily meetings at luncheon in the Secretary-General's suite, with the host generously providing the elegant meal. At these meetings the incoming telegrams from Léopoldville would be discussed, the proceedings and debates in the Council and Assembly reviewed, the information gathered by the participants from delegates or visitors shared. And there would be a running commentary, interspersed with much wit and wisdom, by Hammarskjold himself. Everyone would be encouraged to speak and unburden himself of his ideas. The conversation would sometimes turn to poetry and literature, sometimes to art, and sometimes even to gossip. Nothing and nobody was sacrosanct. But while the luncheon progressed, and beneath the banter and *bonhomie*, there was always a deep undercurrent of consciousness of the grave responsibilities that devolved on those present. At the end of each such meeting, all would disperse to attend to their respective functions somewhat lighter of heart and clearer of mind, with faith renewed, but nevertheless with a certain sense of anxiety and of deep commitment.

Late every evening, when the debating halls were silent and the last of the delegates had folded his papers and departed, after the lights had gone out in the vast glass edifice, Hammarskjold's suite would come to renewed life. Battered after an exhausting day's work, tired but unruffled, the faithful would reassemble, this time around a conference table. There would again be a review of the day's trials and activities, more telegrams would have come in from the Congo posing new and yet more unexpected problems. Decisions would be taken and replies drafted, some dictated by Hammarskjold himself, others by his colleagues, and all would once again be discussed and sometimes revised before dispatch. By eight or nine o'clock in the evening, those with families would excuse themselves, but others would remain with the chief to share with him a well-earned dinner. On occasions of special crisis, the full team would remain and continue its discussions till well after midnight.

I was privileged to have been a member of this famed 'Congo Club', as it came to be called, and during my visits from Léopoldville and my protracted stay in New York before I concluded my assignment, I participated in these diurnal and nocturnal gatherings.

The Secretary-General had set up a Congo Advisory Committee comprising the Permanent Representatives to the United Nations of states that had contributed troops to the Congo. Its membership increased as more states lent their forces, the composition being largely African and Asian, although Canada and Ireland were also members.

Hammarskjold was very appreciative of the political and military support being given to the United Nations in the Congo by the countries of Africa and Asia and he hoped that with their deep commitment to the Operation, they would provide a focus for the reconciliation of divergent attitudes on the part of other international groups of powers. At any rate, he felt that neither of the major power groups would openly oppose a line of policy on which the African and Asian powers were agreed. The Secretary-General's interpretations of the mandate had not been questioned by any member and the situation in the Security Council was, at that time, generally favourable.

With the arrival of Ralph Bunche from the Congo on 2 September and from my subsequent talks with him, I got a still more direct insight into the nature of the problems and atmosphere prevailing in that country. My first shock was Ralph Bunche's physical appearance: he was obviously very tired and he looked much older. He spoke of the great strain under which the Operation was being conducted, and the complex nature of its functions.

Bunche did not find the Congolese in general at all easy to deal with. They were full of fears and mistrust and had little idea about the United Nations or the functions and competences of the Operation. Bunche had a good deal to say about Major-General Alexander, an Englishman, who was Commander-in-Chief of the Ghanaian army. This rather swashbuckling soldier thought that he had answers to the problems of the Congolese army and the maintenance of order and he had taken a strong but mistaken position on the question of disarming the Congolese troops. Bunche also cautioned me about the attitude and activities of some of the foreign missions. It was clear from Bunche's talk, and even more from what I sensed of his mind, that he had no illusions about the extreme difficulty of my future task and the highly uncertain prospect ahead of us.

CHAPTER 2

The Mission

In the broad panorama of history, the Congo passed in the short span of seventy-five years—from 1885 to 1960—from the status of a feudal fiefdom of Léopold II to that of a colony of Belgium and then to complete sovereignty. The entire range of national experience had thus been crowded into three quarters of a century. It seems almost incredible that those whom the Belgians regarded as savages, fit only to labour for the enrichment of their proprietors, were able to wrest, in so short a time, freedom from their Belgian masters, and to assert their rights and dignity as free human beings. But the process was not orderly or coherent. Decisions were taken under the pressure of time and circumstance. The very instrument of governance that Belgium had laid down—the Loi Fondamentale—was replete with inconsistencies and lacunae which gave rise to a disastrous constitutional crisis barely two months after Independence. Nothing had been done to alter the administrative structure or to train Congolese in the arts of governance.

The actual and potential wealth of the country was stupendous. The resources of the Congo had from the end of the last century been harnessed by King Léopold and developed by a small group of Belgian business concerns. In their keeping, the Congo had become one of the wealthiest countries on the African continent, second only to South Africa. Zaïre now produces 75 per cent of the world's supply of cobalt, 70 per cent of its industrial diamonds, more than half of its uranium, 9 per cent of its tin, and 7 per cent of its copper. In 1960— before Independence—the total export of metal was valued at around £100 million. In addition, Zaïre has vast resources of timber, palm-oil, cotton, coffee, and rubber, and immense reserves of hydro-electric power.

Nevertheless, in this country of nearly a million square miles with a population of 14 million, there was, at the time of Independence, not one Congolese judge or magistrate, not one doctor, not one engineer, and only one lawyer.

Hammarskjold had a very human understanding of the desperate plight of the Congolese people whom he was sincerely anxious to help. But he could not understand the attitude of extreme suspicion, almost of hostility, displayed by some of the politicians, notably Lumumba and some of his followers, towards the United Nations. The principal bone of contention between them was the question of Katanga. When the United Nations entered the Congo, Katanga's secession had been proclaimed only three days earlier.

That southernmost province of the country had, in 1960, accounted for 75 per cent of the Congo's mining production, estimated at 11·8 billion Belgian francs.[1] Its contribution to the total resources of the Congo amounted to about 50 per cent of the budget. Seventy-five per cent of the Congo's total foreign exchange earnings were contributed by Katanga. The production of copper approximated 300,000 tons, valued at over eight billion Belgian francs. Cobalt, silver, zinc, platinum, radium, uranium, germanium, and palladium were among the other minerals produced by Katanga. So rich indeed was Katanga in its mineral resources that it was called 'a geological scandal'. The loss of Katanga in economic terms would have resulted in the virtual bankruptcy of the Congo.

The Security Council had not accepted the legality or the finality of the secession; its decisions required the United Nations mission to deal with Katanga as a provincial government, equally subject to its mandate as the rest of the Congo. The entry of U.N. troops into the other provinces was achieved without difficulty. But in Katanga Moïse Tshombe, the President of Katanga province, had declared that since Katanga's 'Independence' antedated the resolution of the Security Council it did not apply to his 'sovereign state', and he would oppose the entry of U.N. troops with all the force at his command. The Central Government of the Congo, for its part, regarded the early liquidation of the secession as one of the primary

[1] Then 50 francs to one U.S. dollar.

responsibilities of the United Nations, to be achieved, if necessary, by the use of force.

Hammarskjold considered that the problem could be solved by a judicious blend of political pressure with a show of force. Since Katanga's pretensions were dependent on Belgian political, financial, and military support, denial of such assistance would effectively undermine secession. But Belgium claimed that her presence and activities in Katanga were legitimate as they had been requested by the Katanga authorities. The Western powers held that Katanga was entitled to determine its own political destiny and its incorporation into the Congo would only spread the area of disorder. In any case they opposed the use of force to end secession.

The Soviet Union and her allies pressed for firm measures against Katanga including the use of force. The African and Asian states urged the speedy end of secession by all available means, but they did not at first insist on force. The Congolese leaders, however, were convinced that political means were inadequate and insisted on the immediate application of military sanctions. The attitude to the Katanga issue, and the means to end it, therefore became the touchstone by which the loyalty of member states to the aims of the United Nations Operation in the Congo came to be judged. Tshombe had, meanwhile, fearing U.N. armed intervention in Katanga, written to Hammarskjold expressing his surprise at the request of the Léopoldville Government for the withdrawal of Belgian troops and the introduction of a United Nations force. Tshombe said that Katanga did not need or want international troops, as peace and order reigned there thanks to the action of Belgian troops invited by his government. He expressed his government's wish to maintain friendly relations with all states and to continue the work undertaken by Belgium. He drew attention to the Charter of the United Nations, which assured to all peoples the right to decide their own destiny.[1] The Belgian Government also issued a statement to the effect that the government of Katanga had proclaimed its independence, that order prevailed, and that economic life was flourishing.

Towards the third week of July, international troops had arrived in sufficient strength to permit their deployment in

[1] CRISP, *Congo 1960*, p. 724.

the five provincial capitals and other centres, and the United Nations turned its attention to the difficult problem of sending them into Katanga. Its objective was to establish a United Nations presence in Katanga, not to end the secession by force. The Central Government had insisted on a U.N. Force being sent into Katanga without delay, hoping that it would be used to overthrow Tshombe's régime. Lumumba had undertaken a long tour which took him to New York, Washington, Ottawa, London, and several African capitals; he had seen Hammarskjold at New York and had urged immediate action against Katanga.

Hammarskjold's approach was that Kasavubu should first contact Tshombe with a view to effecting the entry of U.N. troops into Katanga on the basis of mutual agreement. Hammarskjold had concluded that the problem of Katanga was deeply intertwined with domestic politics and since the Central Government was anxious to retain the initiative in its hands, he felt that United Nations moves in the military and diplomatic fields should be related to the efforts of the Central Government itself. He convened a meeting of the Security Council to seek a clear directive regarding the measures to be taken to overcome Katanga's opposition to the entry of U.N. troops. He was given the formal authority he sought from the Council, which 'called upon Belgium in categorical terms immediately to withdraw its troops from Katanga under speedy modalities determined by the Secretary-General' and further 'to assist in every possible way the implementation of the Council's resolutions'. The resolution also declared 'that the entry of the United Nations Force into the province of Katanga is necessary for the full implementation of the resolution'. To force the issue Hammarskjold flew into Élisabethville on 12 August 1960 with four plane-loads of Swedish U.N. troops. From the airport Tshombe radioed that permission to land would be given only for the Secretary-General's plane. But when Hammarskjold threatened to turn back, all five planes were permitted to land. On the tarmac, Tshombe and his Ministers, wreathed in smiles, received the Secretary-General. Belgium now had no option but to agree to the withdrawal of her troops from Katanga, and Tshombe shrewdly realized that the situation could be turned to his advantage. For he could now dispense with Belgian troops, being assured that law and order would be maintained by a U.N. force. But above all, he felt that with the U.N. Force holding the ring, the forces that he was rapidly assembling would be able to repel any attack which the Central Government might attempt to launch.

Tshombe and his advisers hoped to reduce the United Nations mission in Katanga to complete impotence by raising the cry of interference in Katanga's internal affairs if it tried to apply pressures against it. They were determined not only to preserve intact the economy and administrative structure, but to strengthen Katanga's capacity for resistance and to make it an impregnable bastion with the help of a 'foreign legion' and Belgian technicians.

Hammarskjold, for his part, was satisfied with the results. He told his U.N. colleagues that the operation had been successful all through and the risks taken had been justified. He stated categorically that he had made no concessions nor accepted any conditions and that he did not fear any complications from either the Katangan or Belgian side. He felt that the problem was centred on hate and fear of Lumumba among the Katangan politicians and Belgians. Lumumba, on the other hand, challenged the Secretary-General's interpretation of the 'neutral' role of the U.N. Force in Katanga as enunciated in his addendum to his second report to the Security Council. He insisted that the United Nations Force should be placed at the disposal of his Government 'to subdue the rebel government' and asked for United Nations transport for its civilian and military representatives to proceed to Katanga. He protested that the Secretary-General did not consult his Government and that, on the contrary, he had dealt with a rebel government, to whom he had given certain assurances. He charged that the Secretary-General was behaving as though the Central Government did not exist and was 'making himself a party to the conflict and using the U.N. Force to influence its outcome'. Hammarskjold coldly declined to discuss the 'allegations and objections' to his interpretation of the role of the U.N. Force, adding that he would refer the matter to the Security Council.

The first round in the labyrinthine contest with Tshombe was over, and the United Nations had won on points. But the succeeding stages were even more tortuous and difficult, for while Tshombe was aided morally and materially by Belgium and her Western allies, thus compensating for his intrinsic weakness, the United Nations was denied the political support of those on whom it had counted. Hammarskjold undoubtedly acted prudently in preparing the ground by means of negotiations for the peaceful entry of United Nations troops. The alternative would have been to risk a confrontation if the Force had tried to shoot its way in the teeth of opposition, and the Western powers would have bitterly opposed such a move. The United Nations Force had come as a peace force and it could hardly have changed its character at that stage into a fighting force without first attempting to achieve its aims by pacific means.

But the limited success of the United Nations turned to failure when Lumumba questioned the propriety of the operation and was joined in his attack by the Soviet Union and a number of African states. Criticism of Hammarskjold's methods in tackling the Katanga issue, which was initially confined to differences of method, now extended to his motivations. Furthermore, the break between Lumumba and Hammarskjold put in jeopardy the whole ONUC (Organisation des Nations Unies au Congo) Operation, for without the minimum cooperation of the Central Government, the mission could not function effectively.

Arbitrary arrests of U.N. personnel in Léopoldville now became a daily occurrence. Two U.N. security guards who had taken a letter from Bunche to Lumumba—the latter having broken off personal contact with Bunche—narrowly escaped execution. For the first time, Congolese troops tried to challenge the authority of the U.N. Force when, under Lumumba's orders, they were sent to take over control of Ndjili airport near Léopoldville, but a clash was narrowly avoided by timely negotiations between senior military officers on both sides. There was an unfortunate case of violence against Canadian airmen in the service of the United Nations who were rescued with difficulty from their Congolese assailants. These events and the growing hostility between the Lumumba Government and ONUC were the result of a failure of communication and understanding between the Secretary-General and Lumumba which was brought to a head over the Katanga question. This had its echoes at United Nations Headquarters where there developed an increasing polarization between delegations on the basis of their respective attitudes towards the Lumumba–Hammarskjold–Tshombe triangle.

On grounds of principle and of approach to the problem of Katanga, no common line between Hammarskjold and Lumumba was possible. Lumumba was bent on the use of force, with the help of the United Nations if possible, without it if necessary. Hammarskjold was equally determined to avoid the use of force and to make every endeavour to deal with the problem by diplomatic and political means. Hammarskjold's Katanga strategy might have succeeded if he had received the support of the Western powers, especially of the United States. But the United States believed that to support the United Nations plan to undo the Katanga secession would strengthen the Central Government, which in turn would enhance Lumumba's standing. The American Ambassador in Léopoldville (Clare Timberlake), then on a visit to Washington, had convinced the Administration of Lumumba's Communist proclivities. Denied the political backing of the Western powers in pursuing his Katanga policy to a conclusion, Hammarskjold became increasingly vulnerable to the attacks of his opponents at the United Nations.

Lumumba made a desperate attempt to mobilize African support for military action against Katanga by convening a Conference of African Foreign Ministers in Léopoldville at the end of August 1960. But the chaos prevailing in Léopoldville and Lumumba's impetuous temperament filled his guests with serious misgivings about the whole project. In the end they recommended action through the United Nations, politely declining requests for bilateral aid. When in the face of this rebuff Lumumba launched his unruly army against Kasai and Katanga, the enterprise ended in a hopeless fiasco, the troops falling on the unfortunate Baluba tribe in Kasai, who were mercilessly butchered, the objective of Katanga's overthrow being drowned in tribal warfare.

The problem of Katanga was to remain a running sore for two and a half years. Until the cancer was healed or excised, the task of the United Nations could not be completed. The poison it spread paralysed the country and seriously affected the health of the United Nations mission, compelling it in the end to resort to violent measures to eradicate it.

The immediate task of ONUC, as it appeared to me on my appointment as Hammarskjold's Special Representative in the Congo, was to ensure the earliest possible withdrawal of the Belgian troops that had intervened (a process that had been unconscionably delayed), to assist the Congolese Government in the maintenance of order and security, and to build up the technical and administrative services which had broken down with the departure of Belgian officials and experts. It was therefore a mixed peace-keeping and technical-assistance programme, with, till then, no sharp or controversial political overtones. Though functioning erratically, the Congolese Government was still in existence, the U.N. presence in the country had been established, and the Operation had in some measure the support, or at least the acquiescence, of the great powers and other members of the Security Council. But there was a conflict of opinion regarding the handling of the problem of Katanga's secession, which some regarded as an internal political matter to be settled by political means by the Congolese themselves, others as a product of foreign—essentially Belgian—intervention, which called for more energetic action by the U.N. Force.

I had thought that I would assume responsibility directly from Bunche, but was told in New York that there would be an interregnum of a few days. I was somewhat surprised to learn, however, that Andrew Cordier, Executive Assistant to the Secretary-General, had been sent to Léopoldville to fill the gap. Cordier was well known for his role in the Secretariat but he had not been responsible directly for the conduct of any U.N. field operation.

On my arrival in the Congo I found that the Headquarters of the U.N. Mission were in a glass and concrete apartment building called 'Le Royal', a miniature of the glass house on Turtle Bay. There the sixth floor was occupied by the top echelon, the lower floors in succession by the military command, the civilian affairs organization, and so on down to the basement which contained the stores, stationery, and other paraphernalia which supplied provender to the floors above. My executive assistant was an experienced and dependable senior permanent official, John McDiarmid. The legal adviser was another senior official, William Cox, whose fine legal mind and serenity, as well as his capacity to simplify the most intricate problems, were a great asset to the mission. Cox was succeeded by Vladimir Fabry, a man of great legal insight, who later met his death in the plane crash with Hammarskjold. My political adviser was Brian Urquhart, the *alter ego* of Ralph Bunche, a skilled draftsman with a penetrating intellect, enormous courage, and delightful wit. His colleague, F. T. Liu, endowed with uncanny dexterity and subtlety, was the soul of discretion.

The military organization of the mission had at its head the Supreme Commander of the U.N. Force, Major-General Carl von Horn of Sweden. Von Horn had suddenly been diverted to the Congo from Jerusalem, where he was head of the U.N. Truce Supervision Organization which had well-defined functions and an elaborate set-up. But the Congo, where much had to be improvised, and where the situation was often unfathomable, was a little too much for the General, whose ways were set and ideas orthodox. He was constantly engaged in a petty vendetta with Ralph Bunche. Knowing his sensitivity, I was especially careful not to ruffle his dignity and we managed to get on well enough together. Von Horn was succeeded in January 1961 by Major-General Sean McKeown, Chief of Staff of the Irish Army. McKeown was in every way very different from his predecessor. Conscientious to a degree, he was never ruffled and he quickly adjusted himself, without fuss or demur, to the ways of the Organization. The Deputy Supreme Commander, Major-General Kettani of Morocco, had distinguished himself with the French army in World War II and in other fields. He had the air of a *grand seigneur* and he lived like a pasha. But he had a keen political eye and was a martinet for discipline. Brigadier Rikhye, the Secretary-General's military adviser, who had been sent to assist in liaison work, and for whose courage and capacity to get things done Hammarskjold had much admiration ('digestive qualities', as he called them), was also included in my military team.

The civilian affairs operation was headed by Sture Linner, a Swede whom Hammarskjold had met while Linner was working for a mining company in Liberia, and had chosen to look after the United Nations technical-assistance programme in the Congo. After the crisis he was appointed to supervise the now vastly expanded programme, a vital part of ONUC's functions. He was assisted by a team of a dozen senior consultants, experts in fields such as administration, finance, education, public health, industry and commerce, agriculture, and civil aviation. Robert Gardiner, a distinguished Ghanaian civil servant, had the unenviable task of recreating the administrative structure, a responsibility that he discharged with remarkable tact and patience. The financial consultant was an eminent Swiss banker, Victor Umbricht, who had the stupendous task of sorting out what remained of the Congo's finances and imposing some semblance of financial discipline on the Congolese authorities. There were teams from UNESCO, WHO, and FAO, whose aims were to establish and maintain practical policies in education, health, and food distribution.

In each of the six provinces there were U.N. political representatives, supported by technical-assistance advisers and a small staff. They maintained close links with the commander of the U.N. troops in the area to ensure the fullest coordination of policy and action.

At my morning conferences in 'Le Royal' which came to be known as 'prayer meetings' there would be first a situation report given in detail by the generals and their staff officers with the aid of a large map. Then the telegrams that had flowed in from New York and the provinces through the night would be taken up and discussed, and draft replies prepared or instructions issued. As new situations and crises were constantly arising, there would be a discussion as to how each should be tackled, followed late in the evening by a general round-up of the crowded day's events.

The Public Relations Officer kept the committee informed of the reactions in the world to the debates in New York and to the activities of the Operation in the field. This was perhaps the most depressing part of the morning, as it was difficult to believe there could be such misunderstanding and criticism of a mission on which so much disinterested toil and sweat were being expended.

In contrast to the rather sombre morning meetings, the evening session would be gay with an almost desperate abandon. The experiences of each trying day would be recounted, impressions and news exchanged, all enlivened by a sense of humour sharpened by an ever-present sense of crisis. I would then dictate a report to the Secretary-General, a sort of round-up of the day's events, in which the atmosphere of the scene and the subjective reactions of the participants would be conveyed. Hammarskjold, for his part, also sent me daily telegrams containing his feelings and observations at the end of each long day. These spontaneous exchanges were rather lively and personal and, by way of emotional release, witty, as the situation in the Security Council or the Congo worsened. They are a valuable chronicle of events during those momentous days and provide considerable insight into the inner workings of the mind of their authors. I have drawn heavily on these exchanges as they provide the most authentic record of the policies being pursued and a running commentary on events.

My first task on arrival at ONUC Headquarters in Léopold-ville was to set my own house in order. I allocated a room to each official, set up a conference room with the usual paraphernalia of maps, charts, and blackboard, drew up a roster of duties and fixed working hours. True, events in the Congo did not await the movements of the clock. But there seemed little reason for the entire senior staff—on whom the brunt of the burden lay—to be up and about all twenty-four hours, often doing nothing but snatching a little sleep on a sofa. I appointed duty officers who would alternate during the night, and issued instructions that the senior officers be called up at any time to attend to most immediate telegrams or crisis situations. I tried to organize a commissariat, which later developed into a flourishing PX. And I insisted on officials and staff taking some relaxation and exercise. There were swimming-pools available and good facilities for tennis and golf and even for riding. I set the example myself by going riding or swimming whenever I had the time and, when hard pressed, by taking a vigorous walk along the bank of the River Congo.

It was obvious that the Operation would be prolonged; it was already taking a heavy toll on the health and morale of the staff, and there were several cases of nervous breakdowns. I encouraged the staff to take leave out of the Congo, and we arranged facilities at a beach in the more placid atmosphere of Congo (Brazzaville) and sometimes even in Angola, if not beyond, in Europe. For the greater part of my stay I was housed in the guest-house of the Union Minière set in a large garden with the Congo River at the back. This was a tiled affair, somewhat Victorian in style and rather frugally furnished and equipped. I wondered if the directors of that great company did indeed have such a parsimonious outlook on life. While the bedrooms were air-conditioned, the large living-room was not. The house, despite its inadequacies, was a sharp transition from the austerities of 'Le Royal', and I still remember it with gratitude though not with nostalgia. Neither I nor my wife, who was to arrive later, really liked the atmosphere of the place. For one thing the proximity of the Congo River was not reassuring. Some rivers are friendly, others are not, and the Congo, with its thundering cataracts and its sheer immensity, was awe-inspiring. The swish and swirl of the muddy waters could be heard all the time, accentuated at nightfall by the roar of the cataracts below. Great tangled masses of water hyacinth littered its oily surface. After nightfall the bats would emerge thick and fast from the tiled roof and eaves of the house, performing aerial acrobatics in the rooms. The evening before Hammarskjold arrived from New York to stay with us, my wife and I spent an energetic hour with bamboo and duster trying to clear at least one room of the bats' unwelcome presence. But there was nothing we could do to prevent their night-long scratching on the plank ceiling, to silence their shrieks and squeals, or to rid the place of their omnipresent odour. Other nocturnal visitors, equally unwanted, were streams of buff-coloured beetles which flew in from the riverside and which showed extraordinary tenacity in exploiting every fault and tear in the wire-meshed doors to make their entry. These insects, we learned with disgust, were a form of cockroach.

The river provided other sources of unasked-for excitement besides. One morning there was a great commotion among the Congolese servants and gardeners in front of the house near a leafy tree where my car was generally parked. A python had crawled up the river-bank and was vainly trying to make itself invisible in the shrubs surrounding the tree, and an altercation was going on as to the respective shares of its twenty feet of length among its clamouring claimants. The generous offer to me of the lion's share was gratefully declined.

To offset the abnormal conditions in the country, we ourselves tried and encouraged our colleagues to lead as nearly normal a life as possible. We frequently entertained at lunch, cocktails, or dinner and attended numerous parties given by the various units comprising ONUC. Ghanaians, Canadians, Indians, Pakistanis, Moroccans, Tunisians, Malayans, Indonesians, and many other nationalities were there together or in succession, and we made it a point to attend their national day and other functions. We often invited Congolese personalities to our house, some of whom responded, generally without their wives, excusing the latter on the ground of household duties or sometimes frankly admitting that they were not yet used to 'social life'. But as the political difficulties in the country intensified, Congolese participation at social gatherings correspondingly diminished. This was indeed a pity, since the formality of an official meeting is not always the best way towards mutual comprehension..Nor did the Congolese leaders —with certain exceptions—offer any entertainment themselves. Some of them said with disarming candour that they were not well enough organized or equipped to invite foreigners to their homes.

We were always acutely conscious of the grave developments at New York, where Hammarskjold, who enjoyed great personal devotion among the personnel of ONUC and was regarded as the very symbol of the United Nations, was battling for his political life. There was among all of us immense faith in what the Operation was trying to accomplish and little doubt that what we were doing was right.

CHAPTER 3

The First Three Days

The moment I had set foot on Congolese soil on 5 September 1960, I felt an oppressive sense of tension, as before a tropical storm. At 'Le Royal' there was a restless stir of movement and ONUC officials appeared anxious and preoccupied. There were elaborate security precautions around the building.

I asked Cordier about the excitement and gathered from his remarks—for he was a man of few words—that President Kasavubu had decided to dismiss the Prime Minister, Lumumba.[1] The President had had enough of his Prime Minister and was exercising his prerogative as Head of State to make a change of government. An announcement was expected in a few hours and ONUC had to be geared to meet the shock. Cordier's main anxiety was to ensure that the change took place peacefully, without street fighting or other disorders. He was particularly concerned about the danger of armed interference by Congolese troops loyal to Lumumba. If units from Stanleyville—Lumumba's political stronghold—were to be flown in, there would be the certainty of a clash. But Cordier was in a mood of confidence combined with watchfulness. He had alerted the U.N. Force, which, he felt, could hold the ring. At all events, he said, the United Nations was responsible for maintaining law and order, and it would take appropriate measures, depending on the situation, to fulfil its duty.

What I learnt from Cordier was something totally unexpected, of which there had been not the faintest indication in my talks with Hammarskjold and Bunche. Information about the sudden turn of events had not reached New York before my departure, for it would have immediately been passed on to me. If it had, I would certainly have deferred my departure

[1] For an account of Lumumba's career, see Chapter 17.

to allow an interval for realigning my sights. I found myself thrust into the middle of a situation from which it was impossible either to retract or to advance. ONUC, I feared, would now have to adjust itself to events rather than help in shaping them.

In the course of that eventful day and subsequently, I pieced together in greater detail precisely what had happened. On 3 September Cordier had called on the President at his request, when Kasavubu unburdened himself of his catalogue of complaints against his Prime Minister. Kasavubu spoke of Lumumba's erratic behaviour and his propensity to take decisions without reference to the Head of State or Cabinet. Lumumba, he charged, had Communist advisers who were misleading him and he had created a reign of terror against his opponents. Kasavubu feared that unless Lumumba were stopped in his tracks, he would become a dictator. Lumumba had brought ruin to the Congo and was now embarked on a fratricidal war in Kasai with the aid of Soviet planes. He had set himself against the United Nations, and so long as he was in office there could be no fruitful cooperation between his government and the U.N.

Cordier listened silently to the indictment. At the end he offered a brief comment to the effect that the President had no doubt weighed the consequences of whatever action he proposed to take and that before taking it, he would make sure of his ground. There was no discussion and no advice was asked for or given. Kasavubu was evidently trying to gauge Cordier's reactions; Cordier was measuring Kasavubu's determination. In the end, neither of them got anything definite from the other. But Cordier had heard enough to realize that something was brewing, although he was not sure what precise form it would take. The only tangible result of the interview was an invitation to lunch at the President's house the following day, a Sunday.

The meal was an intimate family affair, but although Cordier kept an attentive ear for further enlightenment on the previous day's conversation, Kasavubu said nothing. Nor did Cordier think it prudent to question the President about his intentions. Host and guest eyed each other warily, waiting for a sign from the other. But no sign came and the Sunday luncheon ended pleasantly enough, undisturbed by any political talk.

On Monday morning, 5 September, a few hours before my arrival, the President sent for Cordier and, repeating his accusations against Lumumba, finally said he had decided to remove him. He would make an announcement from the Léopoldville radio station at 8.15 that evening and asked for U.N. protection at the radio station and at his residence. He also wanted U.N. assistance in arresting Lumumba and twenty-five other persons, including a number of Ministers. Cordier told the President that the United Nations wished to keep out of the whole affair. It would have nothing to do with the arrests as they were not its concern, nor did it have the legal competence to carry them out. But Cordier agreed to the provision of U.N. guards at the radio station and the presidential palace.

Cordier told me he was certain that Kasavubu would make his broadcast that evening, counting heavily on the element of surprise. But he wondered if Kasavubu had worked out his plans and whether he was clear about his further steps, as the ingenuity and agility of his opponent could not be underrated. Cordier had informed the Secretary-General by telex of his talk with Kasavubu. The instructions he received were that ONUC should not intervene in any way in the constitutional crisis and, keeping close to its mandate, limit its role strictly to the maintenance of public order. Cautioning against any action that would appear to favour one particular side against another, Hammarskjold left it to Cordier to exercise his discretion in regard to the measures that ONUC should take. On the constitutional issue, Hammarskjold said he would get the matter examined by his legal experts. But should Kasavubu's venture fail, he warned against a situation where an ineffective constitutional government would be confronted by an effective *de facto* government.

Cordier's view was that President Kasavubu must make his own decision, without any commitment or responsibility on the part of ONUC. The Mission's responsibility was confined to preventing violence from interfering with the consequences of the President's decision, the parties being left to work out the issue between themselves. If ONUC were compelled to take any independent measures for enforcing peace, and if such measures influenced the outcome of the political conflict in favour of a particular party, that would only be incidental to its overriding responsibility for the preservation of order and would by no means deter it from what was its evident duty.

Kasavubu's expectations were different. He had nursed the hope that, as Head of State, he would receive the full backing of the United Nations. The serious differences between Lumumba and the U.N. were common knowledge, and there were rumours that a change of government would be welcomed by the harried U.N. officials. Indeed, the Western embassies had been openly urging Lumumba's overthrow.

ONUC officials had recently been seeing the President on current business during Lumumba's protracted absence on his tour abroad. The Secretary-General had directed them not to deal exclusively with the Prime Minister but to develop contacts with the President and other responsible ministers as well. That was an entirely correct procedure that should have been followed from the outset. But because of the well-known unpredictability of the Prime Minister and the difficulty of getting prompt and sensible decisions from him, the directive was generally construed as implying a lack of confidence in him. Kasavubu had therefore assumed that his initiative for the removal of Lumumba would at the very least have the tacit approval of ONUC. But if he did not receive open support, he still hoped it would be given in sufficient degree to tilt the balance in his favour.

All the senior ONUC officials gathered on the sixth floor of 'Le Royal' were keenly conscious of the gravity of the moment. One of the critical issues was whether the President was exceeding his constitutional authority by removing a prime minister who continued to enjoy a parliamentary majority without giving him an opportunity to test his strength in parliament, as enjoined by the Loi Fondamentale. The legal adviser, William Cox, was of the opinion that while the President had the authority, under Article 22 of the constitution, to appoint and remove prime ministers, that authority could be exercised only if certain mandatory provisions spelt out in the constitution were followed. For example, a prime minister could be removed if parliament, by a vote of censure or by turning down important legislation, had demonstrated its lack of confidence in him. But he would still continue as head of a caretaker government until the new cabinet had presented itself to parliament and been given a vote of confidence. These procedures had not been observed.

But Cordier did not think it was ONUC's responsibility to interpret the Loi Fondamentale, and he seemed to attach greater weight to the powers of removal vested in the president than to the restrictions limiting their exercise. It seemed to me quite extraordinary that a constitutional president, deriving his powers from a parliamentary and not presidential form of constitution, should act in the way that Kasavubu had done. To substitute the broadcasting station for parliament was anything but constitutional procedure. Since the President had informed ONUC of his intentions and asked that it take certain supporting measures, surely it would have been in order for Cordier to have advised Kasavubu to make certain that his actions did not transgress his constitutional powers? The legal government of the Congo had invited the United Nations to its assistance, and the United Nations had every interest in ensuring that whatever government followed would at least be legal, if not viable. It was of course up to Kasavubu to accept or reject the advice that was offered, but the responsibility for subsequent events would then have been entirely his. Kasavubu may well have hesitated to act, or may have deferred his action if doubts about the legality of his proposed move had been sown in his mind. That would at least have given him time to reflect on the constitutional question and served as a warning that the United Nations would not unhesitatingly accept the validity of his actions. ONUC would have had a fuller opportunity to survey the ground and to determine its own stand; valuable time would have been gained, a factor of supreme importance at that moment. But the opportunity was not taken.

Later that evening, Van Bilsen, a Belgian adviser of President Kasavubu, arrived to see Cordier. Van Bilsen was the bearer of a letter from the President that made ten demands of the United Nations. These repeated Kasavubu's previous request for assistance in making a number of political arrests, including that of Lumumba, and the immediate closure of the radio station and airports. Van Bilsen confirmed that the President would be making his announcement at the appointed hour. Cordier again refused to carry out any arrests, but confirmed that U.N. protection would be provided at the presidential palace and radio station. He gave no undertaking regarding the closure of the public facilities asked for, explaining that ONUC would take whatever action it considered necessary in the interest of public order. He added that while ONUC would take note of the President's requests, its decisions would be based on its own mandate from the Security Council.

Kasavubu's broadcast was now due at any moment and great was the excitement and anticipation on the sixth floor of 'Le Royal'. The assembly in the room grouped around the radio was all attention. At 8.15 p.m. Kasavubu's voice came through in a monotonous drone. Addressing his compatriots, he said he had an important announcement to make. Lumumba, 'the First Burgomaster'[1] whom the Belgian King had appointed under the provisional constitution, had betrayed his trust. Lumumba's actions had provoked discord in the Government and among the people. He had governed arbitrarily and had deprived a number of citizens of their basic liberties and was plunging the country into a frightful civil war. Therefore, by virtue of his constitutional powers, Kasavubu continued, he had considered it necessary to dismiss the Government and to appoint Joseph Ileo as Prime Minister, and had charged him to form a new Government.

Soon thereafter Lumumba's voice, sharp and strident, was heard on the radio. Referring to Kasavubu's declaration, Lumumba denied 'on behalf of the Government and the entire nation' that the Government had been revoked. The Government had been elected democratically by the people, whose unanimous confidence it enjoyed, and who alone had the power to remove it. The Government would therefore remain in authority and would continue its mission to defend the people, the unity of the country, and the integrity of its territory.

Lumumba had obviously been caught unawares. His first response had been moderate and reasoned, without a word of vituperation. But he returned to the radio within the hour with a much stronger and accusatory statement.[2] This broadcast showed unmistakably that Lumumba was determined to

[1] In his nervousness Kasavubu fumbled, wrongly describing Lumumba as 'First Burgomaster' instead of 'Prime Minister'.
[2] CRISP, *Congo 1960*, ii, 820–1.

fight back hard with all the force and energy at his command. The anxiety and concern in 'Le Royal' deepened, for if Kasavubu was unable to follow up his announcement by energetic action, the situation would get infinitely worse. There was fear that Lumumba's popular appeal and parliamentary strength would be rallied to turn the tables on Kasavubu. But there was no indication of what, if anything, Kasavubu now proposed to do. Cordier became alarmed that Lumumba's broadcasts would stir up the populace to militant action leading to civil war. What particularly worried him was the possibility of Soviet planes, known to be in Stanleyville, being used to ferry troops to Léopoldville to try conclusions with Kasavubu and his supporters.

Cordier consulted von Horn about the closure of the airports to contain the disorders he felt were bound to ensue if Lumumbist reinforcements were flown in. Much concerned about the effect of any widespread upheavals on U.N. operations and lines of communications, von Horn was categorically in favour of closure. Cordier then took his decision and issued orders to von Horn, who promptly had them relayed to U.N. troops all over the country. Cordier felt there was no time to consult the Secretary-General in view of the supposed imminence of the danger and took full responsibility for the decision. The orders did not apply to U.N. flights, and Cordier announced that the closure was temporary, solely in the interest of preserving peace and security.

Another problem was how the Léopoldville garrison could be prevented from joining the struggle on behalf of one party or another. The matter was debated by Cordier with the leadership of ONUC's military command. Kettani suggested that the Congolese troops would be kept off the streets if they were paid their arrears of salary. They were notoriously divided and unruly and they were now also starving. Cordier first telephoned the U.S. Ambassador, Clare Timberlake, about funds and Timberlake replied reassuringly that there would be no difficulty. Then Cordier sent a cable to U.N. Headquarters asking for the early remittance of one million dollars. It was, however, impossible to obtain the funds immediately, and when they arrived a week or so later, the situation had radically changed.

The Secretary-General's comments on the general situation likely to follow Kasavubu's action arrived late at night. On the constitutional issue, Hammarskjold felt that the United Nations would be compelled to deal with the Head of State as the only clear legal authority. As for the Prime Minister's attempt to dismiss the President, it was unquestionably unconstitutional. Hammarskjold directed ONUC to maintain an attitude of strict non-intervention in the political conflict, reserving to itself the right to take necessary measures for the preservation of peace in conformity with the mandate and United Nations principles.

Cordier issued orders to the U.N. Force permitting the use of arms in legitimate self-defence and to retain positions held by U.N. troops against attack. Unit commanders were authorized to intervene if their men were in jeopardy and take necessary action to preserve law and order. On reviewing the directions, Hammarskjold objected to the use of the word 'intervene' as going beyond the 'self-defence' formula, since it implied taking an initiative in the use of force. He regarded the military strength of the U.N. Force as largely symbolic, as opposed to its moral force which he considered as more effective and appropriate in view of its peace-keeping role.

Meanwhile, Colonel Joseph Mobutu, who was the senior Congolese officer present in Léopoldville, sounded the alarm at the A.N.C. garrison. Assembling the 4,000 troops there, he appealed for calm and discipline. He had been advised by General Kettani to keep the A.N.C. out of the political crisis. Mobutu tried to do what he could. The troops were persuaded to deposit their arms in temporary custody with the United Nations, in the hope that their return would be deferred until the end of the crisis. But Mobutu remained nervous about the mood of his soldiers and, as a matter of domestic precaution, moved his family into General Kettani's safe-keeping.

The U.S. and British Embassies were keeping up an incessant telephonic barrage, enquiring by the hour how the situation was developing. Timberlake was pressing Cordier to get into action by first arresting Lumumba. Cordier firmly refused. Then Timberlake telephoned him 'to fight it out', much to Cordier's annoyance, but without disclosing precisely whom ONUC was expected to fight.

Earlier in the day, the British Ambassador, Ian Scott, had made an urgent call on Brian Urquhart, a senior Political Adviser of ONUC. Urquhart was sitting at his desk dealing with official cables. Scott asked him petulantly what ONUC was doing about the outbreak in the A.N.C. barracks. Surprised, Urquhart asked: 'What outbreak?' Scott demanded if ONUC did not know that the A.N.C. soldiers had planned to break out of their camp at that very hour. Urquhart, admitting ignorance, asked Scott how he knew. Scott said he had his own sources of information. 'What, may I ask, are these?' was Urquhart's reply. Scott whispered in confidence: 'My Military Attaché overheard a conversation between Congolese soldiers as he moved about inconspicuously among them.' 'Oh, I see,' exclaimed Urquhart, as he returned to contemplation of his papers. The Military Attaché referred to was Lieutenant-Colonel the Hon. John Sinclair, six feet three inches in height with flaming ginger hair and moustache, who habitually wore a Scottish kilt. That was the only light interlude in a long and agitated day.

Early next morning, on 6 September, I had a talk with Cordier over a hasty cup of coffee. He asked me when he should return to New York. I said that a very difficult situation faced ONUC and the outlook was cloudy. The next few days would be critical. Cordier had dealt with events and knew the personalities involved and at that stage continuity of leadership was essential. He had made his own assessment of the situation in the light of which he had taken certain decisions. It would not be right to change horses in mid-stream. Whatever lay ahead on the other bank would probably be equally difficult, but it would at least allow me some time to gather my breath. Cordier agreed to stay in command, I felt, with some relief, for he had himself thought it advisable to see matters through.

All day a procession of irate visitors, most of them adherents of the ousted Prime Minister, invaded 'Le Royal' protesting angrily at Kasavubu's decision and demanding U.N. intervention to reverse it. It was fast becoming apparent that Lumumba could not be so easily set aside. It was evident also that Kasavubu lacked the decisiveness and sense of purpose to push his initiative to a swift and workable conclusion. There was no news of Ileo or of what he was thinking or doing.

The Congolese Cabinet had held an extraordinary three-hour

meeting in the course of the night, and at about half-past five on the morning of 6 September, Lumumba announced on the radio the text of the Government's communiqué, followed by his own comments. It discussed Article 22 of the Loi Fonda-mentale under which the President had purported to have acted, along with other related articles, and concluded that the President's action went beyond his prerogative and was therefore null and void. The President's person being invio-lable, it was the Government that was responsible to Parlia-ment, which alone could call it to account for its actions. Any action of the President's had to be countersigned by a minister accountable to Parliament. The President's verbal order was accordingly ineffective. The President was accused of high treason and declared deprived of his functions. The communiqué strongly criticized the points made by Kasavubu in his broad-cast, refuting them one by one, especially his call to the A.N.C. to lay down its arms. It saw in this a danger of foreign military occupation and abandonment of all hope for the liberation of Katanga by the National Army. Referring to Kasavubu's appeal to the United Nations, the communiqué interpreted it as a request to the Organization to intervene in a conflict of a purely internal nature. In conclusion, the communiqué ex-pressed the fervent hope that neither the United Nations nor any country would lend assistance to those who stood in the way of the exercise by the Government of its sovereignty. Thir-teen of the twenty-three Ministers who comprised the Cabinet participated at the meeting.

Other parties also made broadcasts on the morning of 6 Sep-tember strongly criticizing Kasavubu. Meanwhile, the Cabinet had agreed on a number of emergency measures, including a curfew. Orders were issued to the security agencies to impose strict control over the borders and on all communications whether by land, air, or water. But these orders remained inoperative as the Congolese Government lacked the means to block the land routes or the only seaport, while the United Nations was already in control of the principal airports. There were some incidents of lawlessness when opposing groups of Jeunesse Lumumba clashed with the Jeunesse Abako,[1] while rumours of all kinds continued to circulate.

[1] The Lumumbist and the main Bakongo political party's youth organizations.

Cordier became particularly worried about the inflammatory effects of the broadcasts and the possibility of partisans of opposing factions trying to gain control over the radio station. He therefore decided to suspend all broadcasts and issued orders to U.N. troops to take over the radio station. The duty fell to the Ghana contingent then in Léopoldville. The operation was carried out with unexpected success, the Congolese soldiers on guard offering little or no resistance to their expulsion and disarming. It was again announced that the measure was temporary, to avoid the risk of bloodshed and civil strife. But because the radio station was in the city and therefore rather exposed, a U.N. expert had been ordered to render the apparatus ineffective by removing a vital part. Cordier again did not refer his decision to the Secretary-General for prior instructions in view of the rapid march of events.

Various politicians who, unaware of the U.N. ban on broadcasting, hastened to the radio station to air their views, were turned back. They streamed into 'Le Royal', angry and frustrated, to make noisy protests. Attempts were made to pacify them by telling them the ban was in the interests of peace and order and applicable to all, including the United Nations. But unknown to ONUC, Kasavubu was able to circumvent the ban by coming to an arrangement with his kinsman, Abbé Fulbert Youlou, President of Congo (Brazzaville), to broadcast his statements through the much more powerful Brazzaville transmitter across the river, to which the Congolese habitually turned when their own station was silent or inaudible. Soon Kasavubu's unchallenged broadcasts were filling the Congolese air, while his opponents were silenced. After this it became difficult to assert to Lumumba's supporters that the closure of the radio station was, indeed, a neutral act.

The Secretary-General, reacting to the closure of the airports, observed that the step could probably be justified on the ground of a liberal interpretation of the mandate in a state of emergency. But when he heard of the closure of the radio station, he described it as 'a quite extreme move', 'a regrettable fact', which could be defended only on the ground that it had been taken 'to forestall a radio fight for the minds', with the risk of serious disturbances. Hammarskjold continued to urge the importance of finding 'a proper balance between strictly legal and extraordinary emergency latitudes', taking into account the local atmosphere and conditions. With an undertone of warning he made the seemingly flippant remark that 'responsible people on the spot may permit themselves, within the framework of principles which are imperative, what I could not justify doing myself—taking the risk of being disowned'.

Cordier took the position that the emergency steps were necessitated by the situation, complicated by the possible intervention of Stanleyville troops lifted by Soviet planes. Kasavubu remained the supreme constitutional authority and he had chosen 'to follow the U.N. line'. While ONUC's actions were in conformity with its mandate, there should be no objection if 'they contribute to the objectives desired by the constitutional authorities'. Lumumba, as Prime Minister, had also insisted on ONUC's taking action to further the objectives of his Government. ONUC was therefore, Cordier explained, in a position of careful balance and was maintaining its position of non-intervention in the political conflict 'despite appearances to the contrary'.

News soon came that General Lundula's Ilyushin plane from Stanleyville had circled Ndjili airport and had been prevented by the U.N. Force from landing. The President of Léopoldville Province, Cléophas Kamitatu, on tour in his far-flung bailiwick, had also been unable to return by air to his headquarters. Kasavubu followed up his advantage by asking the Public Prosecutor's office to issue a warrant for Lumumba's arrest on the ground that he was inciting the population to violence with a view to overthrowing 'the established authorities and the lawful régime'.

Although there was no immediate disorder in the city or elsewhere, tension was rising steadily. Politicians of different persuasions, fearful of arrest or personal violence and emulating the example of the Head of State, made frantic appeals for United Nations protection, which they were generally afforded. Throughout the day there was a flurry of activity among the agitated politicians while the President, having struck the first blow, sat awaiting the reactions.

Lumumba's response came on 7 September, when sessions of both Houses of Parliament were convened in a highly charged atmosphere. Some 90 of the 137 deputies were present in the

Chamber, many having been unable to come because of the closure of the airports while some may have decided discreetly to absent themselves. News of the debate came through to 'Le Royal' during the five hours of the meeting of the Chamber of Representatives. It was evident from the speeches that deputies of different affiliations were present, although the supporters of Lumumba predominated. Members were generally highly critical of the President's action. But some were also critical of the Prime Minister and of his conduct of public affairs, charging him with making arbitrary arrests and violating the immunity of parliamentarians.[1]

Lumumba made a long and impassioned speech in reply to the accusations made against him. He proceeded to repudiate every one of the criticisms made against him, claiming that opponents to his government had been imprisoned only to safeguard the security of the state. He claimed that his dismissal by Kasavubu had been illegal and suggested that a joint governmental and parliamentary commission should be set up to review the whole situation. It was an eloquent, constructive, and well-reasoned speech.[2] Lumumba had skilfully marshalled his facts and used them with telling effect. It was about the last speech in Parliament that he was to make and of which there is a record. It brings out Lumumba's character and personality and shows the heights to which he was capable of rising, but not always of sustaining.

A motion proposed at the conclusion of the session annulling the revocation of both President and Prime Minister was adopted by a vote of sixty to nineteen, Lumumba himself voting with the majority. It was undoubtedly a triumph for him, and it became clear that so far as Parliament was concerned, he was irresistible. The Senate, which was meeting concurrently, adjourned till the next day after a long discussion on the legal effect of the President's action and whether the Lumumba Government would continue as a caretaker government until the Ileo Government was invested.

When the Senate reconvened on 8 September, the Foreign Minister, Justin Bomboko, and Albert Delvaux, signatories of the Presidential Ordinance dismissing the Prime Minister, made a

[1] CRISP, *Congo 1960*, ii. 828.
[2] For the full text of this speech, see CRISP, *Congo 1960*, ii. 829–48.

number of accusations of arbitrary and illegal actions against
Lumumba to which he replied in a bitter and vituperative
speech. Of the eighty-four members of the Senate, between
fifty and sixty were present, many Senators being grounded
by the blockade, while others belonging to Tshombe's and
Kalonji's parties preferred to stay away. The Senate voted
by a majority of forty-two votes to two, with six abstentions,
in favour of the Government and against the President's dismissal of the Prime Minister. The Chamber also met and
decided to set up a Commission of seven members drawn from
different parties to attempt a reconciliation between Kasavubu
and Lumumba.

Prime Minister Lumumba had sent repeated word to Cordier
through emissaries asking him to a meeting at his house which
Cordier had avoided on the ground that he was not available
or was away. I was to have called on Kasavubu that day, but,
to restore the political balance, the meeting was cancelled.
For four days there was no personal contact between ONUC
and the two principal contestants.

The situation in Léopoldville was now extremely tense as de-
monstrations and counter-demonstrations were being planned.
Colonel Mobutu called on ONUC in a rather distraught state
as Lumumba's emissary, with strong instructions to protest
against the closure of the radio station and airports and the
prevention of General Lundula from landing at Léopoldville
airport. Mobutu also complained against the presence of a U.N.
guard at the post office. It was arranged that as a compromise,
U.N. troops would be on guard outside the radio station while
Congolese troops would be inside. At the post office the order
would be reversed. Mobutu confided that he intended to resign
his office next day as he was under great pressure from different
sides. To redress the grievance about General Lundula, Brian
Urquhart, who had been sent to Stanleyville to report on the
situation there, brought back the General in a United Nations
aircraft.

Three days after Kasavubu's broadcast the situation was
more confused than ever, but there was still no serious public
disturbance. Lumumba and his supporters were extremely
active in Parliament and outside rallying their supporters.
Kasavubu relied on presidential communiqués and radio state-

ments, but his supporters were far less vigilant and, in the case of Ileo, both inert and invisible.

It was now time for Cordier to depart and Hammarskjold advised that there were 'strong reasons' for him to leave. The Secretary-General undoubtedly felt that if Cordier remained longer in Léopoldville, I would be identified with a policy for which I had no personal responsibility. Hammarskjold had clearly indicated his strong reservations about the two initiatives Cordier had taken which were already being severely criticized by a number of countries on whom Hammarskjold relied heavily for support for the Operation. He also thought that since Kasavubu's move had lost its momentum, a restoration of ONUC's position of equidistance between the opposing factions could best be effected by a change in ONUC's leadership. In any case I had been designated to the post and my position at ONUC, lacking both responsibility and authority, was becoming highly equivocal. I therefore assumed charge of the Operation on 8 September to the relief of Cordier, whose eight days in the Congo had been both tumultuous and controversial.

Hammarskjold had been alarmed by the effusive Western reactions to Lumumba's dismissal, but even more by their enthusiastic approval of ONUC's actions during the crisis and the supposed connection between the two.

The first round in the gladiatorial contest had been inconclusive. Constitutionally, both sides had acted in a manner not laid down in the Loi Fondamentale, yet both relied on it to justify their actions. Lumumba was right in saying that the President's powers of removing a prime minister could not be exercised except in accordance with various other provisions of the constitution which limited them by requiring preliminary parliamentary action. And the President was right in saying that Parliament could not declare a presidential ordinance dismissing a prime minister invalid, but it could censure the Ministers countersigning it and also deny its confidence to the new government.

The Loi Fondamentale was not very precisely worded, and there was no means of getting an impartial or objective interpretation in the absence of a constitutional court and indeed of a judiciary. The judges, all of them Belgian, had fled the country soon after Independence. There could have been re-course to the Supreme Court at Brussels, but there was no time to make a reference which in any event was out of the question, as diplomatic relations with Belgium had been severed. So long as the argument remained confined to the two Chambers and to statements advocating or refuting one or other point of view, there was some possibility of a way out being found by means of conciliation.

ONUC's legal advisers, after carefully examining the constitutional provisions, had little doubt that the President's action virtually amounted to a 'constitutional coup'. Kasavubu and his advisers had clearly acted on false premises.

The President did not lack advisers, nor did the other Congolese politicians. But the advice came from dubious sources. Kasavubu's preference was for Belgian advisers; Lumumba gathered his indiscriminately from miscellaneous nationalities. Advice was a plentiful commodity in the Congo as it cost little and could reap rich dividends. Advice was even available without consent. The secret advisers, 'conseillers occultes' as they were called, sought every opportunity to insinuate their way into the confidence of the inexperienced politicians, who sometimes succumbed to the sheer persistence of their self-appointed mentors.

But more decisive than the advisers in their impact on the Congolese were the foreign interests which were deeply, though furtively, entrenched in the political and economic life of the fledgling state. There were representatives of the vast commercial and industrial trusts, whose arms were long and whose touch was golden. There was an extensive network of foreign intelligence agencies catering to all tastes and needs but inspired by the single purpose of subverting as many Congolese politicians as possible to their particular aims. Deftly adapting their methods to the changing scene, their agents, sometimes sordid, sometimes glamorous, eagerly sought their clientele among the impoverished or inhibited Congolese politicians. In a situation where political loyalties were lightly held, where changes in allegiance were far from uncommon, the field was ripe for a rich harvest.

Among the foreign envoys in Léopoldville, I happened to know the three who represented the Western great powers.

Clare Timberlake, who presided over the U.S. Embassy, had formerly been Consul-General in Bombay and I looked forward to renewing our previous association. Ian Scott had belonged to the Indian Civil Service and I hoped our common background would help to establish a bond of mutual understanding. The French Ambassador, Charpentier, was a diplomat of skill and finesse who clothed his official views in language of admirable subtlety and restraint. My expectations, however, were soon to meet with disappointment, as the international issues seemed too intricate and the prejudices and predilections of the envoys too ingrained to allow them to relate their activities to the disinterested endeavours of the United Nations.

In the fluid and changeable conditions that prevailed, the foreign embassies found exciting opportunities for the exercise of dubious skills, which in normal conditions, where the main activity is routine rapportage interspersed with dull negotiations, generally lie dormant. Here the very malleability of the situation offered a standing temptation to the adventurous, not always within the bounds of diplomatic propriety, to attempt to mould the pattern of developments in accordance with their narrow concept of their particular national or ideological interests.

The Belgians were greatly embittered against Lumumba, particularly because of his speech on Independence Day, which they regarded as an unforgivable affront to their king. And although Lumumba—and Kasavubu—had tried to calm the mutinous Congolese soldiers, the blame for the misfortunes of the Belgians was unfairly laid only at Lumumba's door. Even the expulsion of the Belgian envoy, which was taken by a Cabinet decision with which the President was in full concurrence, was attributed to Lumumba's personal spite. Lumumba's statements against the great trusts and monopolies, whose activities he proclaimed his intention of curbing—a promise more easily made than fulfilled—was regarded as a threat against legitimate Belgian economic concerns in the Congo. And Lumumba's determination to liquidate the secession of Katanga, whose cause the Belgians had espoused, was to them unpardonable. Although the Belgians were backing up the secessionist Tshombe and his accomplice Albert Kalonji, head of the dissident state of South Kasai, they characterized the assistance that

Lumumba was to receive from another foreign source—the Soviet Union—as clear proof of his ideological affinities. If Belgian assistance to Katanga and South Kasai was intended to sustain their illegal independence, it could be argued that Soviet assistance to Lumumba's legal Government went towards strengthening the unity and independence of the whole of the Congo and of its legal government.

But in the game of power politics logic and consistency are often at a discount. The Belgians were determined, with the resources at their command, both diplomatic and financial, to oust Lumumba. Although formal diplomatic relations had ceased, the Belgian presence was ubiquitous, and it took many and variegated forms. Apart from Kasavubu's and Tshombe's advisers, there were still in Léopoldville and in the provinces representatives of the great commercial and industrial houses whose money and influence, sometimes discreetly, sometimes more openly applied, could be very effective.

Brazzaville was the focus of activity against Lumumba, his Government, and the Congolese people. There the expelled Belgian Mission continued its activities and planned its strategy. It was not difficult for its emissaries to come daily across the river, sow their tares, and retreat to the privileged sanctuary of the French shore. All disgruntled Congolese found a ready refuge in Brazzaville, and Abbé Fulbert Youlou and his French advisers were always available for help and counsel. Tshombe and Kalonji were in close contact with elements in Brazzaville, all of them violently hostile to Lumumba and subsequently also to the United Nations.

The Western embassies, particularly the American and British, were convinced partisans of the Belgian position and they actively joined in the denigration of Lumumba and his Government. The United States Government had no coherent policy in the Congo for, surprisingly enough, it had expected Belgium to provide leadership and guidance to the Congo even after Independence. When the situation changed, it was compelled to improvise and innovate, its sympathies falling heavily on the side of the Belgians despite its own anti-colonial tradition.

This miscellany of influences bearing upon the Congolese politicians, some more susceptible than others, seemed inspired by every conceivable consideration other than the welfare of the Congolese people and the integrity of their state. ONUC therefore found itself rather isolated, battling with the problems crowding in upon it, attempting to hold fast to its lifeline—the purposes and principles of the Organization.

To the difficulties in the field, ONUC was now saddled with the charge of involvement in the Congo's political affairs. It was blamed for bringing about the fall of a nationalist Prime Minister and accused of acting as an agent of Western interests. Hammarskjold had not willed the events or given his prior consent to Cordier's initiatives. True, he had welcomed Lumumba's dismissal, but he had cautioned ONUC against any action which would have given an advantage to one faction against another in the constitutional struggle.

On 8 September, after I took charge, my first concern was to see how I could, after a decent interval and with plausible reason, rescind the orders which had evoked so much controversy. In one of my earliest telegrams to the Secretary-General I subconsciously used the phrase 'regrettable necessity' thrice in referring to those orders. Hammarskjold promptly wired back pointing to the repeated use of the expression and inquiring if he should conclude that I disagreed with the decisions. I sent back a non-committal reply to the effect that while the action was taken in good faith to avoid violence, its further necessity was in doubt and I was discussing the matter with the Congolese leaders with a view to taking corrective action. Hammarskjold agreed, leaving the timing and other connected matters to my discretion. Subsequently I asked him on two occasions whether there were any decisions taken by ONUC during my tenure or previously about whose wisdom or legality he was in doubt. Hammarskjold immediately said, on both occasions, that he was unhappy about the closure of the radio station and airports and considered both their legality and necessity doubtful.

Throughout my tenure in the Congo the consequences of those decisions were to cast a malevolent spell over the Operation and it became a Sisyphean task to undo their damaging effects. Although the restrictive measures were withdrawn within a week, they had contributed to a radical change in the political situation. Attempts to correct the balance brought immediate and vociferous charges of partiality from the countries and interests that had favoured the *coup*. Those who had applauded what they regarded as ONUC's decisive contribution towards bringing Lumumba to heel viewed any attempt on the part of the Operation to resume its even course as an act of partisanship. Yet despite the pressures and criticisms, it was essential for ONUC to return to the path of legality and even-handed justice.

CHAPTER 4

The Next Seven Days

The Congo was like a storm-tossed ship, drifting aimlessly on the turbulent waters. Abandoned by its Belgian crew and full of panicky passengers on board, it was a danger to itself and to other ships in the area. The United Nations had rushed in to help the Congolese to man the engine-room and pumps and to steer the ship to calmer waters where the Congolese could themselves take over control.

The situation that faced me was a critical one even without the developments of the last three or four days. The problem of Katanga's secession clouded the horizon. The province of South Kasai had declared its independence and a savage tribal conflict was raging there. The remnants of Belgian troops were dragging their feet in withdrawing, while many of their officers were active in Katanga building up a gendarmerie. The Congolese army, scattered over different provinces, was like a rogue elephant, rampaging wildly over the countryside, unresponsive to the command of its officers and resisting the efforts of the United Nations to calm it. The administration was in hopeless disarray; the seats of the departed Belgian officials either lay vacant or were assumed by their former clerks or assistants. The judiciary had disintegrated, and there were no Congolese with even a smattering of judicial training to run the courts. Most of the Belgian doctors had abandoned their patients and the hospitals were carrying on as best they could with medical assistants and nurses, some of whom were gallantly but unskilfully performing serious operations. The schools, fortunately closed for the vacations, could not be reopened because of the precipitate departure of the thousands of Belgian teachers. The customs services had virtually ceased to function, and the docks and shipyards lay idle. The airport control-towers had been forsaken by their Belgian technicians, and air travel had become hazardous in the extreme. River and rail movement was fitful. The supply of goods and services, because of the breakdown of the agencies of distribution, was causing serious shortages, and famine had made its appearance in certain parts of the country. The sanitary services were disrupted and there was no means of combating epidemics of diseases, some of which were endemic. Electric and water supplies were precarious. In the remote countryside, the people could perhaps revert to their traditional ways, but what of the towns, where some order and organization were essential to sustain urban life? There was a prevailing sense of fear, in which tribal hatreds and local feuds, and even personal differences, could break out unhindered into hideous forms of violence.

Bad enough though the situation was at the centre, in the provinces it was worse. The provincial ministers were quite unaccustomed to their new responsibilities. Many of them had not much education and little or no contact with public affairs. They belonged to different parties and sometimes to rival ethnic groups. There was no clear political platform, no programme of action. Office assistants and book-keepers had taken over the responsibilities of their highly trained and experienced Belgian predecessors. They had no knowledge of official procedures or financial discipline. The treasury was practically empty and taxes remained uncollected. Yet heavy payments had to be made to keep the Congolese officials at work, the various public services from complete collapse, and the soldiery from repeated mutiny.

But there was occasional relief from the general anarchy. Some Congolese officials, either self-appointed to their higher responsibilities or drafted by their colleagues, tried with unexpected success to emulate what they had seen their Belgian superiors do in court or office. Court assistants became judges, and clerks magistrates. Some hospital attendants managed to keep their forsaken patients alive, while foremen and junior workmen were sometimes able to maintain one or other facility in function. These were indeed remarkable instances of devotion to duty and to the service of their fellow citizens. But such examples unhappily were all too few.

Among the Belgians private medical practitioners often stood their ground, and some planters, merchants, and businessmen either remained or returned. The Catholic Sisters, true to their vows and their religious duty, stayed to look after the mission stations, leprosaria, and other charitable and religious institutions after many of the monks had fled. They were often insulted and molested, but nevertheless continued to minister to the sick and the needy. Their example was moving, and indeed inspiring.

The yawning breach left by the Belgian officials, experts, and technicians the United Nations attempted to fill by organizing a massive technical-assistance programme launched with the help of its specialized agencies. For the first time every specialized agency contributed, under the banner of the United Nations, its share in a joint enterprise. They all functioned under the direction of the Special Representative and his staff with a rare harmony and united will. Every Central and Provincial Government department had its United Nations expert to advise and guide the Minister, to help organize the work, and discreetly to train. Behind all the life-giving activities in the Congo there was at some point an international expert manning the controls. It was this dedicated band of men drawn from many countries and conditions that helped to resuscitate the stricken body of the Congo, to pump new blood into its dry veins, and to nurse it back to life. The foreign experts worked in wholly unfamiliar and often perilous conditions, where even their personal safety could not be assured.

I began a series of meetings with Congolese leaders, starting with Bomboko, followed by Thomas Kanza and other ministers and parliamentarians, some of whom came singly, but the majority in groups. There was no abatement in criticism of the United Nations for its alleged interference in the internal affairs of the country. ONUC was also charged with departing from its declared principle of impartiality by permitting Ileo to fly in a U.N. plane to the provinces to canvass support for his Government. Another grievance was that the Élisabethville airport and radio station continued to function despite the ban. When questions were asked by journalists about Ileo's supposed travels, ONUC had vigorously denied the accusation and I had personally confirmed the denial after making necessary enquiries. The rumour about Ileo's movements got currency as he was nowhere to be seen in Léopoldville, and it may have been thought that he was travelling about. In fact, when Ileo met the press later, he said he had been in contact with various politicians in the provinces, and this was mistakenly thought to mean that he had physically met them, using U.N. transport for the purpose.

So far as Élisabethville was concerned, the United Nations had little more than a token military presence there at the time, and was not in physical control of the airport, where only a small contingent of Swedish troops was posted, largely on observation duty. The U.N. also had no control over the Élisabethville radio station, which continued its anti-Lumumba broadcasts uninterrupted. Although ONUC's orders should have been universally applied, the failure to extend them to Élisabethville promptly was due solely to a lack of the necessary means. Corrective measures were soon taken to restore the equilibrium.

The Western ambassadors called to offer their warm support for what they regarded as a courageous initiative on the part of the United Nations in the interests of law and order. They had no doubt whatever about the duty, and indeed the obligation, of the Organization to intervene on Kasavubu's behalf, and they dismissed as legal quibbling any opinion to the contrary. Some of them made it plain that since their countries paid a large contribution to United Nations funds they had a right to expect their notions of what ONUC should do to guide the Operation.

There were visits also from envoys of African countries, some half a dozen of whom had by that time set up missions in the Congo. They seemed to feel that they had been let down by the United Nations. They were convinced that the President had acted unconstitutionally and was badly advised by his foreign counsellors and Western embassies. They appeared certain that Lumumba enjoyed the confidence of Parliament and would be able to regain his position. Some of them conceded that Lumumba was inclined to be erratic and unbalanced, but all agreed that he was a true patriot, working, according to the best of his lights, in the interests of his country.

The African envoys were, on the whole, not too exigent. They had no exaggerated notions of the weight their countries pulled at the United Nations, although most had contributed troops to the Congo Operation, many at great sacrifice. They looked up to the United Nations for even-handed action, and they did not doubt its purposes, although they questioned some of its decisions.

My first impressions of the Congolese politicians who had called on me were rather mixed. Many of them were in their early thirties, some were even younger and looked it. They were well-dressed, some foppishly, but all expensively. They had an eager air about them and talked incessantly, often simultaneously, and it was sometimes difficult to make out what they wished to convey. They never paused for a word or to marshal their thoughts, speaking fluently in French, although in their own style. Bomboko, the Foreign Minister, was barely thirty-two, with a good mind and an easy manner. He was one of the few Congolese to have graduated from a Belgian university and carried with him an air of self-assurance. He was given to good living and expensive tastes and was popular with the Western missions, which he much frequented. Thomas Kanza, the Minister Delegate at the United Nations, was one of the earliest Congolese graduates from the University of Louvain and one of the handful of Congolese politicians who also had a good knowledge of English. He spoke in measured and earnest tones, without flamboyance or exaggeration, and during the short time that he had been at the United Nations, had acquired a useful knowledge of the powers and limitations of the Organization. While party politics is inevitably one-sided, the majority of Congolese politicians seemed unable to rise above their own predilections and narrow concerns. Their general concept of the United Nations had little to do with the realities of the situation or the powers of the Organization. Having had to struggle with the colonial power for their most elementary rights, they were inclined to overplay their hand when a little moderation would have sufficed. And they were not beyond uttering threats of one kind or another if they felt dissatisfied at the response.

Meanwhile the struggle between the divided Congolese politicians continued unabated. Lumumba made a declaration to the effect that unless the United Nations relinquished control of the airports and radio station, he would demand the withdrawal of all United Nations troops. He also cabled the Secretary-

General to urge the Security Council to hold its next meeting in Léopoldville.

I made arrangements to call on the Head of State and the Prime Minister, and I was given appointments to see them on 10 September. The visit to Lumumba, intended largely as a courtesy call, was the first and last official visit that I was to pay him. It took place at the Prime Minister's residence, a large villa formerly the residence of the Belgian Governor-General. I had been asked to come at noon, but I waited in the anteroom for almost an hour, as I was told that the Prime Minister was addressing a public meeting. When he arrived, surrounded by a large retinue, he greeted me and led me to his study, a spacious room with glazed windows. There was a big desk in the centre with a lot of books and papers lying around. Lumumba ushered me to a sofa, sitting beside me, while a political officer from ONUC Headquarters, who acted as interpreter in case of need, was also present.

Without much ceremony and before I could utter the words of courtesy usual at a first meeting, Lumumba launched into a tirade against the United Nations for arbitrarily taking over control of the radio station and airports. He complained that he had been prevented from addressing his own people, an intolerable situation for the Prime Minister of a country. The United Nations had been invited to help the legal Government but instead was trying to usurp its powers and functions. He insisted that ONUC issue immediate orders for the withdrawal of the U.N. guard, otherwise he would be compelled to remove it by force. He handed me an aide-mémoire which accused the United Nations of flagrant intervention in the internal affairs of the Congo, and challenged the authority of the President to remove him from office. I told Lumumba that I had just taken over and had been closely studying the situation since my arrival. My predecessor's actions had been necessitated by the unfortunate circumstances that had arisen and were of a purely temporary nature. They had been taken to avoid any outbreak of violence and the restrictions would be withdrawn as early as possible. I explained that the Security Council and Secretary-General were fully informed of the situation and it would not be possible for me to issue any orders until I received appropriate instructions from New York. I said it was a question of a day or so, and I pressed Lumumba not to precipitate the issue.

But Lumumba refused to pay heed and kept repeating that ONUC must issue orders the same day. I said that I sympathized with his position, but for the moment I was unable to take any action even if I wanted to, and asked for patience. But Lumumba continued to press his demand, adding, '*Aujourd'hui, pas demain*',[1] a phrase which he kept repeating.

I was then compelled to speak firmly, hoping that Lumumba would take note of my warning. I said, 'Mr. Prime Minister, I represent a peaceful organization which is here at the request of your own Government to help you in your difficulties. An unfortunate constitutional dispute has arisen which it is of course for the political leaders of the country to resolve. The United Nations was regrettably compelled to take certain precautionary measures solely in the interest of preventing violence and disorder. Those measures are of a temporary nature and will be withdrawn at the earliest possible moment. The United Nations has no aims of its own in the Congo; it has come into the Congo for one purpose only, namely to carry out the mandate of the Security Council, and it will be only too happy to leave when its task is done. Please do not speak of the use of force in compelling a decision, for that would only add to the difficulties. Also please believe me when I say that I shall make every endeavour in my power to bring the present situation to an early end.'

Lumumba thereupon slightly shifted his stand, and while pressing for immediate action, said he would not be responsible if the populace, in view of the strong resentment aroused by the unwarranted silencing of the radio station, would themselves seize it by force. I replied that surely the Prime Minister commanded sufficient influence and authority with his own people to prevent such recklessness. Lumumba's rejoinder was that as a popular leader he could not stand in the way of the people giving vent to their feelings. I was now left with no option but to tell him that much as I personally detested the use of force—and neither I nor the United Nations was in the Congo to use force against the Congolese people or leaders— yet if force were used against us, we would have no choice but

[1] 'Today, not tomorrow.'

to meet force with force. I offered to come again to discuss the matter further, adding that talks with Vice-Premier Gizenga were already in progress. I still hoped that Lumumba would not pit his will against the power of the United Nations or attempt to alter by force what could be achieved by negotiation.

I then changed the subject and said that since this was our first meeting, the Prime Minister would perhaps be interested to know me a little better since I hoped we would be working closely together. Mr. Nehru had himself asked me to accept my present appointment because of his sympathy for the Congo in its difficulties and the sense of solidarity felt by the people of India with the Congolese people. Whatever experience I had of the problems facing a country at Independence, I would place unreservedly at the disposal of the Congolese Government. Lumumba thanked me, adding that he very much appreciated my coming and hoped that we could work together harmoniously and sincerely.

As I stood up to leave, Lumumba said, almost as an afterthought, 'Mr. Ambassador, let me, on behalf of my Government and myself, wish you a warm welcome to the Congo.' I replied spontaneously, for I had had a gruelling two hours with him, 'Mr. Prime Minister, thank you for your statement. I have had not only a warm welcome but, if I may say so, a hot one.' At this Lumumba burst into peals of laughter in which I heartily joined.

Lumumba had an arresting personality. He was tall and slim, with earnest bespectacled eyes and a small beard. Quick and intelligent, he appeared to be driven by an almost desperate courage. In his impatience to get things done, he seemed possessed by some inner force which made him tense, like a coiled spring. Yet he could be charming and likeable. I had been impressed by the manner in which he had been fighting back. But a man fired with such dynamism and feverish energy stood in danger of becoming the victim of his own restless nature. I came away hoping that Lumumba would not get himself into the unequal situation of using force against the United Nations. But he had made it an issue of prestige and of commitment to his followers. I regretted his commitment, for the Ghana troops who were at the radio station would, I knew, faithfully carry out their duty.

A letter from President Kasavubu awaited me, declaring that the Lumumba Government had ceased to exist and that ONUC should have no official dealings with it. The same day the Bureau of the Chamber informed the Secretary-General that any question relating to the interpretation of the Loi Fondamentale was the exclusive prerogative of Parliament and protested against the Secretary-General's statement on the legal efficacy of Kasavubu's order. It insisted that the Lumumba Government was still in being and that ONUC should continue to deal with it.

The Secretary-General had said in the Security Council, 'I do not want to analyse the complicated constitution and the complicated constitutional situation, but let me register as a fact that, according to the constitution, the president has the right to revoke the mandate of the prime minister and that his decisions are effective when countersigned by constitutionally responsible ministers.' He added, 'In this situation—where there was on the one side a Chief of State whom the United Nations must recognize and whom the statements of the Prime Minister had not deprived of his rights, but when there was, on the other side, a Cabinet which continued in being, but the chief of which had put himself in sharp opposition to the Chief of State—the instructions to our representatives in the Congo were to avoid any action, directly or indirectly, open or by implication, that would pass judgment on the stand taken by either one of the parties to the conflict.'

This statement was somewhat premature and not in keeping with Hammarskjold's habitual sense of prudence. If it had been confined to the president's constitutional status, which had not been affected by the recent events, it would have been unexceptionable. But when the Secretary-General expressed an opinion regarding the legality of Kasavubu's action, affirming his legal right to remove the prime minister, he made an implied commitment in support of that action. However, Hammarskjold soon realized that he had expressed a controversial opinion and he did not repeat it subsequently.

In Léopoldville the political struggle took the form of statements and counter-statements and feverish parliamentary activity. The protagonists were still trying to justify to the public and to the United Nations the legal and constitutional validity of their respective stands. So long as this war of words went on, the issue seemed open to argument and reason. A new government was announced by Ileo between 11 and 12 September, but it was never presented to Parliament, and it remained a disembodied spirit.

On 10 September I paid my first call on the Head of State at the presidential palace. The President was affable and relaxed though not very communicative. I tried to ascertain what action he proposed to take to introduce greater clarity in the situation, but I got no coherent answers. Presently Ileo, who had been sitting inconspicuously in the crowded amity of the dinner table, emerged to take his seat with us, smiling diffidently. He said he was announcing his Government and hoped he would receive support from the various political parties. Before leaving I told the President that I looked forward to fruitful cooperation with him in the interests of his country and people, that I hoped I would merit his trust and understanding, and that he could count on me to be always available to him. Kasavubu graciously nodded his assent.

Efforts to resolve the political crisis, to which the President had hardly referred at my meeting with him, continued in Léopoldville, with the politicians engaged in an endless round of conferences and meetings. Various groups of politicians came to 'Le Royal' seeking advice, of which our supply, though abundant, was monotonously uniform. Our line with all politicians, whatever their persuasion, was to advise national reconciliation, a responsibility which no outside authority could usurp. But our good offices were always available if asked for by either side. Knowing their extreme sensitivity to any suggestion of interference in their internal affairs, I refused to adopt any view in regard to the rights and wrongs of the political differences.

To the African ambassadors I conveyed my full moral support for their efforts at conciliation of which they kept me informed. Another attempt at reconciliation, initially a piece of private enterprise, was undertaken by Jean David, a U.N. consultant from Haiti, who claimed to know the Congolese leaders well. In fact it was Cordier who, alarmed at the storm that had burst in New York immediately after the Kasavubu *coup*, had encouraged David in his efforts. I therefore gave David a free hand but asked him to keep within the bounds of discretion to guard against any subsequent charge of improper interference in the political affairs of the country.

But if the peace-makers were slow in their progress, events were not. In my round of talks with parliamentary leaders I received a call from Joseph Okito, Vice-President of the Senate, of which Ileo was President. Okito, an elderly man by Congolese standards, was obviously much affected by the crisis and his face was drawn with anxiety.

Suddenly, with tears coursing down his face, he left his chair and fell at my feet, sobbing uncontrollably, and begged me to help the Congo in its travail by lending my good offices. Greatly taken aback and much moved, I pleaded with Okito to compose himself. I helped him back to his seat and did what I could to comfort him. All I could do was to urge Okito to use his authority and, without losing heart, to continue his efforts towards reconciliation between the rival factions.

Okito received my words of advice and consolation gratefully and I wished him well in his patriotic efforts. On leaving, Okito said that he fully agreed with me and would discuss the matter with his colleague, Joseph Kasongo, the President of the House of Representatives, and asked if they could both come around later to see me. I gladly agreed.

But when an hour or two later Okito reappeared with his colleague Kasongo, a tall man in a red fez, the nature of the conversation was entirely different. While Okito sat quietly, Kasongo, much to my surprise, lashed out in anger, protesting against what he described as my presumption in trying to interfere in the country's internal affairs. He said it was none of ONUC's business to offer political advice to the Congolese leaders as they were the best judges of their own interests. I tried to protest, vainly explaining that my advice was not gratuitous but had been earnestly sought by his colleague, and that I had said or done nothing which could reasonably provoke his ire. Meanwhile Okito sat benignly without saying a word. And so, Kasongo leading, they stomped out.

Bewildered by this strange experience, I warned Jean David to be extremely prudent in his efforts at reconciliation. I found the experience with Okito and Kasongo, on the human plane of mutual comprehension, most discouraging.

While still recovering from the effects of my high-level visitation, I received another unpleasant piece of news. Contrary to my advice, Lumumba had after all tried to enter the radio station by force. That afternoon, accompanied by a civilian guard and some ten armed soldiers, he arrived at the radio station and forced his way in despite the warnings of the Ghana guard. A member of Lumumba's bodyguard drew a pistol at the Ghanaian non-commissioned officer, but the latter succeeded in disarming his would-be assailant. Thereafter the U.N. guard ousted the entire party from the building. About half an hour later General Lundula appeared at the studio with a company of soldiers in trucks. The Ghana Brigade Commander, Colonel Joseph Ankrah, and his Brigadier, Joseph Otu, rushed to the scene and started a long argument with General Lundula, whose troops fortunately remained in their trucks. With commendable skill and firmness the Ghanaian officers convinced Lundula that a further encounter would be much more violent and would redound to nobody's credit; it was also unnecessary, as action was already being taken by ONUC to resolve the matter. Thereupon General Lundula and his troops withdrew.

Lumumba reacted to his expulsion from the radio station by addressing a telegram to the Secretary-General demanding the installation of a powerful radio transmitter to enable the Government to reach the people. On the ground that since the United Nations was not prepared to intervene for the re-establishment of 'calm and legality' in Katanga he demanded twenty aircraft with crews, along with a large quantity of arms. In case his request was not accepted, he warned that his Government would seek assistance elsewhere. The message hardly called for a response and Hammarskjold ignored it. But the same day Lumumba, while trying to muster support for himself among the troops at Camp Léopold, was arrested, apparently on the orders of Colonel Mobutu, but was released after a few hours on the intercession of General Lundula. This was followed by President Kasavubu's issuing an order dismissing General Lundula from command of the army and appointing Colonel Mobutu in his place.

On 12 September, I took action to remove the United Nations guard from the radio station with an appeal to all concerned that they use its facilities to promote unity and not hatred and conflict. In vacating the studio we also tried to avoid a struggle between the two rival governments for its exclusive possession, an attempt in which we largely succeeded. Both factions were now free to use the radio to air their views. Lumumba made a broadcast to explain his stand while his opponents promptly announced their intention to arrest him and place him on trial.

To assist a return to normality, I next issued orders for restoring the airports to 'all peaceful civilian and humanitarian traffic'. The stoppage of air traffic was causing unnecessary hardship to the population and was impeding parliamentary action for the solution of the crisis, as many of the politicians had been marooned in the provinces.

On 13 September the presiding officers of the two Chambers convened a joint session of both Houses at which the President of the lower House addressed a fervent appeal to Kasavubu and Lumumba 'to put an end to their quarrels and to reunite in a spirit of patriotism, sacrifice, and mutual concession'.

The appeal received applause from all sides. Lumumba stated that he was ready for reconciliation and suggested that the Chambers appoint a parliamentary commission to work alongside the Government. The joint session adopted a resolution voting full powers to the Government to deal with 'the alarming situation' and set up a parliamentary commission to supervise the actions of Government. In my report to the Secretary-General I said the joint session had 'conferred full powers on the Prime Minister in a vote which was somewhat uncertain both as to substance and count'.

Kasavubu's reaction to the joint session was to issue another communiqué challenging the legality of the meeting and declaring the resolution null and void. But Parliament had shown its determination to assert itself by not recognizing the dismissal of Lumumba. As it was also certain to reject the Ileo Government, Kasavubu issued an Ordinance adjourning Parliament for one month to prevent any further acts of defiance. The Presidents of the two Chambers promptly reacted by informing the President that his Ordinance had been countersigned by Ileo, who had not received parliamentary investiture and was therefore without force.

Kasavubu's attitude during the days immediately following destroyed any possibility of achieving a compromise through the intermediary of Parliament. He continued to treat with the peacemakers, but he was full of evasions and subterfuges. Under the constitution, a government that had been dismissed would continue to function until a new *formateur* announced the composition of his Cabinet, which Ileo did after a period of five or six days after his nomination. During the interim, the Lumumba Government must be considered to have been in existence. But Kasavubu insisted that the dismissal became effective from the moment he pronounced it on the radio like a sorcerer's incantation. Thus while he refused to admit the further existence of the Lumumba Government, the government of Ileo remained an elusive phantom. The future disasters that were to befall owed a great deal to the President's own contribution.

There was one good result from the dissolution of Parliament. Lumumba had rashly entered into an agreement, without taking the advice of ONUC or of his colleagues, with an American businessman, Durtweiler, for the development of the Congo's resources. The contract had been signed but not ratified. It had given Durtweiler a concession over vast tracts and extending over a long period of time in exchange for a nominal royalty. It was reminiscent of the concessions given in King Léopold II's time, and it was fortunate indeed for the Congo that it remained a scrap of paper.

Politics, like nature, abhors a vacuum. And into the political vacuum created by Kasavubu stepped Colonel Joseph Désiré Mobutu, Chief of Staff of the Congolese National Army. Mobutu had been extremely unhappy at the state of affairs in the country. The army was little better than an 'armed rabble', and Mobutu trembled before the incendiary force under his uneasy command. At first he was anxious that it be properly disciplined and trained. But he could do nothing to get the officers and soldiers to submit to training, still less to obey their superior officers. General Kettani of the United Nations had been specifically deputed to train the troops and he was a friend and confidant of Mobutu.

During his visits to the U.N. Military Command Mobutu often dropped in to see me, generally in the evenings, when he spoke with sadness, not unmixed with bitterness, of the state of his country. He said that he owed everything to Lumumba, whom he regarded as his patron. Like most Congolese, he hoped that the rift between Lumumba and Kasavubu would be settled by reconciliation. He lamented the egotism of the political leaders which was destroying the country. He promised full support to the United Nations, which he was convinced could help in putting the country on its feet. He was one Congolese of note who till that time had refrained from any criticism of the United Nations and made no unreasonable demands on it.

At these meetings I used to give Mobutu what encouragement I could, asking him not to lose heart, to work for national reconciliation, and above all to do his best to discipline and control the army. Mobutu was, however, most fearful for the safety of his family. The United Nations had provided a guard at Mobutu's residence and he himself was always accompanied by a United Nations escort when he moved about the army camp or in the city. My first impression of Mobutu was of a rather diffident but patriotic man who felt powerless in the face of events that he could neither fully understand nor influence.

Mobutu would sit in his chair dressed in a khaki military shirt carrying the insignia of his rank, and shorts—the Belgian colonial uniform—and in dark glasses which he habitually wore day and night. He was a fairly tall and slim man with a sensitive face and nervous temperament. His manner was of one seeking sympathy and understanding; everyone at 'Le Royal' felt sorry for this young man who was so troubled by his unfamiliar and onerous responsibilities and overwhelmed by the problems of his country. Mobutu gave the impression of a Hamlet torn between opposing loyalties, unsure of himself, and full of doubts and fears. His mobile face was gloomy and preoccupied, his dark glasses adding to his mournful appearance. To set him at ease I always offered him whisky, which he took in generous draughts, brightening up visibly as the evening advanced. Without appearing to be unkind, I had often to remind him when it got particularly late, that it was time for him, after a hard and harassing day, to return to the soothing company of his wife and children, to whom he seemed much attached.

Late on the evening of 14 September, when I was at my desk, I received a message from the U.N. Military Command that Colonel Mobutu, who had been visiting them, wished to see me. I thought nothing of it, as it was the Colonel's habit frequently to drop in on me. I moved over to the adjacent reception room, where the Colonel was ushered in. As he took his seat, I noticed that he was more nervous than usual. I hoped that he would relax after having some refreshment, but he continued to fidget in his chair, conversing at random. This went on for half an hour or so, and I asked if he had anything on his mind.

After some hesitation Mobutu said he had come to inform me of a decision that he had been compelled to take. Kasavubu and Lumumba had brought the country to the verge of ruin. There was no government and he was convinced that neither Lumumba nor Ileo could function as Prime Minister. Reaffirming his continued loyalty to Lumumba, he said he had not wished to arrest him in Camp Léopold a couple of days earlier and had allowed him to be released. In fact he had taken Lumumba into temporary custody for his own safety, as Lumumba was impulsive and often exposed himself to danger. Mobutu said he was opposed to all political arrests and lamented the excesses being committed by both sides. He was convinced that the rift between Kasavubu and Lumumba was too deep to be bridged. In the circumstances, Mobutu announced in the same flat tone, he had decided to neutralize both the Head of State and Prime Minister!

I could not immediately fathom his meaning and I asked Mobutu what precisely he had in mind. He replied that if the two leaders were 'neutralized', there would be a chance of reconciliation. The army was not taking over the government, and what he proposed to do would be only for a temporary period till the end of the year. I asked how he was setting about his intentions and whether he had considered the consequences. I warned against the army entering politics as that would make matters far worse. He again tried to assure me that his action was intended solely to bring the quarrels of the leaders to an end so that after a period in cold storage they would be forced to make up. His sole aim, he repeated, was to promote a government of national reconciliation and he had no intention of usurping power. He added diffidently that he was making a broadcast to that effect.

By now I had become quite alarmed and asked when he would go on the air. He said it would be at 8.30 that evening. It was now almost a quarter past eight and I told him that if that was his intention, he should leave forthwith, and should not be seen at the United Nations Mission. I accompanied him to the elevator and took leave of him hurriedly. Soon after I heard Mobutu's broadcast statement, which he had previously recorded.

At an impromptu press conference at a local hotel later that night, Mobutu claimed that he had put his proposal to Kasavubu and Lumumba and that both had agreed. In answer to a question and almost as an afterthought, Mobutu declared that he would demand the recall of the 'Communist ambassadors' in the Congo.

I gathered my advisers together for urgent consultations, for we had all been caught off guard. I had heard nothing that day or previously of Mobutu's plans, and when he spoke about his desire to 'neutralize' the President and Prime Minister, it was not clear what he meant, for in a sense the two had already neutralized each other. What in effect had happened was a military *coup d'état*, despite Mobutu's denial. I wondered what Mobutu's object was in coming to see me at that hour, for he seemed to have every intention of being present at 'Le Royal' while the broadcast went on the air. Had he been present with me during the broadcast, no amount of explanation would have convinced the world that the United Nations was not behind his *coup*. As it was, the visit to 'Le Royal' came to be known—though not his call on me—and suspicion fell on General Kettani and the U.N. Military Command. Kettani, however, was no more privy to Mobutu's action than anyone else in 'Le Royal'.

We could hardly believe, as Mobutu had claimed, that Kasavubu and Lumumba had given their blessings to him, for they did not have that sort of self-abnegating spirit. It soon became evident that the two leaders also had no inkling of what was coming. The following day a communiqué was issued by Lumumba's Cabinet strongly attacking Mobutu. Kasavubu, for his part, reacted in an interview a few days later when he said that 'the neutralization of the Head of State did not make any sense'.[1] That, coming from the placid Kasavubu, was a strong statement indeed.

Andrew Tully states categorically that the Central Intelligence Agency had already spotted Mobutu as their man and had been building him up,[2] a statement which has been accepted by many writers on the Congo including the careful Catherine Hoskyns.[3] Tshombe's biographer, Ian Colvin, a journalist who was in the Congo at the time and continued there for years, states with considerable conviction throughout his narrative that Mobutu had the full backing of the C.I.A. He actually identifies the C.I.A. agent as a Lieutenant-Colonel Laurence Devlin, who was the United States Military Attaché in the Congo and who stayed there for a considerable period, returning in 1965 just before Mobutu's second *coup*.[4] At 'Le Royal' we had no doubt that Mobutu's own weak will had not provided the driving urge. We had our suspicions which did not point to the C.I.A. alone. But convincing proof was hard to find.

It was no secret in Léopoldville that, although Mobutu had been appointed by Kasavubu to replace the dismissed Lundula, his influence with the Congolese army even in Camp Léopold was confined to certain tribal elements from his own province of Équateur and to some from the Lower Congo region. But unless the troops were paid, even tribal considerations would be of no avail. Here again certain actions taken by ONUC with laudable motives unconnected with the *coup* were to come to Mobutu's aid. General Kettani's proposal to invest one million dollars to pay the penniless Congolese troops in order to pacify them had a sound purpose and had been relayed to New York. The sanction arrived right in the middle of the political stalemate. A parade was held at Camp Léopold on 10 September where, in the presence of General Kettani, some of the money was disbursed to the troops. At that time there was of course no indication of what Mobutu would do four days later. The payment was undoubtedly effective in keeping the Congolese troops in their barracks for a time. But for ONUC it was politically damaging.

[1] CRISP, *Congo 1960*, ii. 870.
[2] Tully, *CIA: The Inside Story*.
[3] Catherine Hoskyns, *The Congo since Independence*, p. 215.
[4] Ian Colvin, *The Rise and Fall of Moïse Tshombe*, pp. 37, 146–7, 207–8, 218.

I later learnt from the U.N. Military Command that Mobutu had himself supplemented the money received from the United Nations by contributions of his own. When asked where the money came from, Mobutu explained to ONUC's senior military officers that when the Belgians had fled the country, they had been searched and their funds and valuables seized by the Congolese troops and deposited. Those funds had now been used to complete the payment. This was indeed a surprising explanation, as it was inconceivable that the starving soldiers would not have helped themselves to the money and valuables purloined from the Belgians. Significantly enough, Mobutu never asked the United Nations again for funds. And since the treasury was empty and was to remain chronically in deficit, one may well wonder at the source of his overflowing cornucopia. While the teachers, medical assistants, and other Congolese functionaries remained starving and unpaid for months, Mobutu's men continued regularly to receive their inflated salaries, becoming by far the most affluent soldiers in Africa.

ONUC's financial experts who had been struggling with the Congo's rickety finances and were the only people who knew anything about them, were unaware of Mobutu's source of funds. ONUC's liaison officers attached to Mobutu used frequently to report on the constant comings and goings of some Western military attachés who visited Mobutu with bulging brief-cases containing thick brown paper packets which they obligingly deposited on his table. We could not tell what they contained, but could not help making guesses.

Neither the payment to the troops, nor the fact that Mobutu was unchallenged in his rank after Lundula's dismissal, won him their total allegiance. The Léopoldville garrison was like a time-bomb which could detonate at any moment. Mobutu retained his United Nations guard and escort and, for greater security, moved into General Kettani's adjacent house in Camp Léopold with his whole family. Kettani put up with this imposition for a considerable time, hoping that this propinquity would make Mobutu more amenable to ONUC's influence.

One day in October Mobutu, during one of his nocturnal visits to 'Le Royal', seemed more troubled than ever and asked ONUC's military liaison staff if he could see me. He came upstairs, accompanied by a couple of ONUC's senior officers, and said he had not been able to sleep for a week as two attempts had been made on his life and he was in great danger. He pleaded that he was completely exhausted and on the verge of mental and physical collapse. Could he spend a night or two at 'Le Royal' quietly and unobtrusively? I was in a quandary as, apart from one or two rooms downstairs still occupied as living quarters, the rest of our accommodation had been converted into offices. But Mobutu, a picture of despair, begged for sympathy. I hurriedly consulted my colleagues, to find out what we could do to provide Mobutu with a bed and food.

Eventually I received word that a bedroom had been rigged up and I told Mobutu he would be welcome to it. Mobutu then asked if he could bring over his wife and children. This seemed rather difficult, for we really lacked boarding-house facilities. But Mobutu would not take a refusal, and we eventually managed to set up a dormitory. The final addition was Mobutu's sister-in-law, who, he said, was required to minister to the family's needs. From one or two days the stay of the Mobutu family stretched out to seven or eight, straining both our resources and our patience. Polite hints were cast about the presumably improved state of the Colonel's nerves and the need for him to resurface. His hideaway had been kept a close secret known only to the top personnel of ONUC. Although we strongly disapproved of Mobutu's *coup*, we could not deny him the shelter he sought. An Indian proverb says: 'Hospitality is commanded even towards an enemy who comes to your house. The tree does not withdraw its shade from the woodcutter.'

CHAPTER 5

Reaping the Whirlwind

Mobutu had rudely crashed through the constitutional mesh, scattering the brawling politicians in confusion. The clamour of factions was momentarily stilled by a wave of resentment as they peered through the tangled debris. Through the dust loomed shadows of new perils and pitfalls. The situation had been difficult enough with two pretender governments stridently claiming recognition. But now there was a third and a wholly illegal one. It was obvious that ONUC could have no truck with a régime whose only sanction was force. The A.N.C., the prime cause of the country's woes, had broken through its restraints, free to rampage at will. Would Mobutu be able to control it and for how long? And could ONUC keep a restraining hand on Mobutu himself? Would the reality of coherent power, which till then only ONUC possessed, inevitably run into a collision-course with Mobutu as he tried to build up his own independent authority?

Mobutu continued his daily rounds to our headquarters, and for a time his manner was almost penitential. He tirelessly repeated his assurances that his only aim was to put the politicians on ice so that their personal ambitions might have time to cool. He denied any ambition of political power and swore that he would keep the army out of politics. But public business must be carried on, and since the politicians had been set aside, he would set up a Collège des Universitaires to run the government departments. He was recalling a number of Congolese students from foreign universities who would join their colleagues from the Université Lovanium near Léopoldville. He asserted that the provisional arrangements would be withdrawn by the end of the year, by which time the politicians, sobered and repentant, would be allowed to return to power.

For a while we were beguiled by Mobutu's disarming words. Indeed, some of our military colleagues were moved by his sincerity and convinced of his self-abnegation. The best we could do was to try and keep him to his word. General Kettani told us he regarded Mobutu almost like his own son, and we hoped that the son would keep to the path of filial duty. But I was afraid that the appetite might grow by what it fed on. I strongly advised our Command to keep him on a tight rein, and this I hoped the top brass of the U.N. Force and our military liaison officers had the influence to do. General Kettani renewed his efforts to persuade Mobutu to submit his troops for training, but he succeeded only in training a parachute unit on which Mobutu had set his heart.

On 15 September, the day after Mobutu's nocturnal bombshell, we had every reason to redouble our vigilance. The African and Asian envoys were even more bewildered at the latest turn of the wheel than were the Congolese politicians. Ambassador Djin of Ghana, who had only a few days earlier shrilly demanded the reopening of the radio station, now pressed for its immediate closure. He also asked for the doubling of the guard at Lumumba's official residence as well as at his own. He was particularly anxious to ensure that Ndjili airport remained firmly in U.N. hands, as that provided his only means of escape from the Congo. Some of the visitors wanted ONUC to arrest Mobutu, although they should have known that we had no power of arrest, not even of a felon caught *in flagrante delicto*. But the Western ambassadors, with a finer appreciation of the actualities of power, were flocking to Mobutu's door.

Meanwhile I bent all my energies towards promoting some form of reconciliation, or at least a *modus vivendi* between Kasavubu and Lumumba. I encouraged Okito, President of the Senate, and Kasongo, President of the Chamber of Representatives, to continue their efforts. Parallel to this the African envoys were also in frequent contact with the two chief protagonists and their supporters. I allowed our U.N. consultant to the President, Jean David, to continue his efforts discreetly, but without crossing any wires with the other conciliators.

On 15 September Colonel Joseph Ankrah, who commanded the Ghana battalion at Léopoldville, rushed in to see me with a very strange tale. Lumumba had been forced to seek shelter at the Ghana Officers' Mess in Camp Léopold, where he had been followed by a mob of angry Baluba soldiers bent on having his blood. The only way in which the assault could be called off would be to get an order from President Kasavubu in his capacity as Supreme Commander. I had great respect for Colonel Ankrah, who was a courageous and honourable man, entirely loyal to the U.N. Command, whose orders he implicitly obeyed against the pressures of the Ghana Ambassador and his own Chief of Staff at Accra, the British Major-General Alexander. He and the other senior Ghana officers, Brigadiers Michel and Otu, used to refer to us for orders countermanding the direct instructions that, contrary to United Nations practice, they received from Accra.

Ankrah was accompanied by a Baluba soldier in a state of indignation, speaking rapidly in his own language, blaming Lumumba for the suffering of his tribe in Kasai and demanding instant retribution. Only if 'King Kasa', as he described the President, would give assurances that Lumumba would be held answerable for the slaughter of his people, would the siege of the Ghana Officers' Mess be called off. Ankrah warned that the pressure on the Ghana guard at the Mess was increasing by the hour and it could not hold out for long. It was clear that we could not possibly allow the Mess to be overrun and Lumumba lynched while under the shelter of the United Nations flag. Without further ado, I rushed to the President's house, accompanied by Colonel Ankrah and the Baluba soldier. Brigadier Rikhye and an interpreter completed the party.

At 7.30 on the morning of 15 September—the day after his *coup*—Mobutu had assembled the troops at Camp Léopold, to whom he explained his aims, having taken the precaution during the night to call in a squadron of armoured cars from Thysville, where he regarded the garrison as more reliable than the rag-tag-and-bobtail troops at Camp Léopold. Mobutu and Lumumba met and spoke to each other in the camp, after which Lumumba held a meeting with the A.N.C. officers, which ended a little after noon in utter confusion. A large crowd of soldiers had burst in, demanding pay, better living conditions, and better weapons. Some of the men got up to Lumumba and spat on him, others hit him. He rushed to the Ghana Officers' Mess near by, pursued by the riotous soldiers, where he asked for and was given sanctuary. Colonel Ankrah and his officers, acting as go-betweens, carried messages from the soldiers to Lumumba and back, trying desperately to stave off an assault on the Mess. Lumumba said he had accepted Mobutu's terms and would meet Kasavubu and Ileo, leaving it to Mobutu to arrange the meeting. But this was not enough to pacify the mob, most of them Baluba, who clamoured for vengeance for the Kasai massacres. By 2.45 p.m. the situation at the Mess had become extremely serious despite the strengthening of the guard, and messages were pouring in by field wireless that the U.N. troops would soon be compelled to use force in self-defence.

When we burst in on the President's house, Kasavubu seemed extremely ruffled at our sudden intrusion. I told him hurriedly what had brought us there and asked for the word which the Baluba emissary wanted. Kasavubu began with a querulous note of complaint that no one informed him of anything. He said there was a warrant of arrest against Lumumba and suggested that the United Nations should arrest him. We said that was impossible, as we did not have the legal right to make arrests; besides, we politely reminded Kasavubu that he too was under a heavy United Nations guard.

While these exchanges were going on, the Baluba soldier, standing at attention behind us, kept up an incessant chatter, punctuated by sudden outbursts of anger. At one point he pressed Kasavubu for a reply to his question about what should be done to Lumumba. When Kasavubu hemmed and hawed, the Baluba exclaimed, 'Are you our King or are you not?' Slowly came Kasavubu's delphic reply: 'When you trap a wild animal in the bush, do you tear him limb from limb?' All this time messages were being brought in by a young British lieutenant in charge of the President's U.N. Ghanaian guard from which it was clear that the Mess could not hold out much longer. For the third time I got up to leave after announcing that if the President would not act, I could not continue to sit there while the lives of U.N. troops—as well as of their unwanted guest—were in such serious jeopardy.

We got word that the Congolese troops had begun digging themselves in and were surrounding the Mess on all sides with mortars and machine-guns. We had been three hours with the

President and dusk was falling. Soon it would be dark and the modern glass-and-cement building that housed the Mess would be a death trap for our troops. It was certainly not intended to resist a siege. Disengaging myself from Kasavubu, who continued to prevaricate, with such firmness as protocol and circumstance would permit, we asked our Danish chauffeur to drive us as fast as he could to the besieged Mess. By now our fears that the Mess might have been overrun had risen, as messages had stopped coming through.

Driving through the leafy park in which the Mess was situated, we saw a mass of angry humanity, many with lighted bramble torches, screaming at the top of their voices and stamping menacingly around the flimsy structure. On nearing the seething mass, I shouted at the mob with as much authority as I could muster for them to make way. Startled, they did. We jumped out of the car to be met by three concentric rows of United Nations troops—Swedes, Moroccans, and Ghanaians —with bayonets fixed, holding off the angry mob. The din was indescribable. Fortunately the place had not been overrun or fired upon. But we could see that we were surrounded, and the gleam of the muzzles of assorted weapons in the hands of the rabble was an urgent reminder of the peril in which we all stood.

On entering the foyer, which was full of U.N. troops, our eyes fell on half a dozen screaming Congolese soldiers who were being held down by our own men. They had been let in when the pressure outside became too great on the promise that they would be allowed to meet Lumumba, who was in a room on the upper floor. Two of their companions had gone in and they were trying to force their way to join them. On reaching the locked door of the room in which Lumumba was sheltered, I saw another group of Congolese soldiers struggling to get in, but the U.N. security guard, Sergeant Victor Noble, was gallantly holding them off. I somehow managed to squeeze into the room through the noise and confusion, followed by Ankrah and Rikhye.

The scene inside will always live in my memory. There was Lumumba in his shirt sleeves in a chair in a corner while a seemingly demented Baluba soldier was shouting and stamping in front of him. A couple of Ghana officers, a Moroccan captain, and some other military personnel were there to prevent any physical harm being done to their unexpected guest. Lumumba was shouting out his replies in a Congolese language, obviously without carrying much conviction with his angry questioner. It was impossible to do anything in that bedlam and I ordered the Baluba to be taken away. He was bodily carried out, struggling vigorously.

Lumumba got up to greet me, holding my hand firmly in both of his and thanking me for coming. I told him how sad I felt at seeing him in that plight, but he could rest assured that come what may, we would not allow the soldiers outside to lay hands on him. I said I hoped this terrible ordeal would convince him and other Congolese leaders of their primary duty to their country and their people to compose their differences and to lead them to orderly progress. If ugly fratricidal quarrels continued, the country would fall apart and lose its independence. Lumumba said he valued my words and was anxious for a settlement with Kasavubu whom he wanted to see, but had received no response. He had agreed to the demand of the Baluba soldiers to return them to their homes in Kasai. He would uphold the law and the constitution, and he expressed confidence in the support of Parliament. From my position of vantage and that of Lumumba's discomfiture, I tried to extract promises from him which, I felt, would be of help in dealing with the constitutional crisis. These I got, but as events were to prove, the initiative had already passed out of his hands. At that time, however, neither he nor I knew it.

Soon an unexpected visitor appeared in the person of Ambassador Andrew Djin of Ghana, who had somehow managed to inveigle his way into the building. Djin began by blaming the Ghana officers for holding Lumumba in custody and for not taking adequate precautions for his safety. Taking the cue from him, Lumumba burst into a diatribe against Colonel Ankrah and his men. He had come to the Mess to make a telephone call, he said, and had been detained by the Ghana officers who had confined him to a room. As Prime Minister of the country, he demanded an explanation for his treatment.

Colonel Ankrah could take no more. He shouted at Lumumba, calling him a rat, and threatened to leave with all his men. Djin chimed in and an unseemly altercation began. I put a stop to this and asked Djin to leave. I said I knew that Ankrah had not had a morsel of food or a drop of water since the morning and that for three hours he had been with me trying to get President Kasavubu to call off the Baluba soldiers. And now we had come, at great risk to our own lives, to save Lumumba. If the ambassador did not leave us to handle the situation, I would depart along with the United Nations troops and he could deal with the matter as he thought best. At this Lumumba clung on to me, thanking me profusely and saying he had nothing against the Colonel and his men who had done all they could for him.

With Djin's departure, I conferred with Ankrah and others about what could be done to get Lumumba away, for by now the night was far advanced and the noise outside was becoming deafening. If we delayed longer, the preparations for siege would be complete and then all of us would be in much graver danger. The plan was that I would go out through the front door with much noise and ceremony to divert the attention of the besiegers while Lumumba would be spirited away by a back door through the kitchen.

Leaving Ankrah behind, I came out accompanied by Brigadier Rikhye and the interpreter. The concentric ring of U.N. troops opened up to let us reach our car while the Baluba soldiers crowded around us. The bubbling mass of Congolese, hurling imprecations at us, fortunately let the car pass through. As we moved away, we could see dark figures digging trenches all around the Mess and setting up mortars and machine-guns.

On arrival at 'Le Royal' we waited impatiently for news. It came soon after. The ruse had worked. Lumumba, surrounded by U.N. troops, had been smuggled out through the back door, pushed into a waiting jeep and driven off at high speed followed by another with a U.N. armed escort. By the time the Congolese soldiers had realized what was afoot the jeep with its burden had picked up speed. They tried to pursue it and someone grabbed at Lumumba's shirt, tearing it from his back. When news got around that the prey had escaped, the siege of the Mess was lifted, to the intense relief of all of us at ONUC Headquarters.

Hammarskjold's prompt reply to my cable informing him of the day's events cheered us enormously. He himself was under strong attack in the Security Council for the failure of ONUC to prevent the overthrow of the constitution. Said Hammarskjold: 'We have followed with crossed fingers and deep engagement your road through another day of sound and fury, so typical of all the facts you mention in your cables and so remote from even the wildest imagination of those in the Security Council who believe that they know everything about the Congo.'

Late that night I was paid a visit by the Soviet Ambassador, Yakovliev, white-haired and distinguished, who had held high office in his country before being sent to the Congo. He had seen me once previously and had asked if I knew what was going on in the country. When I turned the question back on him, he said he was extremely puzzled. He complained of the treatment Soviet doctors and specialists had received in Orientale Province, many of them having been beaten up by the Congolese. They had been sent on a mission of mercy as part of Soviet bilateral aid to a province thought to be friendly. When they protested that they had come as friends, the Congolese had beaten them all the more saying that they were in any case white men. The mistake they made was to dress up in Belgian colonial style in shorts, thus making themselves indistinguishable from the detested Flemish. The doctors soon withdrew from the perils of the bush to the haven of Stanleyville, where they sat around impatiently while the considerable number of crates of medicines and stores they had brought with them remained largely unopened.

On the present occasion, however, Yakovliev had come with a specific request. That morning he had received a curt letter from the President informing him of the severance of diplomatic relations between the two countries and demanding his departure within twenty-four hours, after which diplomatic immunities would be withdrawn. His repeated attempts to call on the President had been brusquely rejected. The Embassy of Czechoslovakia had been given a similar ultimatum. I expressed shock at the discourteous treatment of the envoy of a great country and asked the Ambassador if I should try to intercede on his behalf, at least to allow him a little more time to make his preparations. But the Ambassador had made up his mind, and I subsequently learnt that all day long smoke had been billowing from the Embassy chimney as documents were being destroyed. All that Yakovliev asked for was United Nations help in allowing two Soviet planes to land at Ndjili airport that night to fly him and his staff home. He also hoped we would provide United Nations troops to protect the Embassy and ensure that there were no ugly incidents at the airport at the time of departure.

I readily agreed and issued the necessary orders. The Ambassador then asked for permission for a plane to evacuate Soviet personnel from Stanleyville, which also was promptly given. I enquired about the remaining Soviet planes which had been sent to Stanleyville and which the Congolese were claiming as part of Soviet aid to the country. Yakovliev said they had not been given, only lent, and that they would be flown back. I then asked about the medicines and other stores and pressed that they be left behind as a humanitarian act since the United Nations was in very short supply. Yakovliev agreed. The crates came in very handy subsequently as many were found to contain considerable quantities of vodka, which proved to be a blessing to our hard-pressed Ethiopian troops in Stanleyville.

Lumumba, who had meanwhile gone to earth, probably at the Ghana Embassy, sent me a letter asking for permission for A.N.C. troops to be flown in from Stanleyville 'for the security of the country and of persons'. He also wanted the Stanleyville airport to be put under the control of the 'Government'. But which Government? We did not reply to or act on the letter except to make sure that Stanleyville airport was securely under U.N. control and we sent instructions to the Ethiopian Commander accordingly. But the episode showed that while Kasavubu, Lumumba, and Mobutu all professed their anxiety to end the crisis by compromise, they continued to work against each other and to seek the use of force to worst their opponents.

Mobutu's illegal seizure of power had spread a wave of criticism in many countries against Hammarskjold's handling of the situation. The Security Council was in session at the time and the news electrified the debate and sharpened the rift between the Secretary-General and the Soviet Union. It also raised serious misgivings in the minds of the African and Asian countries. Nehru sent a critical letter to Hammarskjold saying that the situation in the Congo seemed to be extremely unclear and asking what the U.N. Force was doing if the constitutional processes could be so easily subverted. Hammarskjold cabled the letter to me with the following comments: 'I think it will carry additional weight if I could transmit your own comments. I will add mine but [they] would be more on the political margin, while you are at the centre—and how! (Thank God.)'

I replied with a strongly-worded assessment of the situation which placed the responsibility where it belonged, namely on the Congolese leaders themselves. At the same time I drew attention to the controversy raging around the questions of intervention and non-intervention by ONUC in the domestic affairs of the country which arose out of the limited mandate of the Security Council. Another purpose was to caution the Indian delegation to the United Nations, and particularly its leader, Mr. Krishna Menon, to avoid taking a line divergent to that of Hammarskjold's, in view of India's heavy commitment to ONUC and my personal involvement.

Hammarskjold's reactions to my message were evident from his playful reply:

Last Friday I felt I took a long step towards making governments face the naked realities of the Congo. Today I felt I presented the girl still dressed in thick woollen winter suit. Do you mind my going one step further and stripping her not in order to tease but in order to force governments out of this atmosphere of unreality? Please cable me early whether you would permit me to use—with some slight but unavoidable editing in view of thin skins and sensitive nerves—your reply to Nehru's letter as 'report received from the Special Representative in the Congo, Ambassador Dayal'? (Of course, it would go in your own form uncensored to Nehru.) I know the effect of your words which, as all your reports, convey with such utter precision an atmosphere still unknown to all but Slim[1] who has seen nightmare with his own eyes—although that already still was before what is now happening. I repeat, please send immediately your reaction. I think you can trust our judgement as regards editing.

I demurred to Hammarskjold's request. I pointed out that my comments were intended for his and Nehru's private ear and not for publication or attribution. Instead, I suggested the idea of a report couched in more aseptic language, highlighting

[1] Mongi Slim, Ambassador of Tunisia to the United Nations, who had attended the Léopoldville Conference of African Foreign Ministers held at the end of August 1960.

the practical issues and attempting a clarification of the concepts of intervention and non-intervention.

Hammarskjold wired back, 'I agree with you, on sober afterthought, that your reply to Nehru is too hot to be used without possible damage to our mission. However, I believe your suggestion is excellent both as to type of report and to timing. Therefore, please prepare report of UNOGIL[1] type for publication here say Tuesday or Wednesday next week.'

Thus began the practice of the submission to the Secretary-General by the Special Representative, of formal reports on the situation which were published as official U.N. documents. Hammarskjold thought his arguments would carry greater punch if they were supported by hard facts from ONUC's official reports. The pressures were thus partly diverted from his shoulders for it became easier for critics to turn to the man on the spot, who was no longer clothed in the cloak of anonymity. I realized of course that I would now share the burden with my chief in a more direct and public sense, but I was prepared for the risk if it would afford any insulation from criticism to Hammarskjold personally or to his office, for while the Special Representative was expendable, the office of the Secretary-General was not.

In my First Progress Report (euphemistically so called), published on 20 September 1960,[2] I pointed to the unique character of the mission in the history of international organization, as it had to deal with new problems and situations in the general spirit of the mandate but without the benefit of experience from the past. I presented a detailed breakdown of the difficulties we faced in the field, and of the positive achievements of the U.N. team, every one of which was a vital contribution to the continued survival of the country.

This report, whose publication coincided with the opening of the Fifteenth Session of the General Assembly, was much in demand by delegations and it created quite an impact on world opinion. For the first time, an authoritative account had been given of the appalling problems confronting the Congo and ONUC, and of the difficult choices the mission had to make.

---

[1] UNOGIL—United Nations Observation Group in the Lebanon (1958) of which I was a member.
[2] Security Council Document S/4531.

At the General Assembly session, the document provided much grist to the speeches of delegates who used its authority to press for restoration of the constitution and a return to legality. But the outspoken comments angered Mobutu and Kasavubu; the second report which Hammarskjold asked for some weeks later angered them even more.

CHAPTER 6

Heat Without Light

At New York things had not been going well for the Secretary-General. The sharp decline in the political situation which began during Cordier's whirlwind mission had alarmed the African countries. Most of them favoured Lumumba's nationalist and pan-African ideas, but they realized, as was evident from their stand at the Conference of African Foreign Ministers held at Léopoldville, that Lumumba would have to be yoked down to ensure better cooperation between him and his Cabinet as well as with the President and the United Nations. They felt that this could best be done through institutional arrangements. Hammarskjold was thus under pressure from African—and Asian—delegates to restore the balance and to repudiate Cordier's actions. He decided to forestall a demand for a meeting of the Security Council by calling for one himself.

In his report to the Council, Hammarskjold asked it to 're-affirm its request to all States to refrain from any action which might tend to impede the restoration of law and order or to aggravate differences'. He also asked for a clarification of the mandate to empower U.N. troops to take suitable action for the protection of civilian lives. He drew attention to the difficult financial situation and proposed the establishment of a special fund for the Congo, to which he invited voluntary contributions from governments, exclusively for use in the civilian assistance programme.

The Security Council met on 9 September to hear a statement by Hammarskjold who presented his proposals for financial assistance, followed by a report on the constitutional crisis and the problems of bilateral aid and outside intervention. Hammarskjold explained the events leading up to and following Kasavubu's removal of Lumumba and he offered the opinion that while the Head of State had the constitutional right to revoke the mandate of the Prime Minister and that his decision was effective if signed by constitutionally responsible ministers, the Prime Minister, for his part, had no right to dismiss the President. Be that as it may, the Secretary-General added, U.N. officials in the Congo had instructions 'to avoid any action by which, directly or indirectly, openly or by implication, they would pass judgement on the stand taken by either one of the parties in the conflict'. Hammarskjold explained the reasons for Cordier's action in closing the airport 'so as to be certain that the U.N. would be able to operate in fulfilment of its mandate, whatever happened'. He went on to say that there had been no consultation with the authorities nor any prior reference to him because of the extreme urgency of the problem. He added: 'I assume full personal responsibility for what has been done on my behalf', adding that he would submit the question to the Council for 'its consideration and instruction'. In conclusion, Hammarskjold pressed the Security Council to take a clear line regarding assistance to the Congo.

At the next meeting on 10 September, there was a prolonged discussion regarding the seating of Lumumba's delegation led by Thomas Kanza, or of Kasavubu's team led by Justin Bomboko. While the United States supported Kasavubu, its representative suggested that neither be seated to avoid a fruitless debate. Hammarskjold's comment on the meeting made to me in his message the same evening was as follows: 'I have twice said the Security Council must shoulder its responsibility regarding the airports and radio station. When the Security Council adjourned without saying anything on the issue, and the Soviets did not make their point it means that (1) reason for postponement was not wish by Council to hear Kanza (2) they did not feel obliged to rule on airports and radio. That is the only possible interpretation and it is reinforced by the [Council] President's statement. Your line should be that the Security Council has stepped out of the picture and that the Secretary-General has wished emergency measures be liquidated as soon as possible after negotiating mutually satisfactory arrangements with guarantees of compliance.' Turning to the Congo, Hammarskjold said in his message: 'However, today's military developments plus the fact that Kasavubu has formed his government and broken [*sic*] the Security Council in doing it, mean that you might be tougher, as most definitely we do not wish to upset present developments by steps which suddenly would give one party both propaganda opening and military cover (by possible introduction "faithful" troops); this most definitely would be to play in the hands of one of the parties.' Hammarskjold's message concluded with the following: 'Sorry, this is limit of our wisdom for tonight but I am sure your own political wisdom would fill in the gaps.'

At the 14 September meeting of the Security Council, the Soviet representative, Kuznetsov, was replaced by Valerian Zorin, who was noted for his hard-hitting speeches and matching actions. Zorin made a scathing attack on Hammarskjold accusing him of collaborating with the NATO countries in a colonialist plot to help Belgium remain in the Congo, of failure to consult the Central Government, and of actively working against it. Accusing the Secretary-General of choosing 'specialists from the Western camp' (he named Bunche and Cordier), Zorin said that Hammarskjold was trying to set up a U.N. trusteeship in the Congo.

Hammarskjold made a point-by-point reply, concluding as follows: 'That leads me to end this intervention by quoting a passage from a report received from Ambassador Dayal. Ambassador Dayal took over responsibility eight days ago; he has no responsibility for what happened before that time. As we all know, he is a man of very great independence and we would not have hesitated to take another line if he had disapproved of action taken by his predecessors. This is what he says: "It has been made clear, times without number, that the United Nations is here to help but not to intervene, to advise but not to order, to conciliate but not to take sides. We are holding ourselves scrupulously aloof. We have refused to take any position if it could even remotely be considered as an act of intervention. . . ." '

Hammarskjold's personal reactions to the Soviet attack, which had left him astonished but undaunted, reached me the next day in his cable: 'This is also a meeting in never-never land, culminating in speeches of the delegate of U.S.S.R.— repeating his attacks on us for not consulting the legitimate and only legitimate Central Government of Congo—without a shirt on its back and saved from assassination by those who are now attacked.'

The session of the Security Council ended in complete deadlock. The Secretary-General did not receive the guidance and instructions for which he had asked and was left to deal with the confusion as best he could. The next procedural move was to take the question of the Congo to a Special Session of the General Assembly, a move that Hammarskjold welcomed since he knew that the Soviet attack there would be blunted by a massive vote in his favour, thus further isolating the Soviet group.

In his telegram to me that evening, Hammarskjold summed up his impressions of the infructuous Security Council debate as follows:

Your cable this night . . . arrived as an antiphon to the somewhat unmelodious oratory of the Security Council. The Soviet delegation, obviously completely unaware of the latest developments, ran a harsh cold-war strategy of the oldest type and led the Council to a vote on the Afro-Asian resolution which was in fact supported by the Africans. This was unexpected in view of Soviet sensitivity to African opinion but this round they have proven strangely unperceptive to the currents in the regional group.

The most interesting point is that while your visitor whom you will help out two hours from now,[1] obviously had realized definite changes in situation and therefore bowed to orders from President, the key melody here was pro Lumumba.

If none of the eager conciliators to be gets successfully into action tomorrow, I am pretty certain that Ceylon–Tunisia resolution will be carried in Special Session with overwhelming majority, over isolation of Soviet group plus Guinea, in one single meeting. This will not change anything in your power or your mandate but it would give us the funds and it would give purging to the General Assembly majority of the Soviet accusations against the Command and us all. They started with 'partiality', 'plotting', and 'tool of imperialism' but ended after two days with retreat to 'regrettable errors that should be corrected' after Zorin had heard series of expressions of confidence from African States.

The real game is on your side and I know how well you play it, truly in the U.N. spirit but also truly in the interest of the poor Congolese people and the rest of Africa.

[1] This is a reference to the Soviet Ambassador's expulsion from the Congo.

The debate was now transferred to the General Assembly under the so-called 'Uniting for Peace' resolution. The Emergency Special Session began on 17 September in a tense atmosphere. The Soviet delegation resumed its attack on Hammarskjold in terms of the harshest invective.

Stung by the virulence of Zorin's attack, Hammarskjold, in the course of a brief intervention said: 'The General Assembly knows me well enough to realize that I would not wish to serve one day beyond the point at which such continued service would be, and would be considered to be, in the best interests of the Organization.' He knew the sentiments of the members, particularly the Africans and Asians, and expected to receive a vote which could be construed as an expression of their confidence in him. In that he was not wrong, for Zorin had focused the issue on Hammarskjold's personality and office, and not on questions of U.N. policy and principles.

Seventeen delegates from Africa and Asia proposed a draft resolution which requested the Secretary-General to continue to take vigorous action and to assist the Central Government in the restoration and maintenance of law and order. The resolution was adopted by a vote of seventy in favour, and one against and eleven abstentions, which included the Soviet bloc, France, and South Africa.

Hammarskjold summed up the results of the Emergency Special Session in a cable to me immediately after the vote:

The real significance of today's result in the General Assembly is on general political level more than on yours or ours. It means that a certain big power had shown its hand so badly, especially in attack on Secretariat and Command as stumbling block for certain ambitions, and that in fact, the United Afro-Asians in demonstration vote had to tell them off. This situation, in turn, was registered by the big power beforehand and all got definite proof that if the Afro-Asians stick together, or if only the Africans stick together, they represent a new big power to which certain others have to bow. You know this theory on which I have worked now for two months. Today it was fully vindicated and I regard the fact that the Afro-Asian group in this way stood up to the test, found its own strength and a new cohesion, is more important than any other result. Hope that Nehru, who is coming Sunday, will use this to the full (somewhat in keeping, if I may say so, with the philosophy of my annual report to the General Assembly). Nehru's instructions have been most useful in stabilizing

A disillusioned Bunche briefs a sombre Dayal

Dayal reviews U.N. troops in the Léopoldville stadium on U.N. Day

Hammarskjold in the Congo enlightening Adoula and Gizenga

group action. Alas, if you could get the sense of all this across to some people where you stay! This was a good day our end, but just as at your end, the hurricane may start again tomorrow.

Now that the General Assembly had made a solemn appeal for conciliation the conciliators took fresh heart and redoubled their efforts, which had been bogged down by the difficulty of obtaining any firm commitments from the politicians—especially Kasavubu—to anything. I had cabled Hammarskjold that 'the peace-makers have been busy but they may be counting without their host. The Parliamentary Conciliation Committee ran into a snag, which may have been a trap. The four African envoys with Ghaleb [of the U.A.R.] have also been shuttling to and fro till they ran into a road-block at the President's House when they were kept waiting for two hours without an audience.'

Later, I was told that the African envoys had come very close to bringing about a rapprochement. The Parliamentary group claimed to have obtained the signatures of both Kasavubu and Lumumba to their plan. Hopes had been rekindled of a solution to the political impasse, when suddenly Kasavubu reversed direction. Lumumba gave a press conference at which he flourished a document containing the compromise that had been reached but which Kasavubu later repudiated. He said that the U.N. official Jean David had participated in all the negotiations and could bear witness to the fact.

The document of reconciliation which came into our hands, and which was dated 17 September 1960, sought to establish effective procedures for ensuring full Cabinet responsibility and eliminating all possibility of arbitrary action by the Prime Minister. The document, which was skilfully drafted, took care of all the grievances of the President and it would have provided an excellent basis for the orderly conduct of government business and more harmonious and fruitful relations with the United Nations. Lumumba had made far-reaching concessions in the interest of reconciliation. At ONUC headquarters we felt that the document gave us all that we wanted. The compromise would have taken the wind out of the sails of Hammarskjold's critics for it was exactly what the African states had wanted in proposing their resolution to the General Assembly. And the Soviet charges that Hammarskjold was responsible for

Lumumba's overthrow and for setting up Mobutu's arbitrary rule would have been effectively demolished.

The President's repudiation of such an excellent and entirely workable compromise therefore came to us as a shock. Mobutu had earlier that day (21 September) sent a party of soldiers to arrest Lumumba at his house, but they had been turned back by the U.N. Ghana guard. Mobutu came to U.N. headquarters to complain bitterly and uttered all kinds of threats. I informed Hammarskjold that Timberlake had called on me and said he was 'keeping aloof and had not given Mobutu any funds. I suggested he might caution his other colleagues to show similar restraint.'

As our hopes were drooping, a sudden development took place on 22 September to revive them momentarily. Scared by a mutiny in his own ranks and an attempt on his life Mobutu had turned up at U.N. headquarters 'overworked and bewildered' (as I noted at the time), and asked for a U.N. escort. I reported to New York:

Mobutu suddenly appeared with Kettani to see me with plans for reconciliation. Mobutu was exhausted and unshaven. His plan was to get Kasavubu and Lumumba together under U.N. auspices. The next step would be to have a Round Table Conference. I asked if the parties were agreeable; Mobutu immediately telephoned Kasavubu; he found him evasive but made an appointment for next morning. Mobutu could not contact Lumumba as his line was cut and refused to go to his house for fear of assassination. But he sent a letter to which Lumumba sent back a reply inviting him for tomorrow and asking for the release of Gizenga, Mpolo, and two Secretaries of State (arrested that morning) as a gesture of sincerity. Mobutu is in a dilemma as he had ordered the arrest of Gizenga and Mpolo, and the other two are his friends. But he decided to release all four to demonstrate his 'generosity and fear of God'.

Mobutu was as good as his word; from my office he sent hand-written orders for the release of the four men. I later heard that Kasavubu's followers had tried to spirit them away in a waiting plane to Katanga, but U.N. troops intervened to rescue them. When Mobutu heard of this he was furious with Kasavubu. Kasavubu was also under pressure as several Congolese army officers called on him and urged reconciliation under threats. Kasavubu, nervous and fearful, was anxious to establish contact with Mobutu who alone could save him in an emergency if the officers carried out their threats. He sent for Kettani and asked him to set up a liaison group which would keep him in touch with A.N.C. headquarters through the intermediary of the U.N. When Kettani asked about the plan of reconciliation Kasavubu readily replied that he would send me the text. If I had any doubts about Kasavubu having initially given his agreement to the plan which he later denied, they were now removed. But he bided his time and never sent me the promised plan. Okito and his parliamentarians saw me that day in an optimistic mood as they felt that mutual fear of Mobutu was again propelling Kasavubu and Lumumba towards each other. Lumumba, fearing assassination, also seemed in chastened mood. In his letters to me he was profuse in his thanks for the hopeful trends and promised full cooperation with the U.N. I learnt with relief that his foreign advisers, Serge Michel, a leftist of doubtful vintage, Madame Blouin (whom Hammarskjold had described as the 'Madame Du Barry of the Congo'), and a Belgian named Grootout, had all been sent away.

There was, unfortunately, much misunderstanding about Jean David's role in all this. David had convinced Cordier that he had the influence with the President to get his agreement to a form of compromise that would delimit the respective functions of the President and Prime Minister and thus end the constitutional crisis. Cordier therefore gave his *carte blanche* to have a try. When the Congolese parliamentarians and African envoys got into the act without David having been able to produce the promised goods, we cautioned David not to cross wires with the other two groups. When things began to go badly with the peace-makers, they blamed David and the U.N. for interfering with their efforts and misleading Kasavubu. I had always been a little doubtful about David's pretensions and feared that he was more anxious to gain personal credit than genuinely to promote a reconciliation. It was obvious that David's utility to ONUC, especially after his involvement in the political roundabout, had been exhausted, and at his request he was allowed to depart.

Below the surface of the efforts at peace-making, a parallel underhand drama had been going on whose objectives were of a very different order. There were attempts to arrest Lumumba and his associates, stirrings of the A.N.C., and assassination attempts on Mobutu. Kasavubu was alternately leading on the conciliators and dropping them. Meanwhile Mobutu released a series of letters said to have been exchanged between President Nkrumah and Lumumba, including two alleged to have been sent by Lumumba and Gizenga to other recipients. It was given out that the letters had been found in Lumumba's portfolio which he had been forced to abandon when he took shelter in the Ghana Mess. Some of the letters were authentic but two which were extremely damaging to Lumumba and Gizenga were obvious forgeries. They were all published in the Congolese press and created quite a sensation.

One forged letter from Lumumba purported to contain a plan to expel the U.N. and to replace it by Soviet aid, to carry out a large number of arrests and executions and, in short, to set up a reign of terror. I asked our experts to make enquiries about the letter and they were categorical that it was a crude forgery. But many among the Congolese were tricked into believing in its authenticity. It was clear that some foreign hand was behind the conspiracy, for the Congolese did not have the means—or the experience—to produce such a document whose clear aim was to destroy the efforts of the peace-makers.

The sinister influences working on Kasavubu were alarmed as hopes for reconciliation grew, and he was persuaded to resile. Mobutu, who had been frightened by his own soldiers into playing a mediatory role—although a very short-lived one— soon felt himself strong enough to call the whole thing off. There followed two unfortunate incidents for which Lumumba was responsible, but which really had nothing to do with the main issue. One day Lumumba left his house for a drive in the city with escort, after which he gave a press conference; this aroused Mobutu's ire because Lumumba had violated his own 'neutralization'! The next incident was worse. The weekend calm was shattered by an assault on one of Mobutu's Commissioners outside his office by a group of youths who were described as pro-Lumumbist. Mobutu angrily brought the injured Commissioner to our headquarters, and complained that the single Ghana sentry on duty (a rather bewildered young and illiterate soldier who hardly realized what was going on)

had failed in his duty, and he demanded the immediate withdrawal of the Ghana Brigade from the Congo. But what was
really damaging was his firm announcement that reconciliation
was now impossible.

That ended the month-long efforts at political pacification,
but not before the African envoys had tried one final gambit.
They asked me to close down the radio station and airports and
to place them under U.N. control! And they begged me to use
U.N. machinery to set up a 'firm government'. I declined the
temptation to remind them of the events of 5 September and
their aftermath.

The Western ambassadors had remained conspicuously absent while the peace-makers were bustling about. They now
came out with various interesting suggestions. Scott argued
that the United Nations should step in and set up a stable
government. When I reminded him of our limited mandate, he
opined that a United Nations Commission consisting of Africans
and Asians should do it, and, to help Kasavubu form a government under Ileo, Lumumba should be sent abroad as an ambassador. Timberlake told me he felt that a constitutional settlement was out of the picture and he was asking Washington to
allow him to do business with Mobutu's Commissioners. Charpentier, the French Ambassador, took a 'wait and see' attitude
but warned that the Congo should not expect any outside
financial help. When I reported on the motley suggestions
presented by such a wide spectrum of envoys, Hammarskjold
replied, 'Cannot compete with your evensong, but then the
envoys we have around here are not under the salutary influence of the Léo air. I hope that your envoys manage to
transmit to their opposite numbers here the suggestions they
make and our firm and impartial resistance against pressures
to abuse of our powers.'

The only line now open to ONUC was to try and keep the
situation as fluid as possible and to prevent Mobutu from con-
solidating his hold. We also hoped that pressures on Tshombe
would keep him in order till such time as his foreign advisers
could be made to leave. The arrival of the U.N. Conciliation
Commission could perhaps serve to draw attention to the need
for reconciliation, although we had no great hopes of its success.
At best, we would carry out a holding operation.

By now Lumumba had lost heart completely. He first told Ghaleb (the U.A.R. Ambassador) that he wanted to go to Stanleyville, then he changed his mind and said it would be New York where he would present his case personally to the General Assembly. In the event, he went to neither place.

Mobutu now felt strong enough to announce his list of student Commissioners. Kettani reported that Mobutu was getting increasingly arrogant and unresponsive, and suffering from 'illusions of grandeur'. He pressed his demand for the instant removal of the U.N. Ghana troops—to which he now added Guinea. He told Kettani he was too preoccupied to visit U.N. headquarters, as had been his daily practice, as he was busy receiving ambassadors. He stopped making requests for U.N. food and money for his troops, although we knew the Congo treasury was empty. But he did demand a dozen U.N. aircraft to be placed entirely at his disposal, or he would turn to other sources. Hammarskjold's brief comment was that he was 'not impressed' by Mobutu's threats.

I sent the Secretary-General my summing up of the situation and the steps which we in ONUC felt we should take to deal with it. Hammarskjold replied:

Note carefully this worrying summing up and have strongest understanding for the enormous scope of the problems you are facing. We would be happy to be of any assistance but we cannot add anything of value to your own thinking, planning and action. And we *are* happy to know that the team we have on the spot is one in which we have the fullest confidence. We know that you are doing what is humanly possible with the means at your disposal in the mad situation. But my constant prayer is that the people here would start understanding what is really going on and what is the real problem instead of rehashing the question of whether or not the take-over of the airport was within the Security Council mandate and similar exciting problems useful as a munition in the cold war fight about control of the U.N. which disregards the human problem of the Congo just as callously as it is disregarded by the leaders of the country. . . . Action recommended by you seems wise and is fully approved.

CHAPTER 7

The Disunited Nations

The historic Fifteenth Session of the General Assembly which was attended by a glittering array of captains and kings from all corners of the globe commenced on 20 September 1960. The cold war had been raging in all its fury and a summit meeting projected for the summer had collapsed following the interception of an American U2 spy plane over the Soviet Union. Khrushchev then made a proposal that all Heads of State and Government should attend the debate on disarmament at the forthcoming session of the U.N. General Assembly. The idea was spurned by the Western powers but Khrushchev announced that he would go anyway. The leaders of the East European countries also made known their intention to attend. The Western powers thereupon changed their minds, fearful that Khrushchev would, in their default, steal the show. The Assembly also had on its agenda a proposal for granting independence to colonial countries and peoples which was of particular interest to African and Asian leaders. Sixteen new African states were to be admitted to the Organization, which would give it a new colouring and orientation. With the problem of the Congo dominating the activities of the United Nations, the Fifteenth Session virtually became an African session.

Hammarskjold had shown great understanding of the significance of the new trends in his Introduction to the Annual Report, in which he described the states of Africa and Asia as 'powerful elements in the international community' whose independent voice in the world polity was a factor to be reckoned with. The United Nations was to them their 'main platform' and protector as they 'feel themselves strong as members of the international family but are weak in isolation'.

The Assembly met in an atmosphere of expectancy, not unmixed with apprehension, for if there were to be a failure on the part of so eminent a gathering to achieve minimal understanding on the basic issues, the prospects of world peace would be greatly jeopardized. Hammarskjold, however, hoped that in his private talks with the visiting world statesmen he might be able to secure some degree of support for his policies in the Congo which might be denied him in their public utterances. He, therefore, awaited with considerable anticipation the arrival of the statesmen, though not of all with equal eagerness.

Unfortunately it soon became apparent from the speeches of the assembled dignitaries that disagreements would be further sharpened and made more irreconcilable, and the modest consensus recently achieved at the Emergency Session would be watered down. In his speech, President Eisenhower called for non-intervention in the Congo and proposed a five-point stabilizing programme. The plan, as events were to show, remained a dead letter. The next day the debate took a dramatic turn. President Nkrumah made an impassioned speech in which he strongly criticized the United Nations on the question of intervention and non-intervention. He said, 'It is no more possible for a saint to be neutral on the issue of good and evil than for the United Nations to be neutral on the issue of legality and illegality.' He made a six-point proposal which included the setting up of an all-African U.N. Command, and full support to the Central Government.

The next speaker was Khrushchev. He launched a direct attack on Hammarskjold charging him with 'doing the dirty work' of the colonialists. He asked the Assembly to 'call Mr. Hammarskjold to order and ensure that he does not misuse the position of Secretary-General'. He urged that U.N. troops should be drawn exclusively from African and Asian countries. They should function only at the discretion of Mr. Lumumba's Central Government and they should ensure the normal working of Parliament. Describing the activities of the United Nations as 'disgraceful', Khrushchev charged the Secretariat with violating the inalienable rights of the Congolese people. He then proposed that the post of Secretary-General be abolished and replaced by an executive which should reflect the power equations in the world. The United Nations, he said, included states which were members of Western military blocs, socialist states, and 'neutralist countries'. The collective organ should therefore consist of three persons, each representing one group. He explained that each of these groups had a population of one billion and no one individual could presume to speak on behalf of all of them. Khrushchev's attack on Hammarskjold was expected, though perhaps not its virulence. His 'troika' or 'three-headed god' proposal, as Nehru called it, left the Assembly stunned.

Hammarskjold's impressions of the opening round in the General Assembly were conveyed to me vividly in his words:

Round-up of a day in the cold war. I paused yesterday because speeches in the General Assembly did not bring us one inch forward. Today they brought us two steps backward with eloquent interventions transmitted to you in clear. Good when people get to know where others stand. Of course, one speaker[1] made for African leadership with an all-African operation, the potentialities of which, short of support from outside and from U.N., we know. Another one[2] made the same in his way, but with generous offer of outside support. In doing so, he paid greatest compliment so far paid to U.N. in recognizing that we now were the main obstacle to an expansion of empire into Africa. Neither scored much of success. They received ovation from Soviet bloc and Cuba and Guinea. For obvious reasons I did not reply today. Unfortunately, however, U.S. came out, both in debate and press conference, with uncalled for support, tending to personalize issues (although of course they have nothing to do with me or with you or the operation), thus making it more difficult to straighten things out in due time. My excuse for telling you this is that debate undoubtedly will have echoes among peacemakers. My basic feeling, however, is that very venom of certain statements is a recognition of defeat, which again is of interest for ONUC as it means that it is our duty to continue in the interest of those who wish only the best for the people of the Congo.

In a later message Hammarskjold added to his comments on the debate,

African reception of Friday's African leadership speech was just as could be expected. Especially, Afro-Asians resent being recommended to be put under command of British General on African payroll[3]

[1] The reference is to Nkrumah's speech.
[2] The reference is to Khrushchev.
[3] The reference is to Major-General Alexander, serving as Commander of the Ghana Army.

with instructions from a source the philosophy of which is not particularly appreciated.

Have had great fun in preparing proper reply to yesterday's speeches which will be cabled to you Monday. . . .

Looking forward to arrival of Nehru and Nasser. Would have liked to ask you to come back for Nehru's visit. You might find it useful to send personal situation report which I could give to Nehru Monday. His basic reaction is most helpful, but, as many, he is insufficiently briefed on situation.

When Hammarskjold made his reply on Monday after the weekend recess, his voice was calm, but his words were firm and unbending. As he worked up to his central theme that the issue concerned not a man but an institution he began by reminding the Assembly of the facts of the situation. Drawing their urgent attention to the First Progress Report, he said: 'This paper, submitted by Mr. R. Dayal, will, I am sure, be found very helpful by those who want to get a balanced picture of the realities with which the Organization is dealing.'

After outlining the problems spelt out in the Report, Hammarskjold continued: 'The General Assembly is facing a question not of any specific actions but of principles guiding United Nations activities. In those respects it is a question not of a man but of an institution.' He then went on to say:

Use whatever words you like, independence, impartiality, objectivity —they all describe essential aspects of what, without exception, must be the attitude of the Secretary-General. Such an attitude . . . may at any stage become an obstacle for those who work for certain political aims which would be better served or more easily achieved if the Secretary-General compromised with this attitude. But if he did, how gravely he would then betray the trust of all those for whom the strict maintenance of such an attitude is their best protection in the world-wide fight for power and influence. Thus if the office of the Secretary-General becomes a stumbling block for any one, be he individual, a group, or a government, because the incumbent stands by the basic principles which must guide his whole activity, and if, for that reason, he comes under criticism, such criticism strikes at the very office and the concepts on which it is based. I would rather see that office break on strict adherence to the principle of independence, impartiality, and objectivity than drift on the basis of compromise.

Reminding the Assembly of a fact only too often overlooked,

Hammarskjold said: 'Sometimes one gets the impression that the Congo Operation is looked at as being in the hands of the Secretary-General, as distinct from the United Nations. No: this is your Operation, gentlemen.' And he continued: 'It is for you to indicate what you want done. As the agent of the Organization, I am grateful for any positive advice, but if no such positive advice is forthcoming . . . then I have no choice but to follow my own conviction, guided by the principles to which I have just referred.'

Hammarskjold received a thunderous ovation from the Assembly. He had hoped to divert attention from questions of personality to those of principles and institutions. But Khrushchev, exercising his right of reply, soon made it plain that a question of personalities was equally involved with that of structure and he emphasized that the United Nations must reflect the new constellation of forces in the world. This time his attack was biting and personal. Saying that there were no 'saints on earth', Khrushchev taunted Hammarskjold with the praise he had received from the 'imperialist countries' for acting as an agent of their interests, thus qualifying himself to be their 'saint'. Events in the Congo, he said, were 'only the last drop' which filled the cup of his patience to overflowing. No one could tolerate any longer 'the arbitrary and lawless behaviour' of the United Nations troops in the Congo and, expressing his lack of confidence in Hammarskjold ('to prevent any misinterpretation'), he invited him to resign. He concluded, 'If he himself cannot muster the courage to resign, in let us say a chivalrous way, we shall draw the inevitable conclusions . . .,' and he wanted the Assembly 'not to be deluded by the high-flown words' used by the Secretary-General.

Hammarskjold's immediate reaction was to reply forthwith, but he was dissuaded from doing so by the Assembly President, Frederick Boland of Ireland, and agreed to reply later that day. Hammarskjold, in his reply, said that he had been accused of bias against the socialist countries and of using the United Nations to impose 'a new yoke on the Congo'. He had been called upon to resign by the representative of the Soviet Union who had said there was no room for a man who has 'violated the elementary principles of justice in such an important post as that of Secretary-General'. Hammarskjold continued: 'The

Assembly has witnessed over the last few weeks how historical truth is established. Once an allegation has been repeated a few times, it is no longer an allegation, it is established fact, even if no evidence has been brought out to support it. However, facts are facts and the true facts are there for whosoever cares for the truth. Those who invoke history will certainly be heard by history.' He went on to say that the issue had again been personalized: 'The man does not count; the institution does. A weak or non-existent executive would mean that the United Nations would no longer be able to serve as an effective instrument for active protection of the interests of those many members who need such protection.' By resigning at that difficult and dangerous juncture, he would 'throw the Organization to the winds'. He had no right to do that as he had a responsibility to all those member states for whom the Organization was of decisive importance, for 'it is not the Soviet Union or indeed any other big Power which needs the United Nations for their protection. It is all the others. In this sense, the Organization is first of all their Organization.'

Hammarskjold took up Khrushchev's challenge to him to resign by saying that he would remain at his post during his term of office as a servant of the Organization 'in the interest of all those other nations' as long as they want him to do so. He added, 'It is very easy to resign. It is not so easy to stay on. It is very easy to bow to the wish of a big Power. It is another matter to resist. As is well known to all Members of this Assembly, I have done so before on so many occasions and in many directions and if it is the wish of those nations who see in the Organization their best protection in the present world, I shall now do so again.'

The applause which punctuated Hammarskjold's speech and greeted its conclusion, clearly indicated the wishes of the member states, particularly those from Asia and Africa. Not that they regarded Hammarskjold as indispensable, but at that juncture any change in leadership would put in jeopardy the Congo Operation. As for the Soviet proposal, it would destroy the United Nations itself.

Hammarskjold's reactions to the trials of that eventful day reached me in his words: 'The day has been marked by dramatic outburst by Khrushchev who now considers me to

represent the brigand nations in the U.N. and who proposed a
Soviet U.N. if he did not get satisfaction. You know your part
of the world enough to evaluate the effect.'

The general debate had been going on between these stormy
interludes. Mr. Nehru had made a statesmanlike speech in
which he recognized the difficult responsibilities cast on the
United Nations in the Congo where the situation was complicated and uncertain. Disruptive forces had been let loose and
footholds of colonialism remained. He warned against foreign
intervention or encouragement of one faction against another.
The United Nations had a mediatory role to play and it should
help the Central Government to function properly. Emphasizing the responsibility of the Congolese leaders, he said that
leadership could not be imposed from outside, and any attempt
to do so would lead to conflict. He urged the United Nations to
help the Congolese Parliament to meet so that the Congolese
could iron out their own differences. He expressed concern at
the continued presence and activities of Belgian military and
para-military personnel and suggested that a General Assembly
delegation be sent to enquire into the matter. As for the institutional arrangements, he felt that while broad policy directions
must come from the General Assembly or the Security Council,
the executive direction must not be weakened or divided as it
would impair the capacity for rapid decision. But some organizational changes were desirable, particularly in view of the
emergence of the states of Africa and Asia, and he warned
against any attempt at Charter amendment as that would only
add to the present difficulties.

While the General Assembly proceeded in its stately way,
Hammarskjold held detailed talks with a number of visiting
leaders and he cabled me his impressions of some of them.
Nasser was critical in his public remarks but he showed a
considerable measure of understanding in private discussion.
Hammarskjold had informed me he was having Nasser to
dinner on 30 September and enquired if there were any specific matters that he could bring up with him. I reported to him
the Egyptian Ambassador Ghaleb's suspicions about the quarters from which Mobutu was receiving financial and other
forms of support, to which I had added a complaint that we
in ONUC found ourselves in the position of being responsible

for whatever happened, without the necessary authority to take effective action.

Hammarskjold cabled me his impressions of his talk with Nasser:

My guest of honour at dinner tonight obviously has been vaccinated against Lumumbism and may have infection but it has not given him any fever. In fact all he now wants is a strong government without East or West influence, irrespective of who the top man is. I replied that I would be happy enough if there would be any government at all, provided of course that there was no East or West influence.

Assembled personages are not interested in what we may come to do, but only in what supposedly we have not done—or perhaps done —I do not know for certain.

Nkrumah the other day said he was informed resolution of 14 July gave us full authority for take-over. So, in never-never land, you may even have all the necessary authority but no responsibility! To be serious, you state the sad truth.

Ghaleb truly reflects his master's suspicion. Evening's guest of honour asked me several times who paid the troops. I could in greatest honesty be a sheep.

We also sit on volcano—with the pleasant quality that, if it erupts, even the Organization is likely to disappear underground. This may be meagre consolation but it creates the right kind of philosophical approach.

Hammarskjold had a private dinner for Nehru in his suite, and he relayed to me with disarming candour his impressions of the conversation. Hammarskjold was deeply grateful to Nehru for rallying the Asian and African delegations which had been left dazed by Khrushchev's outburst. Nehru had not faltered in his support of United Nations actions in the Congo and had cold-shouldered Khrushchev's proposal to set up a divided executive. In his message to me on his conversations with Nehru, Hammarskjold struck a note of disappointment:

Climax of the day was private dinner for Nehru and Krishna Menon who gave the impression of not repeat not having read your memoranda but certainly had read the one distributed by Gromyko. Questions of temperature fully adjusted to this background. Had therefore to start all over again ABC regarding facts of life, I hope with the result that pupils discovered that they have something to learn before they can read. Frankly, we are hardened but every time you discover again that the word of Mr. Lumumba is regarded as evidence, because he is Prime Minister, while we are suspected to serve God knows what interest and therefore to colour our picture. I wonder how we are able to achieve anything at all. No previous experience which after all extends over years covering also Suez, clearly indicating our aims and methods of work, seems to be remembered the moment what we say does not rhyme with what the modern 'world revolutionaries' want to think. And yet, in this case, guest is one of the best and I have nothing but respect for him.

General atmosphere here now is that the main Secretariat activities cannot be expected to go home without having 'got something' and that therefore majority, with Secretary-General's collusion, should make some concession regarding working methods, checks and controls. I have said clearly that this is not a case for compromises and that such a compromise exposes the Organization to greater risk than the crisis that might follow if we permit white to remain white, and black, black.

Hammarskjold's telegram the next day indicated one of the matters about which Nehru had considerable misgivings which Nasser and Nkrumah also fully shared. The message stated:

Nehru yesterday asked who is now paying the A.N.C., how it is explained that A.N.C. has turned its loyalty from Lumumba and what relationship there is between our financial assistance and Mobutu authority. Implications of their questions are obvious. My reply was to give picture of first payment (of tenth) as it emerged from your reports, with nuances flowing from later additional clarifications, and further to say that as to the situation of today, I simply was not clear on how matters were arranged (this latter part of my reply is, as you know, absolutely accurate, although seemingly evasive) as we have only incidental and spotty information which does not give picture of whether, or to what extent, U.N. funds are directly involved and in what name and how they may have been paid in particular cases.

Hammarskjold asked for a full report on the exact form and channels through which U.N. funds were used to make payments to the A.N.C. and the extent to which Mobutu and others had made payments on their own and from what source. This, of course, related to the one million dollars asked for by Cordier on the night of Kasavubu's *coup*, and which was received some four or five days later from New York. All U.N. funds were in the control of and were disbursed by U.N. financial experts from headquarters through the U.N. military command or other authorized agencies. I accordingly asked General von Horn for a full enquiry and report.

The Supreme Commander's report reached me a few days later and I immediately passed it on to the Secretary-General. Mobutu's troops had not been paid one million dollars after all; they had been paid only 100,000. The objectives of the U.N. Command were to induce the Congolese soldiers to appear for training and to enable Mobutu to replace funds allegedly seized from the departing Belgians for payment to the troops. Also, a sum of $370,000 had been paid on General Iyassou's recommendation to the mutinous A.N.C. troops at Stanleyville, while a further $160,000 had been disbursed in two instalments to A.N.C. troops at Luluabourg who were on the verge of starvation. Additional amounts had been spent at other A.N.C. centres in providing food to the soldiers as a humanitarian act. Von Horn's report differed from his earlier explanation of the expenditure, but I naturally assumed that his latest enquiries had revealed the true and full picture. There was of course no suggestion on the part of any of the critics of misappropriation in aid of a cause regarded by them as unworthy and undeserving.

Hammarskjold had pinned his hopes on support from the African and Asian countries and he found a dichotomy between their public utterances and their private assurances. If they held fast, he would be able to surmount the crisis, but if not, he saw a dark future for the United Nations. He strongly hinted for the first time of the possibility of his own resignation. His anxieties were reflected in his comments: 'There is a world of difference between what is said in public and the views expressed behind closed doors. The Afro-Asian front holds when there is no gallery. The role of Nehru will now be decisive. If he sways, the public Afro-Asian front may break with very far-reaching consequences for the Organization, and, as subordinated matter, for my attitude.'

The message ended on a more personal and relaxed note: 'Weekend mostly quiet and all of us being sleepy I will force everybody not to stay in office for the night as has been the rule for the last three months. Therefore, the late summing-up cable from you will not get as quick a reply as usual.'

Among the gladiators who took the ring was President Sekou

Touré of Guinea. A trenchant critic of United Nations policies in the Congo, he proposed a resolution to seat the representatives of the Central Government in the United Nations. This proposal was to have unfortunate consequences as it provoked the Western powers to press later for the seating of Kasavubu's delegation, a decision which effectively killed all hopes of reconciliation by giving recognition to one faction in preference to others in the struggle for power.

Hammarskjold sent me a cable of his talks with Sekou Touré whom he entertained at a private dinner:

Sekou Touré made his speech yesterday, and introduced a resolution calling for the immediate seating of representatives of Lumumba. His proposal and this vague threat have to be seen together as became apparent yesterday night when I had him to dinner. As to be expected, my guest reflected, all through, stands well known to you from certain representatives in Léo. His perspectives and line of interpretation coincide with that which presumably is Lumumba's. Thus, the Organization and its agents appear to him as playing a highly partial anti-Lumumba game. And, of course, in a delicate operation of this kind, people may easily succeed in putting the interpretation they want into circulation. My guest was convinced that conflict would have been over and resolved in Lumumba's favour if U.N. Force had not been in Congo. This has to be seen together with fact that he seems to consider that it would have been and is legitimate and perhaps necessary for Lumumba to turn Congo into nation through suppression of opposition by actions touching on civil war. I do not believe that he wants to recognize that this latter approach is irreconcilable for U.N. both with Charter philosophy, rejecting force as a means to solution of even external conflicts; with its present mandate to maintain law and order; and with its duty to forestall developments which unavoidably would create a threat to international peace and security.

My guest made numerous innuendoes but refused to be specific on any point. They covered not only all sorts of bribery and corruption presumably through agents of other governments but also similar occurrences within U.N. framework and, I guess, implying general criticism of our manner of using U.N. funds. I could only state my ignorance as to outside briberies and emphatically reject accusations against our own people. He said generously that he would not dig into these matters or 'open dossier' if he got approval of resolution seating Central Government representatives. For this he required my active assistance. Otherwise, everything might have to be brought out into the open. He further wanted my assistance to get immediately a Commission of five Afro-Asians under Krishna Menon's leadership to go to Léopoldville to straighten matters out there, presumably with the aim of establishing P.M. in relation to competitors. My reaction regarding resolution was to state that guest, in every respect of course, was a free man who said whatever he considered it responsible to say, under any circumstances, that further, I did not for a second hesitate to open our dossier, if necessary, although I was not particularly in favour of that kind of public diplomacy, but that, finally, it was for the members alone to decide to what extent they wanted to wash linen in public.

More positive was his clear interest in parliamentary approach although he appeared to consider several members as being bought. Compare in these various respects today's message from Nkrumah which I cable you separately.

Hammarskjold's message worried me as we had a Guinean battalion in the U.N. Force which had loyally carried out its directives and I feared that Sekou Touré's threats would affect its attitude. But much more than my concern about this was my worry about Sekou Touré's innuendoes about the misuse of U.N. funds. For while charges of partiality or misjudgement could be defended, financial irregularities could not. I immediately asked Hammarskjold to send me a team of auditors to examine ONUC's accounts. A team was soon sent and after a thorough inspection reported that it found the accounts in exemplary condition.

Hammarskjold had recorded his views on 'inter-African' politics 'around the Congo' during his visit to that country in August, and he made an analysis of the role of Nkrumah and Sekou Touré in promoting a sentiment of 'strongly emotional pan-Africanism'. He thought that Nkrumah had, more than Sekou Touré, influenced Lumumba in this direction. His observations follow:

He [Nkrumah] would align himself with Guinea on a policy with strong affiliations in relation to Moscow, but with him in the leadership, because of his stronger international position and African support. He would further associate himself with Lumumba on the same basic line as with Sekou Touré. Parallel with these developments he would seek cooperation with those leaders in the south of Nigeria who are of the same temperamental band and opposed to the north of Nigeria. I would not be surprised if he pressed the line even to the point of fomenting domestic troubles followed by a breaking up of the Federation. Were he to succeed he would have anchored Togo so that Olympio[1] would be practically strangled. It would at the same time have got a scissor grip on at least the coastal area of French Equatorial Africa. The line would then be opened for a coastal empire stretching from Ghana down to and including the ex-Belgian Congo with an arm into the Bakongo part of Angola. Guinea would remain the west-side position which, for the time being, would be closely allied—Syria style—without any territorial link.

Of course Nkrumah is aware that this would be strongly resisted not only by the U.N. but also by the Western big powers, while the Soviet Union with the naive support of Israel would be quite willing to play into their hands for different reasons, but in a way which would lend encouragement to such an African drive. Were Nkrumah to succeed, and he would be likely to get support from the U.A.R. not in the beginning and not openly, but as time developed. In this game I hold Lumumba to be an ignorant pawn, in his utter lack of experience of the big political currents, balances and pressures. The perspective is forbidding but real, I have already said that the Congo should not be permitted to become another Korea—nor should it become a Hungary or a Munich.

Nkrumah was somewhat subdued during the General Assembly session at New York as his letters to Lumumba had been seized and broadcast only a few days earlier. I asked Hammarskjold to take up with Nkrumah our complaint about direct instructions to the Ghana Brigade from Accra and I quoted an instance—a rather minor one involving the posting of a U.N. Ghana guard at the behest of the Ghana Ambassador without prior authorization by our military command. Hammarskjold needed some ammunition with which to confront Nkrumah, and he cabled back: 'This cable is a shocker. And Nkrumah is the one to talk about intervention in domestic affairs. I guess he bases his acquiescence in such free-wheeling political initiatives on theory of "legitimacy" of Lumumba, although this theory is, in itself, a case of interference and at best legally inconclusive, as even higher degrees of legitimacy can be claimed by Kasavubu. Having Nkrumah for lunch tomorrow. I will "politely but firmly"[2] take action parallel to the one[3] you

[1] The President of Togo.
[2] This was the expression I used in suggesting that Hammarskjold take up the matter with Nkrumah.
[3] I reported I was taking it up with the Ghana Ambassador.

have in mind. I am afraid that I will not entirely be able to hide my sarcasm.'

While the marathon debate was still in progress, there was a lengthy exchange of opinions between the Secretary-General and me on the line of policy that should be followed in the Congo in the light of the views expressed in the General Assembly, Hammarskjold's private discussions, and my assessment of the local situation. It was fully agreed that ONUC would not give any form of recognition, tacit or explicit, to Mobutu or his student Commissioners, but Kasavubu's position as Head of State would be fully respected and upheld. The U.N. Force would try to keep Mobutu within bounds and Lumumba and other politicians in cold storage. All energies were to be directed towards encouraging the reopening of Parliament with the participation of all six provinces including Katanga. A strong diplomatic offensive would be resumed against Tshombe, taking advantage of his difficulties in North Katanga and his growing irritation with the Belgians for their disinclination to give official recognition to his régime. I did not think much would come out of Mobutu's Round Table Conference idea, although we backed it up to the extent we could. I was also sceptical about the possibility of the U.N. Good Offices Commission being able to achieve much at that particular time as a good deal of advance preparation was necessary. I consulted many of the envoys at Léopoldville and found them in full agreement with our thinking.

Hammarskjold and his advisers had also been making soundings among the visiting notables and members of the Advisory Committee and he informed me of his talks with Nasser and Prince Moulay Hassan of Morocco, whose constructive overtones contrasted with the antiphony of the debate:

The fairy tale continues. However, on this side we seem to be approaching neo-realistic novel with some remaining element of cloak and dagger psychology. Had long lunch with Nasser today and noted with great satisfaction that he had realistic view of the situation as appears from the short summing-up which I feel free to quote: 'All the individual leaders in the Congo are interested in nothing but their own position and none of them stick to a promise or to a view expressed for more than two hours.' Hope he and other African leaders draw the right conclusions; he did at least do so as regards your own difficulties and problems.

I should also mention luncheon yesterday with Prince Moulay Hassan who, although less explicit, seemed on the whole to understand the problem. This leads me to believe that the four extremists may be split among themselves, especially as there is no love lost for Accra these days, to the best of my understanding, in Cairo or even in Rabat. I ask myself if it would not be useful for you to keep in contact with Ghaleb on your own initiative, which seems possible in view of the fact that he has approached you on his own on various occasions.

Hammarskjold followed up his talks by sounding his Advisory Committee and he conveyed his conclusions to me:

Advisory Committee meeting yesterday. As I told you, new current was apparent. This became even more apparent in talk with Nasser today. I promised the Committee to inform you about new trends so that we could profit from your reactions prior to any decisions or initiatives from here. Matters obviously must be treated as top confidential as timing and techniques are extremely important. However, trusting your own judgement you are of course free to try around with the ideas with the right people if you feel that you should do so in order to check your reactions.

The initiative of the Advisory Committee was taken by the Indian and Indonesian representatives. They suggested that the best chance for a return to constitutional authority lay in reconvening Parliament which would enable all the political leaders to meet. Fully endorsing this general line, the Advisory Committee was of the opinion that Tshombe might reconsider his position if the departure of his Belgian advisers and officials could be ensured. Hammarskjold continued: 'The same question came up with Nasser and Fawzi[1] today and I noted with interest that they were on line, which I elaborated yesterday in response to, and based on, Indian and Indonesian interventions. This constellation of three big neutrals is very new phenomenon in U.N. picture regarding the Congo. If it reflects the thinking of the five big neutralists (with the likely exception of Nkrumah) it might give basis for continued rallying for non-committed forces and U.N. Secretariat.' Hammarskjold added that consideration of the question of the U.N. Good Offices Commission had been postponed as 'Fawzi hesitant and Nasser

[1] Mahmoud Fawzi, then Foreign Minister of the U.A.R., whose political judgement Hammarskjold greatly respected.

most sceptical'. In conclusion he said he felt this was the only line which would get 'over the constitutional hump', and related international political complications, and create a setting to reduce the Congolese leaders to their proper size. Referring to Katanga, he stated: 'Key problem is Tshombe and I am considering personal approach appealing to his patriotism and wish for political survival. My wish is for Kasavubu to join in effort to get Tshombe in line with parliamentary approach.'

On the new plans I had already made preliminary soundings in Léopoldville with many of the envoys and with various politicians. I now renewed my efforts to get their more direct approval, without revealing the full picture. Hammarskjold did not inform me if he had outlined his plans to the Western delegations, without whose political support his hands would not be free, particularly in dealing with the Belgian presence in Katanga, and increasingly in Léopoldville. But he had 'run over the ground in a joint exploration of the situation with Fawzi'. He commented: 'I would not talk about enthusiasm, but he [Fawzi] was impressed by Katanga move. Intelligent footwork by Indian friend with cane[1] seems to be gaining ground with Afro-Asians.'

The first step towards reconvening the whole Parliament, including Katanga, was to tackle Tshombe and at the same time to continue diplomatic efforts to winkle out his Belgian underpinning. Hammarskjold prepared a draft letter for Tshombe in his most persuasive manner which he sent for my comments. Addressing the self-styled President of the State of Katanga as 'Dear Mr. Tshombe', Hammarskjold observed that the interplay between international and domestic reactions was moving in a direction of increasing danger to the Congo, heightening the shadow of armed conflict over the whole country. The risks in the situation rested on three factors, namely the disturbing situation in Léopoldville, the continued presence of a considerable number of Belgian military, para-military, and civilian personnel in the Congo and finally, the unresolved constitutional conflict, threatening the integrity of the country which was symbolized by the problem of Katanga. The last two factors were the most crucial and they had a direct impact on

[1] Krishna Menon, who carried a stick to steer himself through the U.N. corridors.

the first. If the Belgian element could be brought 'completely under control and eliminated' and the beginnings of a reconciliation between Katanga and Léopoldville started, the situation in Léopoldville would be straightened out and the road to pacification opened. Basing his actions on the 21 September resolution, the Secretary-General said he was asking the Belgian Government to withdraw its personnel of the defined categories and henceforth to channel its aid to the Congo through the United Nations. The Secretary-General added his conviction that nothing short of the acceptance of these two demands would forestall developments which might make the country 'an arena of conflict of world-wide significance'.

I replied to Hammarskjold that the problem of Katanga could not be treated in isolation. Tshombe's attitude and aspirations were based on four factors, namely Belgian support, Katanga's prosperity, its aversion to the Léopoldville Government and distrust of Lumumba, and the political confusion and economic collapse in the rest of the Congo. To deal with the first, strong pressures should be exerted at the highest United Nations and international levels to exclude the Belgian element from Katanga. But the vacuum thus created should be filled by a definite offer of United Nations technical assistance, in sufficient quantity to prevent a disruption of Katanga's economy and administration. Indeed, Tshombe had been making cautious enquiries about the availability of U.N. aid. Parallel to this, Tshombe's fears about personal reprisals and the political submergence of Katanga had to be allayed by ensuring that Parliament, when it met with Katanga's participation, would be free to transform itself into a Constituent Assembly competent to take up the question of the structure of the Congolese State. To advise the Congolese politicians, a group of three constitutional experts (one each from Nigeria, India, and the U.A.R.) should be set up. Meanwhile, the *status quo* in Katanga should be maintained until the various processes were set in motion. To dislodge Tshombe from his inflexible perch the removal of the omnipresent Belgians was of crucial importance and this needed 'shock-treatment'. Hammarskjold's letter was delivered by Rikhye in person, and its contents enthusiastically received by Tshombe.

Hammarskjold felt encouraged by these hopeful auguries as

he indicated in mid October: 'Rejoicing at results of beautifully harmonized diplomatic actions your side and here. We will keep up appropriate noises and maintain pressure in directions for which we now seem to rally various elements. Sorry in this situation to see manoeuvres like the Guinean[1] resolution which may provoke debate at rather awkward moment. . . . Meeting with Advisory Committee planned tomorrow night at which we shall do our best to introduce sound reactions contained in your various cables.'

But our optimism proved to be premature. The 'beautiful synchronization' of moves of which Hammarskjold had spoken was outmatched by Belgian moves with Tshombe—for all the latter's brave talk. The Belgian Government's reactions to Hammarskjold's parallel letter seeking its cooperation in withdrawing Belgian personnel and bilateral aid from the Congo were of undisguised hostility. Belgium began to marshal the support of the United States, Great Britain, France, and Italy (then a member of the Security Council) and her representative called for a meeting of the NATO Council on 22 October at Paris, where Belgium received her allies' assurances of sympathy and help. The NATO Secretariat-General felt concerned about the role of the United Nations in the world and what it called its interference in the internal affairs of several states. Apparently, the NATO Secretariat considered Hammarskjold's repeated requests to Belgium to comply with the resolutions of the Security Council as interference in Belgium's domestic affairs.

An opulent Katangan office under a plausible Belgian named Struelens was set up on Fifth Avenue in New York which issued a propaganda sheet called 'Katanga Calling' and briskly set to work seeking support for Katangan independence. Many responded to its siren call and Katanga found both paid and unpaid supporters.

No wonder that Tshombe's written reply was tough and unbending for the mouth was 'the mouth of Esau but the hand was the hand of Jacob'. Composed by Tshombe's Belgian advisers, it categorically rejected all the arguments used by the Secretary-General, and made an eloquent defence of the

[1] This refers to the Guinean resolution for seating the delegation of the Central Government in the U.N. in opposition to Kasavubu's delegation.

services of the Belgians and their indispensability to Katanga and, indeed, to the entire Congo.

The parallel moves towards Belgium and Katanga launched with such hope by the Secretary-General ended in failure and frustration. But we set to work to apply what Hammarskjold called 'the cold blanket' treatment to Mobutu and to create conditions for Parliament to meet. When the great of the earth returned from the General Assembly to their respective capitals, we continued to seek a way out of the wilderness. Meanwhile, the General Assembly was to take up the item anodynely inscribed on the agenda as 'The Situation in the Congo'.

CHAPTER 8

More Disunited Than Ever

The renewed debate on the Congo was due to commence in the General Assembly in the first half of November 1960. Hammarskjold was troubled that it would take the same desultory course, without offering any more guidance than the recent mutually contradictory contributions of the world statesmen. To provide some focus for the debate, he asked me to send him a report on the situation which would help guide the discussions. Giving us exactly three days to prepare the draft, he wired on 28 October as follows:

> Poland, this month's Security Council President, has strongly suggested that a new report on the situation in the Congo be made soon. I agree that we should prepare such a report not later than Tuesday. Consequently, I should like to ask you to prepare as soon as possible such a report, paying proper attention to the activities of Mobutu and Commissioners, and your relations with them, particularly in regard to the activities of A.N.C. The Tshombe problem should also be properly presented. I would, with legal comments, add from here the recent notes addressed to the Belgians. All detailed and substantial information regarding the 'return' of the Belgians should be urgently transmitted. To the proper extent, as you see fit, you should yourself include this information in your report, explaining the relationship between the 'return' and the opening created by the passivity in present constitutional circumstances forced upon us by our impartiality.

We at ONUC immediately concluded that the Secretary-General wanted an outspoken report giving the unvarnished facts. He particularly asked for details of the problems and difficulties facing the Operation and the topics he suggested were clearly contentious. But unless the report spelt out the problems in detail and with as much frankness as United

Nations jargon would allow, it would not serve the purpose that Hammarskjold had in mind. That purpose was to direct the attention of the delegations—particularly those which had denounced Hammarskjold officially as well as personally—towards concrete problems facing the Operation, thereby providing some cushioning for his own position.

After fully discussing the Secretary-General's requirements, my principal colleagues, civil and military, legal and administrative, set to work on the report, while I drafted the introduction and the conclusions. When the report was completed all of us were satisfied that the facts and analyses were fully authenticated.

In acknowledging receipt of the draft, the Secretary-General cabled back: 'Submit for your consideration some revisions in Chapter IV [The Question of New Belgian Return] which would seem to me to strengthen the report by eliminating or modifying phraseology which might be vulnerable. The suggested modifications are not intended to question in the least the judgment implicit in the statements affected. Nor is there any wish to soften the case against Belgium. They are concerned rather with the tactic of presentation. My thinking is that since the report, or particularly this Chapter, will be most searchingly scrutinized and is virtually certain to come under attack, it should most carefully avoid the inclusion of anything not fully authenticated or proved. Moreover, the impact will be stronger if established facts are permitted to speak for themselves without intimation of conclusion or judgment. Your views promptly will be appreciated.' Hammarskjold then suggested certain amendments and alterations to the chapter, which we had no hesitation in accepting. His own views on Belgian activities, expressed to us in numerous messages, were much stronger, but of course they were not for publication.

In a survey of the situation during the previous six weeks, my Second Report described the law and order situation as having markedly deteriorated, both in Léopoldville and in the provinces. Pointing to the increasing indiscipline of the A.N.C., I described its illegal and violent acts as the most serious obstacle to the objectives of the United Nations in the Congo. The financial and economic situation had grown steadily worse with the depletion of foreign reserves, the virtual absence of tax collection, and the inability to pay salaries of public servants. I drew attention to the increasing evidence of the return of Belgian nationals in many phases of public life in the Congo.

The constitutional crisis had worsened with rival groupings claiming to constitute the Central Government and by rivalry between Central and separatist 'Governments'. ONUC's dilemma was that it was precluded, in view of its commitment to the principle of neutrality, from choosing between these rival Governments. Equally committed to the principle of legality, it could not give recognition to a régime founded on military force. But its mission could not be accomplished without day-do-day contacts with the ministries. ONUC therefore had been compelled to follow a policy of dealing with whatever authority it found in the ministerial chairs.

Dealing with the problem of the two secessionist states of Katanga and South Kasai, the report spoke of clear evidence of increasing Belgian participation in political and administrative activities there and gave some typical examples of the kind of obstruction to ONUC's efforts which the new Belgian arrivals were offering.

All too often, these developments had coincided with anti-U.N. policies or feelings at the various points of impact and were inhibiting a peaceful return to constitutional government and the implementation of the U.N. technical-assistance programme.

I drew renewed attention to the continued indiscipline and disorganization of the Congolese organs of security which severely hampered the restoration of law and order. The 'usurpation of political powers' by the Chief of Staff had made the A.N.C. more intransigent and defiant, and had drawn it into the vortex of political life despite the assertions of the Chief of Staff of non-interference in civilian affairs. The report quoted chapter and verse on the lawless activities of the A.N.C. and of Mobutu's professed inability to curb or control them. In conclusion, the situation was described as one of great uncertainty and much turbulence, which enjoined on ONUC an attitude of firmness and persistence. It was emphasized that the only two political institutions whose foundations still stood, were the office of Chief of State and Parliament. But the stalemate could provide an opportunity for a fresh start, if individual or factional interests could be subordinated to the general good by the establishment of a single government of conciliation through the medium of these two institutions. That alone could lead the fourteen million Congolese people to a life of peace, freedom, and security.

While the Report was being drafted, Hammarskjold asked me to fly to New York for 'backstage talks' which would certainly follow its publication, prior to the General Assembly or Security Council debate, as there was 'much to be straightened out'. Hammarskjold added that my presence would be particularly useful in maintaining contacts with the African and Asian delegations. I suggested leaving Rikhye or Linner in charge and Hammarskjold replied that 'the question of nationality should be decisive' and accordingly his choice fell on Rikhye, although Linner was the more senior in the hierarchy.

When I took an Air France plane from Brazzaville on 2 November, with its soft music and overflowing hospitality, I felt like a deep-sea diver surfacing after two months in the depths. Even temporary removal of the crushing weight of responsibility was like a tonic and when I reached New York the next day, Hammarskjold greeted me warmly with the remark: 'Raj, you look disgustingly well!' And well I might, for I had been joined at Paris by my long-suffering wife, Susheela, who, by a special dispensation from the Secretary-General, had been permitted to share my life in the Congo instead of having to learn of its perils from radio broadcasts or screaming newspaper headlines. Hammarskjold felt it would be good for the morale of the Onusiens[1] (and not the least, of their Chief!) to have her reassuring presence in their midst.

The publication of my Report the previous day had set the corridors and the Delegates' Lounge at the United Nations buzzing. The Report did much to rally the doubting African and Asian countries to Hammarskjold's side. For with the Secretary-General's imprimatur, it gave an indication of the policy he intended to follow and justification for the decisions of the past. But how would the Western powers react? Even before the ink was dry on the document came Washington's

[1] The term invented for U.N. personnel by the Congolese.

comment from the lips of the spokesman of the State Department: 'We have every confidence in the good faith of Belgium in its desire to be of assistance in the Congo. We are therefore unable to accept the implication to the contrary contained in various parts of the Report.'

I had a long talk with Mr. Averell Harriman, who, though not in office at the time, had visited me in the Congo and was to come again early in the new year. Harriman had been appalled by the shambles he found in the Congo and was not impressed by the calibre of the Congolese politicians. He was very sympathetic to the efforts of ONUC to restore some order in the prevailing confusion and he appreciated the virtue of institutions over personalities in building up the country. He was not enamoured of Belgian policy which was dividing the United Nations and harming Belgium's own interests and he invited me to meet the Belgian Ambassador to Washington and an emissary of the Belgian Government at lunch in his apartment.

The emissary was a Count Dhani, scion of a prominent Belgian family whose forbears had blazed a trail for King Léopold through the Congo where they held extensive investments. Both gentlemen scrutinized me closely for what seemed to me symptoms of cannibalism, but with Harriman's friendly umpiring the conversation began to flow civilly and then warmly. I praised the fine city of Léopoldville and Belgian industrial enterprise, but I wished that Belgian political skill had equalled their other considerable virtues. The measure of success of the U.N.'s efforts would be in inverse proportion to the duration of its mission and I hoped that with Belgian co-operation, the period could be compressed. Surprised by this unexpected line, my interrogators asked why I hated Belgium so much and how I relished being hated in return. Now it was my turn to be surprised and I blandly, but quite sincerely, replied that all former metropolitan powers had an important responsibility to the young states they had created and I hoped that ONUC's efforts would enable the peaceful return of Belgians to serve the Congo as friends and equals.

My next interview was with Valerian Zorin, the Russian Ambassador. Zorin, aided by his deputy, Nesterenko, put me through a two-hour grilling about the objectives of the U.N.

Operation, and he was as dogmatic in his support of Lumumba as his opponents were in their opposition to him. I outlined the situation on the basis of my Reports—of which Zorin seemed to approve—but I held out against supporting any personalities on the shifting Congolese scene. I am afraid my defence of democratic procedures and institutions carried no more weight with Zorin than with my Western interlocutors. The point of total mutual incomprehension was reached when I said that principles must stand above politics. The printed word, however, carried a certain sanctity with Zorin, and my Reports proved to be ONUC's best shield as Zorin's conversation was interlaced with quotations from them. Finally, Zorin said he believed me to be 'an honest man' but what I had said and written did not correspond to Hammarskjold's views and policies. I replied that if Hammarskjold did not agree with me, he would ask me to leave, and if I disagreed with him, I would myself pack up and go.

The delegations from Asia and Africa, especially of countries with troops in the Congo, were in a mood of frustration and puzzlement. They could not understand how the massive U.N. presence had been unable to prevent the anarchy and confusion. They wanted the United Nations to take more forceful action to implement its mandate and not to get entangled in legalisms of its own creation.

My contacts with delegates and the international press had convinced me that the political divisions in New York could, to some extent, be neutralized by positive achievements in the field. ONUC had a sizeable force, but the limited mandate had neutralized it even in spheres where it could be effectively used. The principle of non-intervention should not be carried beyond the point at which the U.N. Force became the laughing-stock of the world. The right to self-defence was too restricted as it did not even allow the arrest of criminals and hooligans or intervention to prevent arbitrary arrest. Nor could the Force interpose itself in incipient or actual civil-war situations. Inactivity on its part in the face of open flouting of law and constitutionality was eroding its prestige and efficacy. A little timely action on its part would prevent increased defiance later. I, therefore, pressed Hammarskjold to ask for an enlargement of the mandate so as more closely to equate ONUC's authority with its wide responsibilities. The U.N. Operation, I pointed out, was, in reality, a massive form of intervention in the guise of non-intervention. On the basis of the principles which had so far been applied, ONUC had been unable to solve any of the major problems. A more forceful approach could retrieve the situation, which, though involved, was still malleable.

Hammarskjold, however, had serious doubts about the wisdom of enlarging the mandate. He felt that a limited mandate, liberally interpreted, was better than a wider one, restrictively applied. He therefore decided not to seek additional powers. Three months later, under the stress of Lumumba's assassination, and at Hammarskjold's behest, the Assembly voted additional powers but by that time the situation had greatly worsened.

It had become clear by now that the Western powers, led by the United States, were firmly opposed to a return to constitutional rule following the recall of Parliament, for to them it meant only one thing—the return of Lumumba. They could not openly take a stand against reconciliation and the restoration of legality. Nor could they formally support the illegal régime of Mobutu and his Commissioners. They therefore seized on the figure of Kasavubu to make their point by bringing him over in person to New York as head of the Congolese delegation. As the undisputed Head of State, he had the right to address the General Assembly. The seating of his delegation, with himself at its head, would not present any problem in the Credentials Committee. That Committee normally had formal functions and it generally met towards the end of the session. Its composition was arbitrary, but at that session it was heavily weighted in favour of the Western powers. True, the United States had, only a few weeks earlier, herself proposed that the question of seating rival delegations be deferred in order not to worsen the situation. But political expediency prevailed over consistency. Besides, Sekou Touré had proposed a draft resolution recommending seating of a delegation representing the Central Government, and the African and Asian delegations could hardly ask for the deferment of a question that one of their own leaders had provoked. Earnest efforts were made by the Secretariat and by delegations

Above:
Kasavubu and
Adoula *(centre)*
with Khiari *(left)*

Left: Tshombe
talks, Adoula
listens

Non-aligned leaders at the U.N. General Assembly session, 4 October 1960: (*l. to r.*) Nasser, Sukarno, Nehru, Nkrumah, and Saeb Salaam (Lebanon)

which feared the consequences of the manoeuvre, to shelve the question for the time being. But to no avail. The Western powers had decided to hoist the Africans and Asians with their own petard.

Meanwhile ONUC reported from Léopoldville that on hearing of Kasavubu's departure, Lumumba had tried to leave for New York but was prevented by the A.N.C. which reinforced its guard around his house. In any case, 'he would not have got a visa from Timberlake'. Thomas Kanza was still the accredited Congolese Ambassador to the United Nations and when he approached the U.S. Embassy for a visa, he was told that the Commissioner for the Interior had withdrawn his passport. The message concluded: 'Timberlake determined not to allow any Lumumbist to enter New York to ensure that Kasavubu has all the advantages.' Hammarskjold wired back that U.N. policy was to facilitate the exit from Léopoldville of top personalities to New York, but the issue of passports was beyond its competence. Kanza had asked if he could be given a U.N. *laissez-passer*. Hammarskjold added: 'On a strictly personal basis, we regret the situation facing Kanza.'

Kasavubu addressed the General Assembly on 8 November. He announced the composition of his delegation which he had come to head. As the representative of the Congolese people whose virtues had been admitted by the Special Representative in his Report, he asked that a meeting of the Credentials Committee be convened to admit him and his delegation.

The debate on the situation in the Congo now began. The representative of Guinea reverted to the motion introduced by his President, and called for the restoration of the Congo's democratic institutions to enable the country to recover its political equilibrium. After Zorin had spoken in support of the Guinean draft resolution which had been co-sponsored by eight powers, including India, the Polish representative spoke. He said that the Report of the Special Representative 'could become a starting point for a basic correction of the state of affairs' in the Congo. All three speakers referred repeatedly to the Report and criticized Belgian activities and the Secretary-General's application of the doctrine of non-intervention, which they argued sought to equate the legal order with a military *coup* based on foreign support.

The co-sponsors of the Guinean draft resolution realized that Kasavubu's personal appearance would strongly tilt the issue of seating in his favour, as some delegations would find it difficult to rebuff a Head of State. Finding themselves out-manoeuvred, Quaison-Sackey of Ghana, on behalf of the eight co-sponsors, sprang to the floor on a point of order. He asked of what avail would a debate be when the Conciliation Commission[1] was about to set out for the Congo, as positions openly taken in the General Assembly would complicate its difficult task. He made an appeal to the members to suspend the debate until receipt of the report of the Commission. After a procedural debate which revealed the positions of the various delegations, a vote was taken by roll call on a motion of adjournment. It was carried by forty-eight votes to thirty, with eighteen abstentions, the Western powers and their followers voting against it.

The counter-manoeuvre was successful. But only for a time. If the Conciliation Commission were to be given a chance to do its job, the Mobutu-Kasavubu combination would not be able to consolidate its strength. The time factor would operate against them as ONUC was gradually restoring a position of uneasy equilibrium by keeping the A.N.C. in check so as to create the very conditions that Mobutu professed he wanted in order to restore the country to civilian rule. Were the Commission to succeed in its task, it could mean only one thing, a reconciliation between Kasavubu and Lumumba. This the Western powers and Belgium were determined to prevent.

The Western powers led by the United States pressed for and obtained a meeting of the Credentials Committee. A bitter debate followed. The United States resolution proposing that the Committee recommend to the General Assembly the credentials of the delegation led by Kasavubu was finally adopted by six votes to one.

It now remained to get a vote in the General Assembly to complete the process. But the Assembly had already decided to adjourn the discussion on the basis of a substantial majority vote. The President of the General Assembly, Frederick Boland,

[1] The Commission, composed of African and Asian representatives of countries with troops in the Congo, had been charged with assisting 'in decisions being reached with a view to the speedy restoration of parliamentary institutions in the Republic of the Congo'. For details, see A/4592.

asked the Assembly to take up the report of the Credentials Committee. This was opposed by the delegate of Ghana on a point of order and gave rise to another long procedural squabble.

India urged that the work of the Conciliation Commission should not be prejudiced before it even commenced. The President put the issue of adjournment to the vote and it was evident that many delegations had switched their votes. It was common knowledge in the corridors and lounges that the intensest pressures had been applied to force countries to change their votes—if not their convictions—from affirmation to abstention and from abstention to negation. A large number succumbed to what is known in U.N. parlance as 'armtwisting'. It was perhaps one of the most glaring examples of the massive and organized application of threats and pressures —along with inducements—to member states to change their votes. It is a sad commentary on the weakness or venality of countries that so many succumbed.

One last attempt was made by the delegate of India to secure an adjournment when he argued that the previous decision to adjourn the debate on the situation in the Congo applied automatically to the report of the Credentials Committee. The President ruled that the two matters were separate on the agenda and asked for formal presentation of the report of the Credentials Committee. Then began the debate which lasted six days. Quaison-Sackey pointed to the incongruity of the situation in the Credentials Committee where six non-African states had taken a majority decision over the opposition of their two African colleagues. But the representative of the Cameroon twitted him and those who thought like him with inconsistency, for while previously they had argued that the situation in the Congo required urgent consideration, now they were arguing for delay.

The Western powers sat back to watch the spectacle of African against African, secure in the knowledge that they had got the votes they needed. The debate ended with a vote of fifty-three to twenty-four, with nineteen abstentions, in favour of seating Kasavubu's delegation. Apart from those who succumbed to pressures, some delegations abstained as they did not wish to appear to be taking sides, others out of respect for an African Head of State. Catherine Hoskyns, in describing the pressures to browbeat delegations, quotes *Le Monde* of 24 November which reported that the vote was 'a success of the American big stick', while the *New York Herald Tribune* noted blandly that now that the Kasavubu delegation had been seated 'some progress towards straightening out the vexatious Congo tangle ought to be possible'.

That night Hammarskjold anxiously reviewed the situation in his suite on the 38th floor. He was appalled at the methods used and the depths to which the Assembly had fallen. He realized that his difficulties had been vastly increased and that it would now be more difficult to hold the scales even, for he would be under pressure to come out more actively in support of Kasavubu and the illegal régime which he had fathered. The U.N. troops were drawn from the neutral countries of Africa and Asia and could hardly be expected to carry out policies of which their governments so strongly disapproved. The only fading hope now lay in sending out the Conciliation Commission as quickly as possible. Hammarskjold had tried to come to an understanding with Kasavubu about ONUC's future course of action, but he found his visitor stubbornly unresponsive.

Kasavubu had his own advisers, mostly Belgian, and in New York there was no lack of the kind of advice and encouragement he wanted. Representatives of powerful countries sought his favours in his sumptuous suite at the Waldorf Astoria. I succeeded, with some effort, in paying him a call, but he was more uncommunicative than ever.

As the resumed debate in the General Assembly was due to take place much later, there was no point in my further stay in New York. Hammarskjold and the Advisory Committee were agreed that everything should be done to prepare the ground for the arrival of the conciliators. But Kasavubu had been unwilling to commit himself to a firm date; he said he would have to study the situation and to consult his colleagues, and in spite of Hammarskjold's personal efforts, he refused to budge.

Bunche suggested that I should have a talk with Dean Rusk before I left New York as it would be useful to have a man of Rusk's standing in our confidence in view of the disarray

which the U.S. presidential elections had caused in that delegation. During my ninety-minute talk with him I tried to explain
that the issues in the Congo were not concerned with ideology
but with tribalism and nationalism. An apolitical solution,
such as the United Nations could provide, would be the best
answer to the Congo's problems. If institutions and not personalities were backed, then only could an equilibrium be
found. Rusk listened attentively and appeared receptive and I
felt encouraged by the meeting. But his attitude when he
attained high office lacked the sensitivity that he had displayed
earlier. It took the Kennedy Administration many vital months
to evolve a coherent policy towards the Congo and it was not
until after Hammarskjold's death that it gave firm support to
the United Nations.

The General Assembly resumed its interrupted debate on
the situation in the Congo from 16 December to 20 December.
By that time, things in the Congo had worsened considerably
and Lumumba was under arrest. The debate was therefore as
bitter as ever, with renewed attacks by the Soviet delegation
and their allies on Hammarskjold and a sense of frustration
among the African and Asian delegations.[1] Zorin demanded
an end to Belgian interference and to the chaos rampant in
the Congo by disarming 'Mobutu's armed bands', the immediate release of Lumumba, the reconvening of Parliament and
establishment of an African and Asian Observation Commission
to control the actions of the Special Representative. The
Soviet delegation introduced a draft resolution incorporating
the proposals made in Zorin's speech.[2]

Mahmoud Fawzi, speaking for the U.A.R., observed that
what was taking place in the Congo was contrary to the
objectives of the United Nations. He questioned the logic of
rendering protection to Lumumba when he was in confinement as not being an act of intervention, but of interference in
giving him protection when he was at large. He noted that
Europeans in Stanleyville were, on the other hand, being
afforded vigorous protection. He asked that 'the money, the
arms, the help and the bribes, which the big, medium, and
small Mobutus get' be stopped. He proposed that a body re-

[1] *GAOR*, 1960, 949th–952nd meetings.
[2] Ibid.

presenting the General Assembly be designated to work in full and close cooperation with the Mission in the Congo. Krishna Menon then presented a draft resolution which asked the United Nations 'henceforth' to implement its mandate fully to prevent a breach of peace and security, and it urged the immediate release of all political prisoners, the convening of Parliament and the prevention of armed units and personnel interfering in the political life of the country.

The Secretary-General interrupted to enquire how the U.N. Force could be expected to disarm and deal with Colonel Mobutu, for had the Assembly or the Council ever permitted him, or the Force, to take the initiative in military action? To this his answer was a categorical 'No'. But a number of speakers continued to press for vigorous action.[1]

Walter Loridan, the Belgian representative, made a vehement defence of Belgian policy in the Congo, seeking to justify Belgian colonialism and its aftermath.[2] The Congo, he said, had been 'the most backward territory in Africa' before Belgium went there as it was 'entirely unexplored', 'inhabited by tribes . . . who had no written language; they did not know how to use the wheel or the plough or to employ domestic animals for transport. Cattle raising was unknown.' . . . 'The population suffered from serious malnutrition. No stone building or monument has been discovered. The country was riddled with disease.' . . . 'Modern civilization existed only in a handful of posts.' . . . 'Belgium had to start from scratch.'

Loridan then extolled Belgian colonial achievements and gave the Belgian official version of the events leading up to and after Independence, including Belgian armed intervention. In conclusion he stated that his Government would support a resolution which upheld the Congo's sovereign rights, called for non-interference in its domestic affairs and abstention from any direct or indirect military assistance to the Congo. It was an unfortunate speech, no doubt inspired by Foreign Minister Wigny, whose interventions in the Assembly had done Belgium's cause more harm than good. Wigny had attacked several states of Africa and Asia and had threatened that Belgium would leave the Organization if criticism continued.

[1] *GAOR*, 1960, 949th–952nd meetings.
[2] *GAOR*, 1960, 953rd meeting.

As the debate proceeded, the polarization of attitudes between the states who wanted to see an orderly transition to constitutional rule in conditions of peace and security and those who, for various reasons, were content to let the situation drift towards even worse chaos and bloodshed, became increasingly marked. The Soviet Union was by now completely isolated along with its allies, as were the Western powers and their friends. The African and Asian states who had a real stake in the operation were divided. But those pressing for moderation did not command the voting strength to see a resolution through.

Hammarskjold made several interventions during the debate, either to restore the discussion to the rails or to answer fresh attacks directed at him. On 17 December,[1] he was provoked to remark that although the item to which the debate referred was called 'The Situation in the Congo', the real issue might better have been called 'The Situation in the United Nations'. Denouncing the methods used in the debate, he warned that the Organization had been brought to 'a point where many may have been tempted to ask whether facts, or truth, or law no longer count. . . .'

Hammarskjold then reiterated the aims of the Operation, the mandate, and the means, pointing out that the discussions had confused the aims with the mandate and had tried to reinterpret the question of means, irrespective of legal considerations. While he did not ask for a widening of the mandate or new means, he did ask for the removal of ambiguities and for an appropriate sharing of responsibilities. In doing so, he would reject anything which could have a touch of control or direction over the Congo's internal affairs. He did not believe that the use of military initiative. or pressure was the way to restoring the political structure, but only the normal political and diplomatic means of persuasion and advice. He urged the restoration of Parliament and the reduction of the Congolese army to its normal subordinate functions as an instrument of the national government. This could be done only by the establishment of a certain balance in Congolese political life which had been tipped in one direction or another. Hammarskjold also asked for support for the efforts of the Concilia-

[1] *GAOR*, 1960, 953rd meeting.

tion Commission. Finally, he drew attention to the deep divisions in the General Assembly. In the earlier stage of the Operation, it had the unanimous support of the Security Council, the General Assembly, and the African group. Now even the African countries were deeply divided. This change would inevitably have dangerous consequences not only for the Organization but also for the Congo itself.

Before the Assembly proceeded to a vote on the resolution, Hammarskjold again took the floor to elaborate on the circumstances which might compel the U.N. Force in the Congo and its operations to be discontinued. If a civil-war situation were to develop with the direct or indirect engagement of outside powers, it would be the duty of the United Nations to try and forestall it by preventive action. But if the situation were of such magnitude as to place the U.N. Force itself in jeopardy, he would refer the matter to the Security Council to decide whether the Force should withdraw. Furthermore, should the involvement of other countries in the Congo's affairs reach the point where the position of the participating states and of the Organization itself were endangered, it would be better 'to look the situation in the eye and to draw the conclusions'. Hammarskjold said that decisions on questions of the type he had posed 'go beyond what reasonably should be put on the shoulders of any one man and his collaborators'.

The eight-power draft resolution was an attempt to mobilize the highest common multiple of agreement among the African and Asian powers, excluding some members of the so-called Brazzaville group who were firmly committed to the Western position. The Soviet draft had no chance of success and would have intensified the split among the Africans and Asians and it was quietly withdrawn. The colourless resolution, sponsored by the United Kingdom and the United States and later by Argentina and Italy, remained. The attitudes of delegations were so far removed from each other that no attempt was made to find any common meeting ground.

The result of the debate was further to weaken the Secretary-General's position, to exacerbate the divisions between member states, to deny the Congo Operation the moral and political support it so badly needed, and to foment dissension in the Congo by giving encouragement to forces that were opposed to the constitution and to legality. The Western powers and their followers had demonstrated their ability to obstruct attempts at reconciliation and the restoration of parliamentary rule, but they lacked the capacity to impose their own solutions. The African and Asian states were splintered into three or more groups.

The powers that had been dissuaded from withdrawing their contingents from the Congo in the hope that the situation would take a turn for the better were now determined to pull out. The Soviet Union and her allies were in open and undiluted hostility to the whole enterprise. The patient work of ONUC to hold the scales even, and by insulating the situation to make it more amenable to correction by legitimate parliamentary means, was undone. This was the harvest reaped by the manoeuvre to force the seating of Kasavubu's delegation. The seeds carried by the winds from New York produced an even more bitter crop of violence, disorder, and bloodshed in the Congo.

CHAPTER 9

No Law, Less Order

My wife, Susheela, accompanied me back to the Congo. She had never been in Africa before and wondered about life and conditions in Léopoldville. On reaching Brazzaville we were received by Brigadier Rikhye and some of our colleagues and flown by helicopter not to our residence, but to 'Le Royal'. There we were ushered into a room that had been hastily set up for our temporary use.

I soon learnt what had occasioned the change in residential arrangements. Brigadier Rikhye and Colonel Lasmar, Commander of the U.N. Tunisian Brigade, told me that a skirmish had occurred between U.N. and Congolese troops a couple of days ago—while we were on our long journey—around the Ghana Embassy which was very close to my residence on the steep banks of the Congo River. The residence had been the target of much firing and was now in the occupation of U.N. troops. Until the situation cleared, it was entirely unsafe for habitation as A.N.C. soldiers were roaming about, waylaying and manhandling anyone connected with the U.N. My wife courageously took her first introduction to the Congo in good heart, and her presence at ONUC headquarters did much to cheer up everyone after their depressing experiences of the past few days.

As a measure of his growing assertiveness, Mobutu renewed his campaign to round up and arrest the politicians. His troops surrounded the house of the President of Léopoldville Province, Cléophas Kamitatu, which was situated between Rikhye's and mine, and arrested him and his family. The family was later released after much scurrying to and fro, and it was forced to take refuge with Nathaniel Welbeck, who had replaced Djin as Ghana's envoy. Kamitatu was released after a few days of palavering and when he returned to his own house he insisted on being provided with a U.N. guard.

Meanwhile, Thomas Kanza, fearing arrest, sought refuge at 'Le Royal', and his father, Daniel Kanza, the First Burgomaster of Léopoldville, an influential member of Kasavubu's tribe and his rival for its leadership, asked for U.N. protection. The Ghana envoy, Welbeck, approached Rikhye for additional U.N. security as he feared assassination. A Ghanaian Second Secretary, Mensah, was arrested and taken to Mobutu in the military camp, where some papers intended for Lumumba were found in his possession. The atmosphere in Léopoldville was full of tension as fear spread among the Congolese politicians and African envoys as a result of the renewed wave of arrests. ONUC headquarters were nervous at having Thomas Kanza as their unwanted guest, but Hammarskjold directed that he must be allowed sanctuary and not be turned over to an uncertain fate.

These arbitrary activities were taking place when Hammarskjold was hoping that the ground would be prepared in the Congo for the arrival of the U.N. Conciliation Commission. He had cabled ONUC that an advance guard, led by its elected Chairman, Jaja Wachuku of Nigeria, would be leaving New York on or about 22 November.

On 17 November Commissioner Nussbaumer called at ONUC headquarters and said that the President had, on 4 October, declared Djin, Welbeck, and Botsio of Ghana *personae non gratae* and had written to President Nkrumah accordingly. Instead of a reply, a note had been received from the Accra Foreign Office to the effect that the letter had not been countersigned by a competent Minister! Nussbaumer insisted that Welbeck—who was still in residence—must leave. Hammarskjold first heard of the expulsion order from news reports and he cabled ONUC to take necessary measures for the protection of Ghana Embassy personnel. Welbeck called on 19 November at ONUC headquarters and said he had heard of his expulsion on the BBC but had received no official notice. If the Embassy itself was being expelled, it was a more serious matter and he would have to ask Accra for instructions and also for an aircraft in case of emergency. He added that he had every intention of staying until the arrival of the Conciliation

Commission. The Congolese protocol department informed ONUC that there was no question of breaking off diplomatic relations. The U.N. position was that a determination by the Head of State that any diplomat was *persona non grata* was entirely a Congolese affair, and ONUC's responsibilities would not be engaged beyond its normal mandate to prevent acts of force being carried out against representatives of governments. The Secretary-General, agreeing with this interpretation which had been given to the Congolese authorities, instructed that 'beyond offering the usual protection to which foreign missions are normally entitled, we cannot intervene in any exercise of the prerogative of Chief of State to declare *persona non grata* personnel attached to diplomatic missions'.

While these exchanges were going on, the position was steadily getting more explosive. The Congolese Chief of Security, Ndele, now took over, and in a call on ONUC, declared that Welbeck must leave forthwith and asked ONUC to advise him accordingly. At about noon on 19 November, a Captain Pongo of Congolese Security served a forty-eight-hour notice of departure on Welbeck. Rikhye reported that 'Welbeck who had been steadily drinking since early this morning and his courage increasing with quantity of alcohol consumed, was incoherent and loud in his determination to remain.' Rikhye and von Horn that day had a 'cordial lunch' with Mobutu at which they found him vacillating, and they thought that an adequate concentration of troops in Léopold-ville and a 'discreet show of force' could keep him within bounds. Mobutu too was insistent that Welbeck must leave but he agreed to allow Ghana to send another ambassador to replace him.

Welbeck called at 'Le Royal' on 20 November in sober mood and said he had received no reply from Accra and as the regular plane for Ghana left only a couple of days later, he hoped to be able to stay on. News soon arrived that the permanent Head of the Ghana Foreign Office and General Alexander were on their way to Léopoldville. A clash that morning with the A.N.C. was averted by ONUC getting an extension of time by twenty-four hours. ONUC reported that it had 'been placed in most embarrassing situation and efforts to create peaceful atmosphere for Conciliation Commission being weakened by one man—Welbeck'. Requesting urgent instructions, the message concluded: 'We are heading for definite clash with A.N.C'.

The Secretary-General's instructions came promptly: 'I have my doubts about wisdom of show of force which may lead to clashes. Such clashes have to be strictly avoided, and I think it should be possible to reach your psychological effect on Mobutu without running risks of the kind you indicate.' To calm things down, Hammarskjold also immediately spoke to the Congolese delegation at New York and replied:

I have just met Bomboko and Cardozo,[1] and informed them of serious developments regarding Welbeck's forcible expulsion and the consequences which could ensue. I pointed to grave dangers which could arise from armed conflict between U.N. and Congolese troops. . . . Bomboko said that a letter had been sent by Kasavubu to Nkrumah early in October to which reply had been received from Ghana Foreign Secretary questioning validity of the action proposed on the ground that Bomboko's counter-signature was not valid. Welbeck had therefore invited the trouble but Bomboko agreed that a clash between U.N. and Congolese forces would be most unfortunate. He was informed that some had actually taken place which he regretted. He promised to inform Kasavubu of the developments and to have a telegram sent to Mobutu immediately for exercise of restraint and for repairing relations with ONUC.

But at the Ghana Embassy in Léopoldville matters had already reached the point of no return. On the evening of 21 November, the U.N. Ghana police guard had been reinforced by ten Tunisian soldiers. When A.N.C. troops appeared on the scene, the U.N. guard was further strengthened. The A.N.C. then brought in more reinforcements. Welbeck had been given an ultimatum to leave the country by a Sabena plane at 4 o'clock that afternoon .and the Commissioners had generously provided an air ticket. But Welbeck held fast in his citadel. Some half a dozen Commissioners called at ONUC headquarters to demand that Welbeck be handed over to them pending discussions with the emissaries from Ghana. This was just before 8 o'clock at night. The angry exchanges were interrupted when news arrived that firing had suddenly broken

[1] A member of Kasavubu's delegation to the U.N. and Commissioner for Education.

out. Colonel Lasmar and Commissioner Nussbaumer immediately left 'Le Royal' to try and bring about a cease-fire, but without success.

What actually started the firing is in some doubt. According to a Tunisian lieutenant posted at the Embassy, talks were going on between the U.N. officers of the guard and Congolese officers when Colonel Kokolo, Commander of the Léopoldville A.N.C. garrison, arrived accompanied by two Congolese civilians and announced angrily that they would attack the Embassy in a quarter of an hour. A little later, the Colonel and his party tried to enter the premises but the Tunisian officer told them that they could not go in armed. Colonel Kokolo refused and struck the officer while some Congolese soldiers fell on him and knocked him down. A Congolese civilian shouted to the A.N.C. to fire and a volley was fired which seriously wounded one Tunisian officer and wounded another lightly. The Tunisians then replied and there was much confused firing in which machine guns and light arms were used.

Another version was that the U.N. troops fired first in self-defence against a charge by Congolese soldiers to storm the building. In the fusillade, Colonel Kokolo fell dead, along with a Tunisian soldier. One dead and four wounded Tunisians were collected by a U.N. ambulance when the firing died down and treated at the U.N. hospital, where Colonel Kokolo's body was also taken. Rikhye tried to maintain contact with Mobutu all through the night to prevent more fighting, but sporadic firing continued till the next morning with more wounded on both sides. General Alexander arrived at the Embassy in the morning and took Welbeck and the entire Ghana staff with him to the airport from where they were flown out.

During the night and on the following day, the Congolese soldiers milled around the city intercepting U.N. personnel, civil and military. Twenty-eight were taken in the first round and locked up for the night in a small room. Over thirty more were seized at various times, but all were released after energetic protests were lodged with the Congolese Chief of Staff. Some residences of U.N. personnel were broken into. Over sixty U.N. vehicles were seized and half of them were never returned.

The gory episode had very unfortunate consequences, as

whatever remained of the professional bonds between the military officers on both sides was shattered and Mobutu broke off relations with the U.N. military command. For the first time, a pitched battle had been fought between the A.N.C. and U.N. troops. The respect of the A.N.C. for the U.N. Force began to evaporate. Life for U.N. personnel in Léopoldville became increasingly hazardous. The death of Colonel Kokolo, a popular figure, was taken badly by the Congolese troops. At New York, the Conciliation Commission decided to defer its departure for Léopoldville.

True, the whole incident would not have occurred but for Welbeck's obstinacy, as other envoys left quietly when they were asked to go. The next to leave was the U.A.R. Ambassador and his entire staff when Kasavubu declared them *personae non gratae*. The Ghana emissaries had arrived and discussions could have been opened with them to prepare the way for their chargé d'affaires' departure. General Alexander, as a soldier, should have known better than to risk a trial of force, for what he did on the morning following the battle, he could have done the previous evening. But the U.N. Command also miscalculated when they felt that a show of force at the Embassy would deter the Congolese from taking forcible action. The 'protection' which the Secretary-General had said should be offered to the Ghana envoy went, in actual fact, far beyond what he had intended or what the U.N. could reasonably have been expected to do.

While these stormy events were occurring, the Supreme Commander of the U.N. Force, General von Horn, was nowhere to be seen. He had been upset that his junior, Rikhye, then a Brigadier, had been placed temporarily at the head of the U.N. mission, and von Horn had begun attending fitfully to his duties. During the crucial days, he remained confined to his house, complaining of an attack of blood pressure. It was clear that the responsibilities were too much for him. He wired the Secretary-General that he wished to return to his less demanding post in Jerusalem,[1] and his wish was speedily granted.

---

[1] Von Horn was the Head of the U.N. Truce Supervision Organization in Jerusalem when he was asked to take over command of the U.N. Force in the Congo.

For a time, General Kettani filled his place until he was replaced by Major-General Sean McKeown, then Chief of Staff of the Irish army. McKeown had come to Léopoldville to inspect the Irish contingent and had called on me. I was impressed by him and asked how he would like to take over command of the Force. He said that the Irish constitution forbade the Chief of Staff from serving with a foreign force, but when I suggested that perhaps the Secretary-General could negotiate the constitutional hurdle with his Government, he readily agreed. I immediately wired Hammarskjold that I had found the answer to his problem, and in a few weeks McKeown arrived to serve with distinction and devotion as Commander of the U.N. Force in the Congo, the pretentious prefix, 'Supreme', having been dropped at my suggestion.

The Ghana Embassy affair sent a shock wave through ONUC and U.N. headquarters at New York. Hammarskjold wired: 'Deeply shocked by the performance of Mobutu A.N.C. This may have most serious political repercussions and may influence whole position of U.N.' Léopoldville was fairly calm when I had left for New York but now it was in turmoil and the U.N. Force was on the defensive. Mobutu was cock-a-hoop with the performance of the A.N.C. and he was not really sorry at Kokolo's disappearance, for the Colonel was genuinely popular with his troops and he could have developed into a serious challenge to his own supremacy. The Belgian-controlled press was crowing about a 'double victory', and the A.N.C. were seeking revenge for Kokolo's death. The situation around Lumumba's house was extremely tense as the A.N.C. had greatly reinforced its strength there. Lumumba himself was in a state of panic, as he feared that he could now be openly arrested.

To add to our problems, the coffin of Lumumba's daughter, who had died of tuberculosis in Switzerland, had just arrived in Léopoldville. Lumumba asked for a United Nations plane to take him and the coffin to Stanleyville for burial but we declined on the ground that our limited aircraft was available only for the transport of U.N. supplies and personnel. U.N. rules forbade the use of U.N. planes for such purposes but we offered, as a humanitarian gesture, facilities for the despatch of the unaccompanied coffin to Stanleyville. This episode has been the subject of some criticism, and much as we regretted the decision from a humanitarian point of view, we really had no choice in the matter, as we had no authority to change the rules. Furthermore, we knew that if Lumumba reached Stanleyville in a U.N. aircraft, we would be blamed for establishing a rival authority and promoting civil war and the disruption of the country. Lumumba then telephoned to say that he would go to Stanleyville on his own, and if he fell, 'he would be a martyr and his blood would be on the U.N.'s conscience'.

General Lundula had, meanwhile, made his way to Stanleyville unmolested and we wondered if Lumumba would follow suit. Lumumba's followers, however, hoped that the arrival of the Conciliation Commission would help them to emerge from their quarantine, otherwise they would build up their strength in Orientale, Kasai, North Katanga, and Kivu. My advice, conveyed to Lumumba and his supporters through the African envoys, was to stay put in Léopoldville until the arrival of the Conciliation Commission, the U.N. Force affording them necessary protection at their homes. But Lumumba sent word that he was suffering from claustrophobia and he felt the urge to renew contact with his people. I could only advise extreme caution as, relative to the A.N.C. in Léopoldville, the position of the U.N. Force was weak, and it could not possibly afford another clash with Mobutu's troops. All that we could do was to hope that our advice would be heeded for while we could give protection at residences there was no question of the provision of mobile patrols which would follow Lumumba or other politicians if they chose to leave their secure havens. ONUC had in fact intervened on 9 October on Lumumba's behalf when there was sufficient legal and political justification. A warrant had been presented at the United Nations headquarters by A.N.C soldiers for the arrest of Lumumba, and a demand made for the recall of our guards around his residence. This we had refused.

My report to New York on this episode said: 'Bomboko - Mobutu combination erupted this morning by trying to arrest Lumumba. There could not have been a more ill-conceived action at this juncture, and we had very little doubt that it should not be allowed. ONUC which has the principal contenders under its protection would have been blamed for allowing an extra-constitutional and illegal manoeuvre of this kind to destroy efforts to find peaceful solutions.'

We were under pressure from the Western ambassadors to allow Lumumba's arrest, and Timberlake asked if there was a change in U.N. policy. Mobutu put up a show of force and then quietly backed down. Our legal adviser, William Cox, examined the warrant which he found *prima facie* illegal since it implicitly derived its authority from the Loi Fondamentale and yet violated it by describing Lumumba as 'Deputy', for even between sessions of Parliament, a deputy cannot be arrested without parliamentary consent. The Commissioner for Defence argued that the warrant had been ordered by Mobutu as head of the military régime. But that also was illegal as it was an act of military force. The warrant itself had cited an article of Belgian law which was not applicable to the Congo. I concluded my report with the following words: 'At this juncture, the arbitrary arrest of politicians would have the effect of torpedoing your efforts to rally the Afro-Asians, your search for peaceful solutions, securing the withdrawal of the Belgians and the unification of the country. . . .'

Hammarskjold fully supported our action and replied:

Absolutely consistent with our 'shameful and disgusting' policy, I firmly uphold your stand on legally invalid warrant of arrest and on continued U.N. protection of Lumumba against actions of political violence such as this—although such protection seems to be against publicly stated will of 'legitimate' P.M. Will try to put Western eager beavers straight on where we stand, an operation which, although subtler and less public, is not less tough than maintaining the front against the other side. I guess you will be attacked for your stand and will therefore take the line that the decision is mine and on my responsibility, as you have submitted question for advice. . . . Bomboko and Mobutu tricks may, if rightly commented upon, help us to throw some badly needed light on principles which have all along guided my actions.

Hammarskjold concluded with the following encouraging words: 'I appreciate very much your wise and effective work on this critical issue which I hope to match by some firm words to those concerned here.' For a time, it appeared that Hammarskjold's efforts at New York to restrain the over-heated envoys in Léopoldville had worked. When Timberlake saw me a few days later, he said his supply of fire extinguishers was exhausted, so hard had he worked to calm down Bomboko! But our respite was short-lived as Mobutu resumed his attempts to arrest Lumumba which ONUC prevented by one means or another while keeping within the framework of the Secretary-General's formula. We had gone as far as we safely could to protect Lumumba and we would have done it again if he had remained at his residence. But he chose otherwise, bringing tragedy upon himself, disaster to his country, and discord to the United Nations.

Hammarskjold summed up his views on the shifting scene, the mercurial Congolese politicians, and the uncertain role of the big powers in a cable:

As regards political situation one major difficulty is that we can never get inside the skin of our Congolese friends or disentangle outside manoeuvres. For that reason also, I find it dangerous to base our actions on anything but rather general concepts as to interplay of forces to extent we find our analysis supported by confirmed facts. Believe that on the whole we will get safer results with this sceptical approach. Believe also that this may save us from danger of getting tied up in Congo-type intrigues which grow like mushrooms and die like mushrooms and mostly, like mushrooms, are rather poisonous. . . . Believe that the real game now, as in fact all the time, is between much bigger powers and personalities than those which figure in the Congo limelight. With all due regard to minor intrigues, conflicts, and alliances, we must never lose our contact with main currents under quickly passing ripples on the surface.

My immediate task was to assure a measure of security for U.N. personnel and to establish some sort of *modus vivendi* with Mobutu and Bomboko. There followed long discussions backed by written demands and protests. Gradually, the road-blocks were removed and some vehicles were restored and the temperature slightly lowered. Mobutu, however, remained alienated from us, and his contacts with our military command became increasingly infrequent. We heard that he was planning formally to take over the reins of government for he had been heard to say that if Nasser could do it, why not he? In fact, the Moroccans reported from Camp Léopold (renamed Camp Kokolo) that such a move was afoot; Kettani tactfully sounded Mobutu, who seemed, however, to have decided that the time was not opportune. But Mobutu's determination not to co-operate with ONUC to the extent he could, remained unshaken, with the bizarre result of an international force which had come to the assistance of a disorganized national army, co-existing in mutual hostility with it.

I did not wish to worry Hammarskjold about the personal danger in which we stood, but he had seen reports in the newspapers which brought an urgent telegram of enquiry from him. In reply, I forwarded him a report from Colonel Lasmar which read as follows: 'Two boats of vedette type were seen on river by our troops posted in residence of Mr. Dayal coming from Kalina side; they were carrying about twenty A.N.C. soldiers armed with machine guns. These boats were patrolling near the residence of Mr. Dayal. Another boat armed with mortars is said to have been seen by Moroccan guard in the same area. One of the boats tried to land the troops but was stopped by the Indonesian guard.'

Some time later, I had a report that the Congolese security officer, Captain Pongo, habitually visited our military headquarters, armed with a loaded revolver which he said was intended for use against the Special Representative who worked two floors above. The U.N. military officers tried to shut him up but he repeated his threats on many occasions. There was nothing that could be done about it as the U.N. had no powers of arrest. I also received many messages reminding me of the 'fate of Count Bernadotte'. But worse were the telephone calls made to my wife containing threats of violence against us, which she dealt with by not picking up the telephone thereafter. We shrugged off these threats for had we taken them seriously, the objective of those making them would have been partially gained.

At the governmental level, the situation was as confused as it could be. Mobutu's College of Commissioners was presided over by that elastic and durable politician, Justin Bomboko, and consisted of fifteen Commissioners General and an equal number of deputies. A dozen among them had university diplomas and another dozen were university students. Three had been Chefs de Cabinet of ministries in the Lumumba Government. Two had worked in the M.N.C. (Lumumba),[1]

[1] M.N.C. stands for Mouvement National Congolais, see pp. 291-2.

one as the party's spokesman and the other as a political adviser. The College had two main tasks, to conduct the administration and to prepare the ground for national reconciliation. There was not a word in a proclamation issued by the College about the United Nations except for a sarcastic comment that the A.N.C. could be counted upon to prevent another form of colonialism being imposed upon the country.

Kasavubu had jumped on Mobutu's bandwagon by installing the Commissioners at a ceremony at his house on 29 September, thus 'fathering a foundling', as I reported to New York. Mobutu was furious with Kasavubu and stated publicly that he had no right to organize the ceremony. The thorny problem of relations between ONUC and the College had been negotiated with Bomboko and an understanding arrived at to the effect that there would be mutual cooperation on a technical plane in the fields of finance, administration, transport, and economy on a day-to-day basis. But there was no question of political recognition, ONUC maintaining an attitude of strict neutrality as regards the political and constitutional issues. ONUC also declined to enter into any formal agreements with the College, business being conducted on the basis of exchanges of memoranda of understanding.

Although we tried to insulate the problems of technical assistance in civilian fields from political complications, some degree of impact was inevitable. The fact that U.N. experts had to do business with the Commissioners without recognizing them as a legal authority would inevitably cause friction and frustration. As the Commissioners gained confidence, their self-assertiveness increased. It was inevitable also that relations between ONUC—which was trying to re-establish legality— and Mobutu, who had overthrown it, would be difficult. Mobutu regarded the U.N. Force as a competitive and rival element to his A.N.C. Our instructions to the international experts were to make every effort to do business with the Commissioners in a spirit of harmony and cooperation, to the exclusion of all political considerations. But without a responsive echo from the Commissioners who were to be helped, the experts found their task not an easy one. There were, fortunately, some notable exceptions which enabled some programmes to be carried out with a fair measure of success. But there were also cases of open sabotage which led to certain aspects of U.N. assistance being terminated.

The administration had been almost completely neglected while the politicians were attacking each other. ONUC's programmes had therefore to be based on the relative urgency of needs and had to be tailored to the situation prevailing in different fields. There were crash programmes such as getting the seaports and the railway network into action. The distribution of food was undertaken as an emergency operation. ONUC'S efforts in these humanitarian fields met with no opposition and they were an outstanding success. The second aspect consisted of the provision of technical assistance in such fields as telecommunications, medical care and public health, education, civil aviation, etc. Here the task was more difficult as it involved the recruitment of large numbers of personnel with adequate experience. On the whole, ONUC succeeded in providing the basic services, although some were at a fairly low level. The third aspect related to long-term planning in the economic and administrative fields. The economic situation was catastrophic and it was essential to stop the drain of foreign exchange, to revive the disrupted tax-collection machinery, to introduce some financial sanity, and to relate expenditure to income. A Monetary Council was set up which did much to stop the outflow of resources by a series of measures regulating foreign exchange transactions and external commerce. Steps were also taken to establish a new National Bank, which soon came into existence, but the issue of bank-notes was, for a time, held up as Kasavubu insisted on his effigy being carried on them. Most difficult of all was the task of preparing central and provincial budgets as very little previous information was available, nor were the Congolese able to make any estimates of their future needs.

Robert Gardiner, the U.N. administrative expert from Ghana, very ably drew up civil service regulations and worked out salary and promotion scales. I had strongly felt that if ONUC could do little or nothing to train the A.N.C., it should at least launch a big training programme for Congolese civilians in various branches of the administration and in nation-building activities. A college for accelerated training in law and administration was started. Some ninety medical assistants were picked out for higher studies abroad and placed in universities in France and Switzerland. I was anxious to ensure that more and more trained Congolese would become fitted to man positions of responsibility in the country, so that by the time the U.N. mission departed, an adequate reservoir of competent Congolese would be available. This was one of the most successful, though not the most eye-catching, of our achievements.

There was also the aspect of finding counsellors and liaison officers for the provincial governments, which were even worse off in the matter of trained personnel than the authorities at the centre. The tendency of the administration to break apart had to be prevented, despite the growing political fragmentation in the country. This we tried to do by linking up the provincial administrations with the centre, the attendance of the Finance Ministers at a Léopoldville conference being an encouraging example. At the same time, we insisted that the financial obligations of the centre to the provinces be honoured. Whenever funds were available in the central treasury, payments of salaries to civilian employees and military personnel in the provinces continued to be made.

The young Commissioners were not used to functioning in an organized way, and it was not easy for U.N. experts to find responsible officials in the chair with whom to work. But more difficult was the problem of gaining their ear. The Belgian influx had been steadily increasing. Some of the Belgian advisers were former colonial officials, others were professors, but a few had little or no previous experience of government.

Hammarskjold's reactions to the reports of Belgian interference came to us in his cable:

Most disturbed by these various pieces of information regarding Belgian policies and Belgian return. It is an absolute must that we stop this infiltration, the basis for which is too easily guessed and the consequences of which are too easily foreseen. . . . One major African leader jokingly said to me that I have certainly not kept the West out to let the Russians in; now I add to this that we are most definitely not 'keeping others out' in order to let the Belgians in. The basic difficulty of course is that we cannot count on good faith on Belgian side or among their Congolese clients. We must pursue a strict policy, strictly our own. For that purpose I consider it necessary to negotiate from strength.

Hammarskjold asked for a comprehensive report which he said he 'would not hesitate to put on the table irrespective of whom it might torpedo', adding that 'there was no treatment reserved for the Belgians' different from that which he had to apply in all cases without exception. He concluded: 'Night thought: it is a miracle that the U.N. operation works at all with no government, at the first and last, really willing to play ball when their interests get involved—and I mean no, repeat no, government.'

The Report, with its addenda, as more information came to light, formed the basis of the Secretary-General's *démarches* to the Belgian Government. But they produced no effect in stemming the influx of Belgians in policy-making positions and in military or para-military capacities. Curiously enough, while the new Belgian arrivals were anxious for the U.N. Force to continue as it gave them a sense of security, they were totally opposed to the continuation of the U.N. technical-assistance programme which they wished to take over entirely. On the other hand, Mobutu and the A.N.C. would have greatly welcomed the withdrawal of the U.N. Force which they regarded as a rival to the A.N.C, but they were most anxious for the U.N. technical assistance to continue as it brought in money and expertise and provided a weapon with which to play off the Belgians in case of need.

Kasavubu was soon due to return from his triumphal visit to New York and it was essential to chart our future course in view of the constellation of forces developing in the Congo. The seating of Kasavubu's delegation at the United Nations had given the President a new standing and it was clear that his 'neutralization' by Mobutu was without practical effect. Relations between Kasavubu and Mobutu had till then been strained, but the situation could now well change. Hammarskjold sent detailed instructions which provided guide-lines for ONUC's future activities:

Result of credentials manoeuvre is so far a strengthening of Kasavubu's hand here and probably a creation of great resistance against all U.N. efforts. Typically, Kasavubu today for a second time raised issue of beginning withdrawal of certain contingents (Ghana and Guinea) and pronounced himself strongly against the introduction of any new troops. My reply was a vote of no, repeat no, confidence in A.N.C.

You will be best judge of repercussions in Léo, one of which is manoeuvres around Lumumba's house. Seating of delegation here, combined with various steps on spot tending to increase Mobutu's self-assurance, may well have created situation where Mobutu feels strongly in the saddle, in fact, protects Kasavubu and under cover of President's new prestige, bases himself on the fictional efficiency of A.N.C. and the real financial strength of certain outsiders. This creates most serious tactical problem for you and for us because on the one side we must work with the realities of the situation, while on the other hand, in the very interests of the Congo and irrespective of various noises here, we must carefully avoid strengthening present tendencies in the longevity of which I find it difficult to believe, knowing the structure of the society and the temperament of its people.

Conclusion is that we, while recognizing new legal situation and what it may imply regarding Kasavubu personally and his position should avoid carefully to build his supporters and those supported. We can contribute to the strengthening of their position not only by participation in their various shows but also by resistance to moves on their side which, due to the fact that we alone play ball, and also to trend in Western press reports, may put us in the wrong and make them successful knights in shining armour. This situation calls for great circumspection in both the directions indicated.

Believe in the possibility to build up over some time valuable working relationship with Kasavubu–Bomboko group, provided that outsiders can be kept low and no illusions are permitted to develop regarding the efficiency of A.N.C. Also due to mistakes on our side things may be played in such a way that we would have to wind up but I shudder at the thought of what that might mean internationally. We would indeed have reasons to rejoice if end result would be return also of Belgian military units with the consequence that what we have avoided for more than four months at great sacrifice will come true!

Kasavubu returned to Léopoldville on 27 November in a chartered Sabena jet and was received at the airport with pomp and ceremony. He took a long time to emerge from the plane while he donned a brand new Field-Marshal's white uniform, complete with epaulettes, gold braid, and sword, which we watched being carried across the tarmac to the waiting plane. That night there was a banquet at the President's house attended by some two hundred guests. Commissioner Ndele greeted the conquering hero as the 'incarnation of the sovereignty and future aspirations of the country'. In a dig at the Second Report, he referred to the 'youth and inexperience' of the College of Commissioners, on which he said that out of deference to age, he preferred not to reply. Kasavubu, in responding, spoke of his experiences at New York but he devoted the greater part of his speech to the question of technical assistance, and while welcoming help from all countries as well as from the United Nations, he added that no interference in the country's internal affairs would be permitted. This remark was received with loud cheers (in which Ian Scott the British Ambassador, sitting near me, enthusiastically joined) which appeared to be out of proportion to the profundity of the observation. Grateful tributes were paid to Mobutu, seated at the high table, by both Kasavubu and Ndele. The occasion demonstrated vividly my apprehensions of a link-up between Kasavubu and Mobutu owing both to the vote in New York and to the recent trial of strength between the A.N.C. and the U.N. Force.

There was a severe tropical storm that night, and while the junketing at the President's house was in progress, a very different drama, unknown to all of us in the midst of the celebrations, was being enacted not very far from there. The story came to light only the next day at ONUC headquarters. Lumumba had fled. The first report was from the Moroccan guard posted at the Prime Minister's residence, who, thinking the house strangely quiet, decided to enter it, only to find it empty. I immediately informed New York that 'Lumumba was presumably one of the three occupants of a large black car which had left the premises in secrecy the previous night. How Lumumba managed to elude the A.N.C. guard shows resourcefulness of his supporters, unless his escape was actually encouraged to get rid of an inconvenient element. Mobutu's men have asked for suspension of all flights, but Lumumba has no doubt contrived less obvious means of escape either to Stanleyville where Gizenga awaits him, or to Luluabourg where Lumumba's daughter's coffin has preceded him. Should Léo-Élisabethville axis develop, Lumumba will set up his own Central Government. We are entering upon a new phase of developments which may radically change balance of forces in the country and next week or two could well be crucial. . . . If Lumumba manages to get to Stanleyville, the whole situation would change in a flash.'

How Lumumba was able to slip through both the U.N. guards—whose duty it was to keep out unwanted visitors—as well as the A.N.C. troops, who were there to prevent his escape, remains a mystery. Normally, the U.N. guard would not concern itself with an outgoing vehicle, but had the Congolese troops been bribed or were they caught napping? We speculated about who could have helped in the escape. Our thoughts turned to Kamitatu, but when he later called at ONUC headquarters and was told of the escape, he was genuinely surprised, as well as terrified about his own safety.

If any of the African ambassadors had helped, it would have been noticed by both the U.N. and Congolese troops. Mobutu told press correspondents that Lumumba had slipped down to the river facing his house and had been rowed some miles upstream where he was then picked up and driven away in a convoy of cars. For a time we believed that Kasavubu's friends might have spirited Lumumba away. But this theory was soon disproved when I received a summons to the President's house, where a highly annoyed Kasavubu received me in the presence of Ileo, Bomboko, and Ndele, all in a state of great agitation. Kasavubu enquired about the circumstances, while Bomboko excitedly suggested U.N. complicity in the affair. I gave details of what we knew with 'a straight face and clear conscience', as I reported to Hammarskjold. My question as to what the A.N.C. guard were doing was received in embarrassed silence. Bomboko said that if Lumumba managed to reach Stanleyville and a civil war were to break out, the U.N. would be responsible.

Meanwhile, all eyes were turned towards the rapidly retreating figure of Lumumba. In 'Le Royal' we awaited news by the hour. The first was that Lumumba had reached Kikwit (Kamitatu's stronghold in Léopoldville province) and was on his way to Port Francqui on the Congo River or to Tshikapa in Kasai province en route to Luluabourg for the burial of his daughter's body. Then followed a rumour that he had crossed the river into Orientale province at Boende. Gizenga had already reached Stanleyville and Okito, Mpolo, and Kasha-mura[1] were on their way. We were under great pressure from different directions either to impede or to facilitate Lumumba's movements. Congolese Security Captain Pongo demanded U.N. air transport for pursuit of Lumumba and this was firmly refused; he then flew with a posse of A.N.C. troops in an Air Congo commercial plane to Kikwit, where he asked for U.N. road transport, which was also refused. In reporting these developments to the Secretary-General, I informed him that 'we have also instructed our units that it is no part of ONUC's functions to provide or transmit intelligence to either side concerning the movements or whereabouts of pursued or pursuers'.

ONUC's legal experts were working on instructions regarding the attitude of the scattered units of the U.N. Force to the various contingencies that might arise in the light of the Secretary-General's recent directive concerning Gizenga when he sought refuge at ONUC headquarters in Stanleyville following a fight between units of the A.N.C. and the local gendarmerie. Hammarskjold had instructed that 'we have for the time being to keep him under our protection in Stanleyville, even if it be in U.N. precincts. But it must be understood that he has to choose either to rely on our protection and to keep out of his tricks or continue with his tricks and forgo all protection.'

Ghana Brigade headquarters had reported their intention to provide protection for Lumumba if requested by him. In our reply, we said that Lumumba 'was under U.N. guard at his residence only and cannot be allowed U.N. cover or protection in pursuit of his aims, and ONUC must be entirely dissociated from his activities. Different rules could apply only if individual lives were in danger in specific circumstances and protection could be given solely as step to restoring peace.' The Secretary-General approved of the formula which would have left the door open for protection in case Lumumba's life was known to be threatened, but which would have dissociated ONUC from his political activities. We thus hoped to keep clear of any charge of illegal interference in the Congo's internal affairs while keeping in reserve the possibility of intervention for the express purpose of preventing danger to Lumumba's life.

Kasavubu's false charge of U.N. complicity had already

[1] Minister for Information in Lumumba's Central Government.

been communicated by certain envoys to New York, for the very next day Hammarskjold wired: 'In corridors here there is a lot of speculation as to the U.N.'s participation in the escape of Mr. Lumumba and there is speculation that he is trying to make his way to Accra or Conakry.'

The chase continued for four or five days. In Léopoldville, Mobutu carried out a fresh spate of panicky and indiscriminate arrests. Pongo, after scouring the countryside in a low-flying aircraft, returned from Luluabourg complaining that the Ghana troops had held up his plane. Ileo charged that Lumumba had been arrested at Port Francqui but released by the Ghana unit. Pongo then flew back with a warrant to continue the hunt.

On 2 December, a flash message was received from the Ghana Brigade at Luluabourg that Lumumba had been arrested some five miles north of Mweka, south-east of Port Francqui, from where he was being taken to Luluabourg en route to Léopoldville. Lumumba could have easily got away to Stanleyville, but he travelled in a leisurely way, addressing public meetings, confident that his personal charisma and the support of the people would be enough protection against his pursuers. There were some scattered U.N. troops in the general area, but he did not approach them for any assistance. Kasha-mura, who was with him, got away, but Okito and Mpolo were arrested. Lumumba was flown by his captor, Captain Pongo, to Ndjili airport under strong guard, dressed in a soiled shirt with his hands tied behind his back. He was roughly pushed into a waiting truck and driven off to a place near Mobutu's residence. There, according to Western correspon-dents who saw him, he was insulted and beaten. After Lu-mumba's flight, Mme Lumumba had tried to board a com-mercial plane to Luluabourg for the burial of her daughter. She and her companions were seized but she was allowed to return home.

Mobutu proudly announced that the forty A.N.C. troops who arrested Lumumba were able to repulse an attempt by Ghana troops to free him. That, of course, was a pure fabrication. Mobutu claimed that he had prevented Lumumba from being shot by the A.N.C. troops who arrested him. The same day I had received a letter from Kasavubu charging that Ghana troops had freed Lumumba at Port Francqui and threatening that he would break off relations with the U.N. Brazzaville radio announced that Lumumba was being taken to Camp Hardy at Thysville. It was confirmed by our own sources that in the small hours of the morning, a convoy of two cars and two station wagons, escorted by armoured cars and jeeps, had left in the direction of Thysville. Later in the morning, Kasavubu himself left with a heavy guard in the same direction and when I tried to make an appointment with him, his household said he would be away for the weekend. I then sent for Bomboko to ask for his comments on Lumumba's reported manhandling and to impress on him the importance of just and humane treatment. Bomboko said that Lumumba's arrest was 'a great embarrassment' and that he was most anxious to ensure that the prisoner received a fair trial. He added that Lumumba's followers were converging on Stanleyville and he feared the start of a civil war.

Hammarskjold shared our concern at the turn of events, and he wired: 'The emotional tension here around the Lumumba case is considerable and if things run wild or summary justice executed, consequences may be very bad also for the Organization and its Operation. We are in the middle of an extraordinarily complicated and indeed politically dangerous situation. I believe all we can do is to fall back on our right and duty to stand firmly on Charter principles as overriding all other considerations, even if this would lay us open to allegations of partisanship—perhaps even from both sides. . . . I know that you will, of course, use all your diplomatic means, as on previous occasions, to see that civilized rules of law are upheld. A case of mob justice, with or without collusion from some authority, would, in present situation, be exceedingly serious in its impact.'

Hammarskjold's message to Kasavubu said that a great number of delegations had approached him expressing their deep concern about the action taken against Lumumba outside the framework of due process of law. The Secretary-General added a strong personal appeal to Kasavubu's 'wisdom and fair-mindedness', with the assurance that he was not expressing an opinion on any internal problem in the Congo. Immediately after this message came another from the Secretary-General in much stronger terms, following a formal call on him by a delegation from the African and Asian group at the U.N. led by the Foreign Minister of Cameroon. Hammarskjold asked that Kasavubu should be informed of the unanimous African and Asian support for his *démarche*.

Kasavubu had promised the Secretary-General and his Advisory Committee that he would definitely send word early in December about the visit of the Conciliation Commission. Hammarskjold cabled me: 'Whatever channel you can find, you should insist on my message getting through to Kasavubu. . . . If he has left without meeting his promise to Advisory Committee, I hope he realizes what that will mean for trust in him also among those who voted in his favour.'

I immediately asked Gustavo Duran, a senior U.N. official who was one of my principal political advisers, to track down the President and personally to deliver the Secretary-General's written and oral messages to him. Duran had been a brilliant General in the Spanish Republican army when still in his early thirties. He was a man of great *savoir-faire* and distinction. He had become an American citizen and was rightly held in high respect and esteem by Hammarskjold and all his U.N. colleagues.

Duran traced Kasavubu to Chela in the Lower Congo region and was able to get an audience with some difficulty. Kasavubu received him and the Canadian Colonel Berthiume coldly, and in an interview lasting barely five minutes, with all present standing, took the Secretary-General's letter. When asked for a reply, Kasavubu said that a written communication would receive a written reply. Pressed to convey some reactions for the information of the Secretary-General, Kasavubu said that he had nothing more to say, and abruptly terminated the interview. The written reply, when it came a few days later, was mean and cantankerous. Kasavubu asked why there was so much solicitude for Lumumba, who was guilty of a number of crimes against the state and the people, including that of genocide, when the U.N. was doing nothing to prevent violation of human rights in Stanleyville. As for the African and Asian countries which had expressed concern, how were they treating their political opponents? The Congo had not adhered to the U.N. Charter in vain and it well knew its obligations which it was faithfully observing.

The Security Council now stepped into the act. At a meeting requisitioned by the representative of the Soviet Union the Secretary-General and his representatives in the Congo were strongly criticized for invoking the doctrine of 'non-intervention', and the representative of Guinea announced his Government's decision to withdraw from the Conciliation Commission and to pull out its troops from the Congo.

Before the Council concluded its session, the Secretary-General made what was for him a long statement in which he took up the various criticisms. Warning against any temptation to withdraw the Operation, he made an evaluation of the danger of unbridled civil war degenerating into tribal conflict. He also appealed to the Council that if it wished an extension of ONUC's mandate, it should also provide the necessary means. But above all, he reminded the Council to take a fair share of the responsibility for running the Operation so as not to weaken the Secretariat by ambiguities and political war waged around its activities. In the event the debate produced no resolution and gave no guidance to the Secretary-General or to his representatives in the Congo; it merely intensified differences among the delegations.

In Léopoldville, we felt orphaned by the attacks on the Secretary-General, because if he, our shield, was so vulnerable, we were defenceless. The Congolese well knew it and did everything to exploit our difficulties to their personal and factional advantage. As Hammarskjold had told us, we were not dealing with individual Congolese alone, but with the far more powerful external forces that were behind them.

When the scramble for power began, the Congolese politicians and Mobutu importuned various foreign powers for help for their competitive causes. Lumumba had first appealed for help to the Americans, then to the Canadians and Ghanaians, and finally to the Russians. The first two would not, and the third could not, provide the kind of help and in the expected measure that he needed. Kasavubu had also joined with Lumumba in an appeal to the Russians, but the break between the two rivals led him to break with the Soviet Union as well. Kasavubu, who in his political life had always fought the Belgians, then turned for help to them and they were glad to win back so pivotal an opponent. Mobutu had been Lumumba's man, but with his patron's removal, he found the path of his ambitions blocked by Kasavubu.

Mobutu had, meanwhile, won the support of the British Embassy. But Bomboko had his own ambitions and he found a receptive ear at the American mission. For a time, there was an amiable rivalry between the two missions as they backed their respective protégés. But British calculations were more realistic as Mobutu had some semblance of military force behind him while Bomboko had only his wits. The same process of finding foreign patrons had led Tshombe, who had little love for the Belgians, to throw himself into their arms, which, in view of a natural conjunction of interests, were readily opened up to him.

The Congolese were shrewd enough to realize that having secured the patronage of various powers and interests, it would advance their purposes to draw their patrons ever deeper into their commitments. The situation therefore arose of great countries getting increasingly enmeshed in the primitive politics of the Congo. The next step was to identify those powers with individual Congolese politicians. The Congolese finally turned the tables by reversing the roles and themselves adopting their former patrons who, in effect, became their clients. Thus, if the fortunes of Lumumba or Gizenga fell, the Soviet Union regarded it as a rebuff; if Mobutu was criticized, the United Kingdom took umbrage; if Kasavubu was not seated at the United Nations, the Americans would feel affronted; if Tshombe's position was threatened, Belgian security was endangered.

So intimate became the identification that it was like a three-legged race in which a great power was linked to a Congolese politician, with the diverting quality that if the pigmy fell, he brought his giant partner down with him. Whether one mercurial politician got the better of his rival was not vital to the larger issues at stake. But, transported to the global dimensions of inter-state relations, the hatreds and rivalries engendered by the Congolese factions posed a real danger to the United Nations and indeed to world peace.

CHAPTER 10

Four Sovereignties

We had come to another perilous crossroads in the tortuous course of the Operation. At the central level, the Ileo 'Government' had not been revoked and was theoretically still in being. But Lumumba and his followers continued to assert that theirs was the only lawful Government. Both pretender Governments had been superseded by Mobutu's College of Commissioners, which was, in a way, in function. But it neither claimed legality nor expected recognition by the United Nations even as a caretaker government. Kasavubu was the legal President, but Mobutu claimed to have 'neutralized' him. Kasavubu had adopted the Commissioners, but his control or influence over them was illusory as they owed their existence to Mobutu. Mobutu, however, still remained Chief of Staff of the army without claiming any political attributes or functions. Kasavubu's delegation's seating at the U.N. had so dispirited Lumumba and his followers that they planned a mass exodus to Stanleyville, the capital of Orientale province. With Lumumba's arrest, dejection turned to desperation. The Lumumbists then decided to proclaim Stanleyville as the seat of the 'legal' Central Government of which the absent Lumumba was the head and Gizenga the regent. They rapidly eliminated political dissidents in Orientale and overcame the resistance of opposing elements in the provincial military command.

ONUC, which had come to establish unity in the Congo, now had the engaging task of dealing with not one but four competing authorities. There was a 'Central' authority in Léopoldville, another in Stanleyville, both claiming sovereignty over the whole of the Congo. Katanga and South Kasai were in open secession. Kalonji soon crowned himself as the 'Mulopwe' or King of the Baluba tribe of South Kasai.

In the raging confusion, it was clear that ONUC would have to rechart its course if it was not to founder. With mutually hostile armies in four centres of authority, the danger of civil war was increasing, seriously threatening the disintegration of the country. The Western powers had given their backing to Mobutu and while they had opposed military measures by the Central Government to end Katanga's secession, they joined with Kasavubu and Mobutu in demanding U.N. military action for the suppression of Stanleyville. They also demanded that the U.N. Force in Stanleyville spread itself over that vast province to protect Belgian plantations and planters who were returning in a flood. But any attempts by U.N. officials to establish working relations with the local authorities in Stanleyville were regarded as giving encouragement to the Lumumbists. These mutually incompatible demands were pressed in New York and Léopoldville at a time when Mobutu's forces and those of the other splinter factions were being steadily expanded, while the U.N. Force was being eroded by withdrawals by several dissatisfied Asian and African countries.

Reviewing the situation in the provinces, I informed the Secretary-General of the new dangers and harassment to which our civilian personnel were increasingly exposed. I also reminded him that the equipment of the U.N. Force was inferior to that of the A.N.C., and that its movements were greatly restricted by lack of adequate transport and by Belgian obstruction in the field.

The Congolese attitude was to pocket the financial and other benefits which suited them and to ask for more, but to offer every type of obstruction to U.N. actions which did not suit them. A proposal was on the anvil to feed some three million dollars worth of United Nations aid into the anaemic economy. I asked for its deferment and suggested that it was time to review the policy of turning the other cheek. The latest attempt to paralyse the U.N.'s military operations was an order issued by Mobutu's Commissioners to the Belgian transport monopoly known as Otraco, to refuse the carriage of U.N. cargoes without the specific authorization of Nendaka, the Congolese Security Chief, a man notorious for his fanatical opposition to ONUC.

Hammarskjold's initial observations reached me within hours of the despatch of my proposals. He said:

I am shocked in particular by this latest case[1] as it aims at one of the U.N. lifelines. Belgian back-stopping or collusion or inspiration is obvious to anyone who cares to see. . . . I do not believe that the Kasavubu-Mobutu-Bomboko trio would be impressed by our threats to react as clearly indicated by their acts of hostility, but I do believe that their supporters, apart perhaps from Belgium, may be a bit worried if we threaten to take the loincloth away. For that reason I think better action would be, with proper documentation, to denounce, in key Western capitals what is going on. . . . We are agreed on a re-appraisal of our technical assistance but when it comes to personnel, we fear that the threat might be somewhat hollow as large number of technicians are in Léo and rather important to ourselves (communications, etc.). It is another matter to put brakes on purely financial operation, as for example the three million one, regarding which the transfer has been stopped in light of your observations (undoubtedly it will prove possible for Congolese to get the necessary money because purveyors are there). From that point of view all we can do is to smoke out the fact that they have such purveyors. . . . Atmosphere here among African delegations is tense and it is easy to tip the scales in extreme directions which may prove irresponsible. I am willing to be very tough but only provided that we have an agreed line indicating what will be the second and third steps after the first. I repeat that basically some plain talk is likely to be necessary with those without whom our Congolese friends would be nothing. . . .

The Secretary-General promised to give his broad policy review after further thought. He had no doubts about Western, and particularly, Belgian backing of the lawless acts of the Léopoldville triumvirate, and I hoped that his diplomatic pressures in the Western capitals would have some effect.

The promised policy directive soon reached us:

I feel we have come to a point where in view of possible drift towards military dictatorship, difficulties with the 'Government', noises here, and our own need to know what we are really doing, we should engage in some urgent stock-taking in order to know where we are and where we go. We are only in first stages of what I would call a good hard look at the U.N. Operation in the Congo but want to bring you in the picture now so as to have a full coordination of views and maximum advantage of your thinking before any steps are taken or I am forced out into the open in some debates here. Following annota-

[1] The order given to Otraco not to carry U.N. cargoes except with the authorization of the Congolese Chief of Security.

tions are only by way of attempt to systematize points for consideration in private tentative agenda.

(A) In the field:

1/ Discontinued protection specifically of Kasavubu. We feel on the one side that Mobutu's and Kasavubu's bragging regarding A.N.C. would be perfectly valid reason for withdrawal of protection; on the other hand, it may be regarded as mean sanction.

2/ A.N.C. training. Disappointment with results so far might well lead to conclusion that time is ripe for liquidation. I am anything but certain of wisdom of such a conclusion. We can estimate extremes, viz. integration of A.N.C. in ONUC or complete withdrawal. I would like us all to give thought to return to my original concept to the effect that our efforts should be concentrated on building up A.N.C., small unit after small unit, using reliable soldiers and getting best possible officers, thereafter agreeing with Congolese Military Command that those units are put in for ONUC functions, but outside U.N. Command, relieving our battalions which, *pari passu*, should be withdrawn. Such an approach would have value of creating rational basis for reduction of ONUC and playing on A.N.C. pride without taking undue risk. Wholesale approach to A.N.C. problem appears to me to be sterile.

3/ Question of reduction of ONUC may come up because of request for withdrawal from three or four nations, or similar request with serious pressure from Congolese side, or finally, of course, by proposal from our side, which, however, at present in my view would be premature and irresponsible. In order to be able to treat this question in responsible terms we must have re-examination of why we are at various points with the specific strength allocated to those points. Obviously, reasons vary, as between North Katanga, Stanleyville, and Léo. What would we do and what would impact be in case of withdrawal of certain national contingents?

4/ Previous question leads straight on to the problem of general policy of gradual withdrawal to which I have registered my reactions above; however, also some financial difficulties come into play and we should have a policy line which obviously should be predicated by conclusions as to ONUC's functions.

5/ In civilian field what does U.N. Operation mean in experts and money? I have asked for text with possible report for stock-taking regarding technicians and disposal of available funds, marking that, with our means, 'this is it', and that remaining gaps would have to be filled by other means (which as you know are unacceptable to the majority of the Assembly). It would be helpful to have your and Linner's cold-headed evaluation of same problems in same terms.

6/ There still remain diplomatic and political problems as well illustrated in recent cables regarding Kasavubu's behaviour to Duran, Mobutu's declarations, attitudes of Western diplomats, etc., all of which will require patient and intelligent action to adjust stands and reactions to policy line which may be derived from discussion of previous five points.

(B) On this side of the Atlantic, I foresee lively discussion . . . in Advisory Committee and, later on, possible discussion on financing in Fifth Committee[1] and the Congo policy in general in the Assembly. All this must be well prepared.

1/ In Advisory Committee I intend to take lead in proposing that presiding officers of Conciliation Commission proceed to the Congo without waiting for President's letter which the good Lord only knows when we may receive. I would also like to give short factual comments on points (A) 6 and 5 and 2, adding your factual information on Belgian set-up and on Mobutu's most recent declarations regarding take-over after end of 1960. However, discussion in Committee likely to concentrate on Lumumba situation.

2/ In Fifth Committee and General Assembly. In Fifth Committee, I would have to pursue harsh line that either they take policy decision on winding up or they provide the necessary advances of money. I would, however, hope that I would reserve discussion of policies for General Assembly where I would try to bring out on record why we went in in the first place, to what extent objectives, as first conceived, have been fulfilled (and that is practically to the full), how 'new objectives' have developed due to internal Congo developments, how the objectives have been handled, the effect a withdrawal would have in the prevailing situation, and finally, the reasons for continuing. Could this be done reasonably well, we may have stabilized the U.N. Congo front from the time of the recess to the reopening of the session, presumably in February. This latter presentation is only indirectly your concern but I would anyway appreciate your advice and comments.

Anything you may bring to our notice by way of comments, analyses, and conclusions regarding this internal agenda, specifically part (A), would be highly appreciated and would facilitate the framing of an active policy which would give us again a lead after the most recent eruptions and their deplorable consequences also for the U.N.

My reactions to the basic issues raised by Hammarskjold were sent to him the same day (5 December). Referring to the drift towards a military dictatorship, I pointed out that a situation

---

[1] U.N. Administrative and Budgetary Committee.

where Mobutu was supreme, the Commissioners were the *de facto* authority, and Lumumba was under arrest, was exactly what certain powers had wanted. If the U.N. military operation collapsed or was seriously impaired, there would be no security left in the country and technical assistance would become impossible. The whole situation hinged on the A.N.C. and Mobutu, who had numerous Belgian advisers and 'plenty of funds from somewhere'. Our proposal for regroupment would reduce the impact of sudden withdrawals of certain national contingents, but we should also ask countries like Nigeria and Ethiopia to raise their contributions of troops. We would have to pull out of a couple of provinces to concentrate our reduced forces at more strategic points where they could also provide protection for U.N. civilian personnel. Hammarskjold observed that 'such action will no doubt evoke anguished cries from Belgians, but they will have to learn to face realities of a situation largely of their own making'. On the technical assistance side, we could either continue our aid as before, or reduce it to cover only the immediate vital functions. We also suggested that in accordance with normal terms of technical aid, the Congo should be asked to defray part of the costs.

On the political plane, I agreed that the issue regarding the arrival of the Conciliation Commission should be forced. The A.N.C. was now supreme in Léopoldville and it was drunk with the heady wine of political power. Mobutu was determined to force out or paralyse the U.N. Force. What could save the mission, however, was a realization by the great powers, however belatedly, that its collapse would imperil the United Nations itself. As a last resort, the Organization could take the line that since its initial duty of effecting the withdrawal of the intervening Belgian troops had been accomplished it was not in a position to undertake the new responsibilities to which the internal situation in the Congo had given rise and that it was leaving the task of maintaining the country's independence to the Congolese leaders themselves. Alternatively, could ONUC dig in at some intermediate point, short of either full activity or total withdrawal?

Hammarskjold commented that he had studied the observations 'with the greatest interest' and that he found 'a striking parallelism of thought', but, for natural reasons, he had placed himself one step further away from withdrawal. The Secretary-General continued his observations:

Your various telegrams. Parallel with these valuable and searching observations of yours, we have been engaging in a kind of dialogue with you through speeches here in the Council and the Assembly. These speeches have exhausted my imagination and our discussion time and we have so far not got beyond points they indicate. However, the immediate follow-up of my statements will be letter to Kasavubu laying down the law as it can be derived from what has happened here. I would try to support that letter by solid talk with Washington and London requesting effective support for our stand in this situation of crisis where they have themselves got committed through their own draft resolution. Hope to cable draft of such a letter tomorrow which, if you approve, should go straight on to Kasavubu. Thus I now follow up your suggestions but with our hand strengthened.

When tonight this part of the Assembly session has ended, we will fortunately have time to concentrate again on essentials but also an opportunity to talk things out with some top men like Fawzi.[1] I am worried by certain under-currents which may take us to a crisis so early as not to give proper time for us to use to the full our means of persuasion. However, there are strong elements of bluff and even of blackmail in the picture and we shall have to call off the bluff and resist the blackmail.

It is as yet impossible to say with certainty to what extent we should take withdrawal decisions seriously apart from the spearhead one by Yugoslavia where we should implement one part as quickly as possible by as smooth arrangements as possible for the return of their people whatever it costs us. I have told Popovic[2] that he will regret it, but their line is firm, determined probably by factors very far from the Congo, and then it is better to liquidate that part of the story without any further notice.

Hammarskjold tried once more to persuade Kasavubu that greater trust and cooperation with the United Nations provided the only way out of the Congo's increasing troubles. In his letter which closely followed the line indicated in his message to me, he especially counselled against the use of force as it would only exacerbate the situation. He took the precaution of showing the letter to the U.A.R. and Indian representatives, but 'more important', he gave copies to the U.S. and U.K. Ambassadors

---

[1] Foreign Minister of the U.A.R.
[2] Koca Popovic, Foreign Minister of Yugoslavia.

with, as he said, 'the explicit statement that I hope this would sober down those who look with favour at military undertakings by Mobutu–Kasavubu; the obvious implication was that I expect London and Washington to exercise influence in direction of the letter'. Hammarskjold ended his despatch with the conclusion that 'we have a period of diplomatic juggling in front of us which may be fairly long unless the Mobutus start moving'.

Unfortunately, the Mobutus and their friends did start moving. A debate had been going on in Léopoldville on the future shape of the central authority which became more pressing as the end of the year approached. Mobutu was implacably opposed to the return of a civilian government, whatever its political orientation. The parliamentarians and political parties which had allied themselves against the M.N.C. (Lumumba) were apprehensive about the indefinite continuance of Mobutu's rule through the Commissioners. While most of the politicians who remained in Léopoldville wanted a return to parliamentary government, others demanded the setting up at least of a provisional Government, with or without parliamentary approval.

Ileo made several attempts to name a Cabinet, in one of which Lumumba was to have been included as one of the three Deputy Prime Ministers; in subsequent lists Lumumba's name was eliminated, although some of his followers were included. Ileo, Bolikango, and other parliamentarians issued a number of statements to the effect that a national Government would soon be installed and would appear before a reconvened Parliament for its approval. Lumumba had also, from his retreat, been issuing statements professing a desire to cooperate, even approving of the project of a Round Table Conference.

Kasavubu found strong allies in Mobutu and the Commissioners, who, for obvious reasons, were opposed to the prospect of a civilian government. Mobutu's veto was crucial as he had the physical means to make his views effective. Furthermore, Mobutu was convinced that the suppression of the Stanleyville régime could be brought about only by force and the imposition of an economic blockade. But he was afraid that the U.N. Force would frustrate his efforts. He tried unsuccessfully to take over Ndjili airport from the control of U.N. troops and to deny them the use of river and rail transport. But Mobutu needed more arms and ammunition for his Stanleyville adventure and these he hoped to get from the former Belgian military base at Kitona, now held by the United Nations. The considerable quantities of arms stocked there were the property of the Belgian Government, which had been extremely tardy in removing them.

On 13 December a couple of Commissioners accompanied by Belgian counsellors had visited the installation ostensibly to call on the Belgian head of the technical mission whose duty was to keep the military stores in proper condition till their repatriation. The Belgian obligingly handed over the keys of the armoury to his Congolese visitors. Next morning, Congolese troops suddenly appeared at the gates of the base and taking up aggressive positions demanded entry. The small U.N. Moroccan guard refused, and appealed for reinforcements which General Kettani promptly sent from a nearby U.N. detachment at Goma. The Congolese intruders were surrounded and talks were opened at Léopoldville with Mobutu. Surprisingly, he blamed the Commissioners for the incident. He agreed to a U.N. emissary accompanied by a Congolese officer proceeding to the scene to enforce the withdrawal of the Congolese troops. On the day of the visit of the Commissioners, a large Belgian transport plane had arrived at Brazzaville which, on investigation by U.N. Swiss police officer, Knecht, was found to contain military stores. These supplies, no doubt, reached Mobutu by devious means, but the large quantities of vehicles, gasoline, and ammunition at Kitona remained firmly out of his reach.

Lumumba's capture radically transformed the situation as a new focus of power developed in Stanleyville, spreading to Kivu, North Katanga, parts of Kasai, with bridgeheads in the Kwilu and Lake Léopold areas of Léopoldville province. The writ of the Central authorities in Léopoldville ran only in the city and the Lower Congo region and Équateur. But even Luluabourg could not be securely relied upon. Not more than one-third of the country remained loyal to the Kasavubu régime.

On 12 December Gizenga finally made an announcement proclaiming Stanleyville as the provisional capital of the Government of the 'Free Republic of the Congo'. This was followed by a declaration that if Lumumba were not released within forty-eight hours, all Belgians would be arrested and some of them killed. Later, the acting President of the provincial

Government, Manzikala, gave a press conference at which he reduced the time-limit to twenty-four hours. ONUC representatives urgently met the local authorities to protest, but were, instead, asked to intercede with the powers at Léopoldville on Lumumba's behalf.

The U.N. Force immediately took occupation of a school building which it used as a strongly guarded refuge for the Belgians, who began flocking to U.N. headquarters for safety. I sent a strong note of protest to the Stanleyville authorities against their threats of reprisals, containing a warning that the United Nations would resist all acts of violence towards persons under its protection. The note also asked that humane treatment be accorded to the Europeans and to all arrested persons and for permission for a visit from representatives of the International Red Cross to Songolo[1] and other parliamentarians who had been placed under detention by the Lumumbists.

The Western envoys were greatly concerned about the Europeans in Orientale and they often came in deputation to discuss how they could be protected. They eventually agreed to advise the repatriation of their nationals with U.N. help, but they were concerned at the economic loss which European evacuation would cause to foreign firms, as 300 million francs worth of cotton and 1200 million francs of rubber and coffee, besides palm-oil, would remain unmarketed.

The problem of what the U.N. Force could do to prevent a full-scale civil war depended on both material and legal considerations. I had, with the approval of ONUC's Military Command, issued fresh instructions about the contingencies in which force could be used, amplifying the principle of 'self-defence', in view of the attacks to which members of the Force had lately been subjected in Léopoldville. Force could be used, keeping it to the minimum required to meet a particular situation, to resist forcible disarming; to oppose attempts to obstruct the carrying out of duly authorized orders; to prevent attempts to force withdrawal from positions already held; and to counter violation of United Nations installations or seizure or abduction of its personnel. But the legal question remained. We discussed the

[1] See p. 170. Songolo, a former Lumumbist, had recently defected to Kasavubu's side and been arrested by the Stanleyville régime while on a mission for the President.

matter with General Kettani and our legal advisers and I posed the problem to the Secretary-General for his instructions. Hammarskjold replied:

A prime concern for us all is to ensure consistency in policy, although policies themselves may occasionally require change in the face of different conditions. . . . Outbreak of conflict between Léo and Stanleyville would, as you indicate, create grave problems of law and order which would inevitably call for emergency measures to extent of capacity of Force. Principle of Operation and consistency dictate continued application of policy of restrictions on troop movements with aggressive intent. But there are important differences in some aspects of situation between September and now, as regards nature of conflict threatened, political conditions, the strength and new aggressiveness of A.N.C., and fact that in a Léo-Stanleyville conflict, major A.N.C. movement would be likely to be by river. These factors and frank appraisal of capacity of Force in employment of force, must of course be taken into account in prolongation of September policy or its modification to cope with changed conditions. Conclusion is that established policy should be maintained but that length to which Force should go to maintain it must be subject to on-the-spot judgement of situation, Force capacity, and reasonable interpretation of use of arms for self-defence only. Would appreciate your comments on these observations which would be helpful to us in clarifying our position.

We had no difficulty in accepting Hammarskjold's interpretation which, indeed, corresponded with our own. The exchange of views concluded with Hammarskjold's message which said: 'I find your conclusions and my intervention in Assembly today well harmonized. Your line of action anyway corresponds to my concept of what you can do. Note however in my intervention I claim certain freedom in interpretation of mandate in situation of duress where preventive action can be justified as taken for protection of life and property.'

The situation in Kivu, the easternmost province, which had till then been relatively quiescent, now took a sharp turn for the worse. On 22 November the A.N.C. garrison at the provincial capital of Bukavu had risen against its officers and arrested a number of them. Commissioner Nussbaumer was sent to Bukavu to detach the military command of Kivu province from that of Stanleyville to which it was subordinate. But he was unsuccessful and the situation rapidly deteriorated, the Government losing all control of both the administration and the A.N.C.

In the middle of December a serious military engagement took place between elements of the A.N.C. and the Nigerian U.N. contingent at Bukavu in which one U.N. soldier was killed and three wounded, while some ten Congolese soldiers were killed and fifty wounded. The incident was typical of how minor episodes in the Congo had the habit of developing quite irrationally into major disasters. An Austrian medical mission had arrived to set up a U.N. hospital which would also serve the general public. Mobutu in Léopoldville and the Kivu provincial authorities had been informed of the arrival of the mission, and there was also an announcement four days earlier in the Bukavu press. Nevertheless, when the mission appeared, the A.N.C. soldiers declared that the doctors were Flemish Belgians, since some of them had been heard talking in Swahili and Lingala, languages which they had taken the trouble to learn. They were marched off to prison and locked up. A Nigerian U.N. escort remonstrated with the A.N.C. officers who agreed to the release, but their soldiers would not obey. Colonel Ironsi,[1] the Commander of the Nigerian troops, thereupon parleyed with the soldiers, then with Miruho, President of the provincial Government, but got nowhere. Meanwhile, the A.N.C. troops were digging in for an attack on the prison which was guarded from the outside by a Nigerian platoon. Firing soon broke out and a battle raged which ended only with the arrival of U.N. reinforcements from Goma. When Mobutu was told of these events, he tendered his apologies to General Kettani, adding that he had forgotten to inform the A.N.C. Commander at Bukavu of the arrival of the Austrians!

To offset the strength of the U.N. Nigerian contingent, President Miruho sent for loyal A.N.C. reinforcements. But on Christmas Day, some sixty gendarmes and civilians arrived from Stanleyville by road with the intention of arresting the Bukavu A.N.C. Commander. When President Miruho went to harangue his own troops, the reinforcements that he had called in arrested him and several of his Ministers and carried them off to Stanleyville. A Lumumbist then temporarily took over the Presidency vacated by the abducted Miruho.

[1] He became General Ironsi, Head of State of Nigeria, after the military *coup*, but was later assassinated.

Léopoldville was thoroughly alarmed at these astonishing developments. Bomboko contacted the Belgian representative in Brazzaville and sought authorization for one company of para-commandos from Luluabourg to land at the airport of Usum-bura in the United Nations trust territory of Ruanda-Urundi, under Belgian administration, en route to Bukavu. In exchange, Léopoldville would agree to the re-establishment of diplomatic relations with Belgium. President Kasavubu addressed a similar request to the French Ambassador in Léopoldville, who watched over Belgian interests. The Belgian Government readily agreed. But the adventure proved to be a hopeless fiasco as the Bukavu A.N.C. refused to recognize Mobutu's authority and arrested the intruders led by Captain Pongo, the captor of Lumumba. The next day, Kashamura, Lumumba's Minister of Informa-tion, arrived from Stanleyville and took over the reins of the Kivu Provincial Government.

I was away on tour in Luluabourg when these extraordinary events took place. I could hardly believe that the provincial Government had been overthrown by a handful of armed men coming from a considerable distance and who were strangers to the province. I reported to the Secretary-General that there had been a triple violation of international law, as a U.N. trust territory had been misused in breach of the Trusteeship Agree-ment; that armed action had been aided and abetted against another state; and that the action had been taken against a state whose integrity and security the Security Council and General Assembly had assured.

Hammarskjold immediately took up the matter with the Bel-gian delegation, which explained that the landings at Usumbura coincided with the receipt by the Belgian Government of Kasa-vubu's request, and that 'Mobutu had jumped the gun'. Faced with a *fait accompli*, instructions were despatched to Usumbura to send the A.N.C. troops by road to the Congo frontier. The Congolese soldiers were provided with trucks and allowed to take their arms with them, and escorted, not to the nearest point on the frontier which was only a few kilometres away, but to a place directly opposite Bukavu, the capital of Kivu province. Hammarskjold observed that 'thus through clumsiness or sup-posedly shrewd planning under cloak of false innocence, Bel-gians have helped Mobutu to achieve exactly what he wanted'.

The U.N. representative at Usumbura was asked to make an investigation and he confirmed that the operation had been planned by the Belgian Resident-General in Ruanda-Urundi with the approval of the Belgian Government. The U.N. also received a report from their man in Brussels that the Belgian Government had in fact received Kasavubu's request twenty-four hours in advance and they had agreed to it as they did not wish to harm relations with him. The Secretary-General made a report to the Security Council exposing the adventure and Belgian involvement in it, much to the embarrassment of Mobutu and his foreign friends.

Équateur province had so far remained comparatively tranquil. The U.N. Force there enjoyed considerable prestige which the Indonesian battalion, by its exemplary behaviour, had visibly enhanced. But ONUC personnel were often threatened, particularly their head, with the increasing arrival of Belgian technicians. The break between Stanleyville and Léopoldville placed the province in the front line of military confrontation, and Stanleyville forces made some forays deep into the interior, which provoked strong anti-U.N. reactions in the provincial capital of Coquilhatville.

The problems with Katanga continued to fester, for in addition to the question of secession, North Katanga was breaking away from Tshombe's rule. That area was populated mostly by the Katanga Baluba tribe which recognized Jason Sendwe as its leader and it was bitterly opposed to secession. Tshombe had welcomed Lumumba's arrest as evidence of Léopoldville's growing affinity with him, but he reacted warily to Kasavubu's and Mobutu's overtures. Mobutu had solicited his help in setting up a common front against the United Nations, but Tshombe had more than enough on his hands to afford adventures further afield. The United Nations had established a neutral zone separating South Katanga—where Tshombe's authority was effective—from the rest of the province which was in virtual revolt. Sendwe, Tshombe's bitter rival, was sent by ONUC on a mission of pacification to North Katanga, further reducing Tshombe's chances of restoring the area to his rule.

But the 'independence' of South Katanga was being strengthened all this time since the United Nations was deeply preoccupied with its own problems in New York and Léopoldville. The Katanga administration continued to be run almost entirely by Belgians; industry was flourishing and there was an air of prosperity in Élisabethville. The Katangan armed forces had been built up to a strength of 6,000 to 7,000, officered by Europeans, and they were amply supplied with Belgian arms which entered by rail through Angola. Katanga, however, was still denied official recognition as an independent state although sentiment in its favour was fast developing in Belgium, the United States, Britain, and France.

The effect of the attitudes of these powers was to neutralize the political pressures applied by Hammarskjold against Tshombe. Furthermore, danger to South Katanga from the Léopoldville Government had vanished, as Kasavubu, Ileo, and Mobutu had been supplicating Tshombe for help. Tshombe had been helping Kalonji of the so-called 'Diamond State of South Kasai' with foreign advisers and military material to build up an army of his own. What kept these two international outlaws together was their common stake in secession, their opposition to the United Nations, and their dependence on Belgium. But Tshombe's refusal to fall in with Kasavubu's plans had begun to create resentment in Léopoldville.

The only provincial capital where the United Nations was not unwelcome was Luluabourg in Kasai. The provincial Government had kept out of the Léopoldville crisis, and its Assembly had addressed a strong memorandum to President Kasavubu rejecting the authority of the Commissioners and asserting the sovereignty of the national Parliament. The Kasai Government had declined any involvement in Lumumba's arrest and, during his flight, it neither helped nor hindered him or his pursuers.

The U.N. civilian affairs officer, Veillet Lavallée, had brought us an invitation from Mukenge, the provincial President, to spend Christmas in his capital. I had not had an opportunity to travel in the country as I had been tied down to Léopoldville and I welcomed the prospect of a brief respite. But there was also a pressing task to which I wished to attend personally, that of speeding up the programme of relief of the over a quarter of a million Baluba who had been evicted from North Kasai, following tribal warfare, and were now starving in South Kasai where they were dying at the rate of over 200 daily. I felt that a mission of mercy would be appropriate during Christmas.

My wife and I were warmly welcomed by President and Mrs. Mukenge, whose Christmas banquet was marked by very friendly speeches and toasts. It was certainly the most pleasant and relaxing evening we ever had in the Congo and it was a strangely unfamiliar experience to find oneself without serious tensions and problems.

On 26 December we left by plane for the Bakwanga air strip, where we were to be met by Caballero, the U.N. 'presence', along with transport to take us to the refugee camps some forty miles distant. We set off from the air strip in a miscellaneous convoy of cars and jeeps, skirting the town of Bakwanga as I did not wish to meet Albert Kalonji, the self-proclaimed king of the secessionist diamond-mining state. But we had not proceeded far when my car, which was at the head of the convoy, was stopped by a heavily armed band of Kalonji's soldiers, equipped with machine-guns and rifles. A sergeant pushed the muzzle of his machine-gun through the open window and asked me who we were and what was our business. I tried to enlighten him, but without visible effect. The menacing muzzle remained pointed in my direction. My U.N. security guard, the only member of our party who had any firearm, tried to get out of the car to deal with the situation, but I called him back, for I could see a quivering finger on the machine-gun's trigger. Eventually we were told that we could not proceed further without the express orders of the Mulopwe ('King'). I decided that discretion was the better part of valour and ordered the convoy to reverse course. At the U.N. camp, we held a hurried consultation, but our decision disappointed the press representatives who were anxious to see some action.

With a Kalonji soldier in my car, I proceeded to the Mulopwe's residence. It was pelting with rain and when I was ushered into the elegant residence, dressed in shirt-sleeves and drenched to the bone, I was accosted by the elegantly dressed Kalonji in dark glasses, surrounded by his equally well-tailored ministers. I apologized for our intrusion and our unkempt appearance. Kalonji replied very politely, although with a trace of sarcasm, that he had been expecting us and would we not share a glass of champagne with him? We declined politely and stated our business. Kalonji apologized profusely for the inconvenience which had been caused to us, which could easily have been avoided had he but known. Of course we would have every facility to proceed on our way and his 'Prime Minister' and other officials would personally escort us. With that, we took our leave.

The road was a quagmire and our cars skidded along the muddy track. Eventually, we reached our destination without any serious mishap. The undulating track passed for miles alongside a high barbed-wire fence which enclosed the famous diamond mines. Only a fraction of the area known to be diamond-yielding had been worked and we were overawed by the fact that we were actually motoring over a mountain of diamonds. The 'Prime Minister' kept up an incessant conversation about how much the Mulopwe had done for the starving Baluba (he belonged to their tribe) but when we reached the refugee area, our hearts sank.

The sight that met our unbelieving eyes was one of utter desolation. Thousands upon thousands of refugees, sick and emaciated, their children with bloated stomachs caused by hunger, were crouching under trees or cowering from the rain in the most elementary shelter. The small hospital barracks, which had beds for two dozen, were crowded with hundreds of seriously ill and dying. The stench was indescribable. Our United Nations doctors were doing a magnificent job and the Indian nursing sisters, the first to volunteer, were like ministering angels to the suffering. Till the arrival of U.N. medical assistance, a couple of Congolese medical assistants had been bravely labouring to give what help they could. But by now international aid was beginning to come in as a result of the world-wide appeal which I had inaugurated.

The newspaper correspondents whom I had taken with me backed up our efforts with their stories, so that within a short time a dozen or more planes were flying in daily with relief supplies. In a few weeks, the problem had been solved, although it had taken a frightful toll. The next problem was the resettlement of the refugees on vacant land and the provision of simple tools and seeds in time for the sowing season. But while help came from far and wide, the opulent diamond-mining company known as Forminière, which reaped such a rich harvest from the soil, had done nothing to help the suffering. Its mining operations were still going on, though at a reduced level perhaps, for I was told that a mysterious four-engined plane flew in once a week from somewhere and took off laden with tightly packed and well-guarded crates to an unknown destination.

On our return to Léopoldville, I received news of the strange happenings in Kivu described earlier. But more reassuring was a cheerful message from Hammarskjold, sending us the season's greetings. When we were in New York, Hammarskjold had told my wife that he would like to spend Christmas in Léopoldville with his U.N. family as he had no other family. A couple of years earlier, he had been to the U.N. Force in Gaza. We were delighted, but Hammarskjold had to defer his trip till early in the New Year because of developments in New York and later in Kivu. His message, which encouraged all of us greatly, said:

Regret very much not to be with you for Christmas holidays of shared hopes and shared worries. Looking forward to seeing you in a week's time. At lunch today trying to compete with Nimba experience of one year ago. Heinz,[1] Bill[2] and I joined in nostalgic memories transmitted to Sture.[3] I am sure that he will manage to infuse the whole Léo team with the right spirit of Swedish irresponsibility for Xmas—which gets reflections even in U.S. press, as for example today when Hearst press hailed McKeown for being a general who 'shoots first and thinks afterwards'. We know that you think first but we also know that with the right cause you do shoot afterwards. All the best to you all from all of us.

[1] Heinz Wieschhoff, Director, U.N. political division and Hammarskjold's adviser on African affairs.
[2] William Ranallo, the Secretary-General's security guard. Wieschhoff and Ranallo lost their lives with Hammarskjold in the plane crash.
[3] Sture Linner, who had been working in a mining firm in Liberia the previous year and was now with ONUC.

CHAPTER 11

Equal Hope and Hazard

We greatly looked forward to the Secretary-General's two-day visit, which he was combining, at the request of the General Assembly, with a call on the Government of South Africa for negotiations on its controversial racial policies. We hoped that the Secretary-General's renewed contacts with the Léopoldville politicians and his personal guidance regarding ONUC's activities would provide the necessary stimulus to propel the situation of uneasy stalemate into more constructive channels.

Hammarskjold looked amazingly fresh and relaxed after his long unbroken flight from New York as he stepped from his plane at Ndjili airport on 4 January 1961. On the drive to our residence, he remarked that he and I had been functioning on the same wavelength because we had almost intuitively arrived at similar conclusions on a variety of matters, as our communications, which frequently crossed each other in transmission, showed. He was in a confident mood and seemed unaffected by the ordeal of the attacks on him at New York. He remarked that principles had a way of asserting themselves, and though we had had our full share, and more, of trials and difficulties, we must firmly adhere to our course. Any concession on principle would be fatal and he felt assured that perseverance, crowned with a little good fortune, would ultimately see us through.

Hammarskjold did not tarry long at the residence and we hurried to 'Le Royal' where the leading ONUC officials were awaiting him. The Secretary-General acquainted himself in detail with the problems, and, always looking to the future, discussed the perspectives. If Kasavubu could be made to stick to the promises he had given at New York of more forthright cooperation with ONUC, the U.N. Conciliation Commission, which had by now assembled in Léopoldville, could provide just the leverage needed to lift the situation out of its present impasse. But Mobutu had to be held in check and Hammarskjold shared our anxiety about the threatened withdrawal from the U.N. Force of important contingents which would inevitably affect its capacity to contain the A.N.C. If the Operation could advance on the political front, it would act as a leaven on the whole situation. But Kasavubu's reactions were an imponderable factor where shrewd calculation and an instinct for survival were the dominating elements. I could not help wondering how the exquisitely balanced reasoning of the Secretary-General and his brilliant exposition of the finer points of international law would stand up to the conditioned reflexes and hatreds of the Congolese leaders and of the various influences behind them. But our almost mystical faith in the Secretary-General's wisdom and lofty idealism as well as our unconditional commitment to our endeavours, filled us with a sense of buoyancy and purpose.

The next morning the Secretary-General was up early, as was his habit, and after attending to the telegrams and messages that had come in during the night, he proceeded to the President's house for his first formal call. The talk with Kasavubu was very much of a monologue. Kasavubu's contribution was largely confined to importunate requests for U.N. action against Stanleyville and Kivu which Hammarskjold declined, explaining in meticulous detail the mandate and the means which inhibited such intervention. Later, the Secretary-General met the Conciliation Commission and gave his views as to its competence and responsibilities, urging the members not merely to study the situation and to make a report, but personally to attempt the task of reconciliation between the politicians so as to prepare the ground for a meeting of Parliament.

In the afternoon, the Ileo 'Government' suddenly assumed tangible shape and had a protracted meeting with the Secretary-General at which some of the Commissioners also participated. The full length of one side of a long table was occupied by the Congolese. The Secretary-General and I sat opposite. Hammarskjold said he had come to see the situation in the Congo for himself with a view to strengthening cooperation between the Congolese authorities and ONUC and he invited suggestions in that regard. The Congolese, ignoring Hammarskjold's cue, raised the question of the situation in Stanleyville and Kivu, complaining that the U.N. Force had deliberately refrained from intervening in both provinces to prevent the setting up of 'rebel' Governments. Hammarskjold explained the legal implications of the matter and the reasons why the U.N. Force could not intervene, drawing a parallel with the case of Katanga. He said the issue raised with him was of a political and constitutional nature and not basically one of maintenance of law and order. The Congolese questioned his interpretation and pressed the point that they, as the only legal authority, were fully entitled to U.N. military support against their opponents. Hammarskjold said the U.N. Force could not intervene in political situations; furthermore political problems should be solved only by political means and he appealed for cooperation with the Conciliation Commission which had the express task of helping the Congolese to find peaceful solutions to their problems. But the Congolese continued to press their charges against the U.N. Force and complained that the Special Representative had personally directed the Kivu U.N. troops not to prevent the abduction of President Miruho. I flatly denied the allegation as no such orders had been issued; besides, I had been away in Luluabourg at the time and had heard of the affair only on my return to Léopoldville. Hammarskjold said that ONUC could not possibly take the responsibility for events in Kivu, or in Stanleyville for that matter. Warning of the danger of civil war, he urged the freeing of all political prisoners, the neutralization of the army from politics, and a search for solutions through parliamentary means.

But the Congolese were not interested. Instead, they blamed Stanleyville for the arrest of Songolo and his companions and asked what the U.N. was doing about it. Hammarskjold pointed out that the Léopoldville authorities were the first to start the practice of making political arrests. The Congolese retorted that there was a valid warrant of arrest against Lumumba which the Special Representative had wrongly prevented from being executed. Hammarskjold said he took full responsibility for the Special Representative's decisions and suggested negotiations for the simultaneous release of Lumumba and Songolo and their respective companions; meanwhile, all political prisoners should receive humane treatment and be permitted to receive visits from the International Red Cross. The Congolese argued that the two cases were entirely different; as for humane treatment, Lumumba was being treated royally in prison while Songolo and his colleagues had been tortured and were in mortal danger. The Secretary-General warned that the Congo would forfeit all international sympathy if the pattern of violence and disorder continued. The Congolese replied that it was the U.N. Force which had been fomenting trouble in the country. As the argument developed, I found my French inadequate to the occasion and the Secretary-General spontaneously acted as my interpreter! But it was not merely a question of a lack of communication. The Congolese spoke from the level of their personal interests; the Secretary-General from that of principles. It was indeed a *dialogue des sourds*.[1]

Hammarskjold received some personal calls that evening, one from the Chairman of the Conciliation Commission, Jaja Wachuku, who interpreted his role, not as a conciliator of Congolese differences, but as an inquisitor into the Secretary-General's and ONUC's supposed inadequacies. A midnight caller was the British Ambassador, Ian Scott, who, in a state of great agitation, came to convey information regarding an intercepted cable from Gizenga to Khrushchev allegedly appealing for help against an attack by Belgian paratroops on Kivu and Orientale provinces. The Secretary-General reassured the distraught Ambassador that there was little physical possibility of any such help coming and he suggested reference to a map of the world. A British correspondent had told me that Léopoldville's attempt to blockade Stanleyville,[2] which was hurting the former more than the latter, had been Scott's brainwave. Hammarskjold later commented that the Léopoldville air had a strange effect on some people.

I held long conversations with Hammarskjold at which we reviewed what had been accomplished and what could be done in the light of the enormous difficulties that the Operation had run into both at New York and in the Congo. Hammarskjold made a cool and objective analysis, and while he recognized

---

[1] Dialogue between the deaf.
[2] Mobutu had taken a motley armada of river boats and rafts up the Congo river to attempt a blockade of Orientale province.

that we were hemmed in in many directions, there was yet a possibility of a break-through if we could somehow manage to reactivate Parliament while keeping Mobutu and Kasavubu in check. I told Hammarskjold that the Conciliation Commission had got off to a very shaky start, largely because of the irascible temperament and uncertain predilections of the Chairman, Jaja Wachuku. When Hammarskjold met the Commission both formally and informally, he tried to bring about conciliation between the conciliators and their high-handed and idiosyncratic Chairman, but without evident results.

I asked Hammarskjold to tell me frankly what mistakes ONUC had made, for in a situation where frequent and hurried decisions had to be taken, we could easily have slipped up. Hammarskjold thought for a moment and replied that the only mistakes were the closure of the radio station and airports, but for those decisions I was not responsible. I was to ask him that question again, and he was to repeat his reply. I then asked in what directions we could improve on our performance. To this he said that things were running well organizationally and if we could keep them that way, we would have a ready and reliable instrument possessing the intrinsic capacity to do its job. But if a number of contingents pulled out and the international situation worsened, or if a fresh wave of insanity seized the Congo, our work would of course be affected, but the fault would not be ours. I then asked Hammarskjold, who had last been in Léopoldville in August 1960, what difference he found in the situation in these five months. He immediately replied: 'Then we were all full of confidence in New York, but things here were panicky. Now, we are panicky in New York, but here in ONUC I find a mood of confidence.'

With Hammarskjold's departure early on 6 January on his long journey to Pretoria in a modest two-engined U.N. aircraft, we returned to our daily problems with renewed heart. My immediate concern was to provide the best possible conditions, so far as it lay in ONUC's power, for the task of the U.N. Conciliation Commission on which so much depended. The departure of the Commission for the Congo had been delayed, first to accommodate President Kasavubu, then the volatile Chairman, Jaja Wachuku. Wachuku, Vice-Chairman Mohamed Sopiee of Malaya, and Rapporteur Andom of Ethiopia, accompanied by their senior U.N. official Secretary, Dragan Protitch, had finally arrived in Léopoldville on 19 December.

Much valuable time was wasted by some irrelevant probings and proceedings on the part of the Chairman, who was only brought up short by the news that Lumumba had been transferred to Élisabethville. Members of the Commission were deeply perturbed, and over the Chairman's objections, decided to question President Kasavubu about it. They met Kasavubu who refused any explanation. Subsequently, when the news became common knowledge, Kasavubu said that the transfer had been made under orders of the Léopoldville authorities for the purpose of ensuring Lumumba's 'safety'. The Commission then drew up a programme for a hurried visit of one day each to the provincial capitals, including Élisabethville but excluding Bukavu, which was still disturbed. I commented to Hammarskjold: 'I wonder what this rushed trip will do. At least two or three days each should have been allotted to Stanleyville and Élisabethville.'

At Stanleyville, the Commission met Gbenye, General Lundula, and the acting President of the Provincial Government, Manzikala. The Commission appealed for cooperation and to prove its credentials produced a secret letter from Lumumba addressed to the Secretary-General in which the former had favoured conciliation and had asked for United Nations assistance in solving the crisis. But Gbenye was inflexible, and the meeting was unproductive. Next, the Commission requested permission to meet the political prisoners in Stanleyville; Songolo and Miruho were eventually brought before them. The Commission found the prisoners in good health but Songolo complained of injury to his right eye as a result of maltreatment. The prisoners affirmed that the only solution was through reconciliation between Kasavubu and Lumumba, and they asked for the disarming of the A.N.C. and release of all political prisoners. General Lundula also advocated disarming all A.N.C. units. But the Commission took no follow-up action as its tight schedule provided no time for negotiations.

At Élisabethville, the next port of call, Tshombe point blank refused to meet the Commission officially but, after some argumentation, agreed to meet the members informally at dinner. Tshombe took the stand that there was nothing to discuss as he had already made his position clear to the Secretary-General. The Commission then asked the Chairman to see Tshombe with President Kasavubu's letter of authority and to ask for a meeting with Lumumba and his colleagues. But Tshombe refused to accept the letter and said that he had no responsibility for the prisoners who had been transferred under orders of the central authorities. The persons actually in charge of the prisoners should be applied to for an interview. Minister Delvaux and the Léopoldville Security Chief, Nendaka, who happened to be on a visit to Élisabethville, were then approached by the Commission but they pleaded that the prisoners were under the authority of the Katanga Government! The Commission then wired Kasavubu to untie the knot but received no reply. Disgusted with the Kafkaesque situation, the Commission flew back to Léopoldville without seeing Lumumba or ascertaining his fate.

On 9 February, President Kasavubu terminated the functions of the College of Commissioners and set up a provisional Government under Ileo, who told the Commission that he would create a broad-based Government, to include representatives of M.N.C. (Lumumba) and the Balubakat.[1] The few remaining Lumumbists in Léopoldville expressed their readiness to cooperate. I had, meanwhile, been meeting various politicians and I felt that there were many common elements which could be put together to produce a coherent pattern. I had an illuminating talk with Cyrille Adoula,[2] in which he mooted the establishment of a provisional Government under a neutral personality (he was perhaps the most neutral at the time). I felt that Adoula's ideas should be followed up and contact with the provinces renewed, for which time and determination were needed. But Wachuku, who was beginning to find the situation far more complicated and exacting than he had bargained for, was not interested in the sweaty task of negotiation. He was already talking of returning to the more salubrious air of Geneva or Paris for the drafting of the Commission's report.

Hammarskjold had been kept fully informed by the Secretariat of the Commission about its activities and he cabled me as follows:

[1] The Katanga Baluba party, led by Jason Sendwe.
[2] Later Prime Minister. He was noted for his moderation, a rare quality among Congolese politicians at that time.

Most disappointed by shortness of stay of Commission in Stanley-ville and Élisabethville which robbed us of valuable possibilities. Pro-longed stay in Stanleyville might have served as valuable brake on present crisis both regarding Western powers interested and Gizenga group. Prolonged stay in Élisabethville in same way might have forced the hand regarding Lumumba. As usual, I find myself in much more advanced position than member countries and without getting the support I should be entitled to. This is, in this case, true both as regards Gizenga and the Lumumba problem.

I hope members are clear on their status, that their report will first of all have to go to the Advisory Committee and from there to the General Assembly. I do not believe that the Advisory Committee has regarded itself solely as an electorate, the child of which is an indepen-dent General Assembly organ once it is born. How otherwise could Advisory Committee have been entitled to formulate the mandate?

The Commission, or some of its members, again met Kasa-vubu to inform him of their talks, but he had nothing much to offer. His irritation became marked when some members asked when they could expect to interview Lumumba. Hammarskjold had already added the weight of his authority to the request when he demanded from Kasavubu facilities for the Com-mission to meet Lumumba.

The sudden news of Lumumba's murder[1] hit the Commission amidships like a torpedo. All the members were aghast at the cynical barbarity of the whole affair and deeply humiliated at the treachery of Kasavubu and his friends who had toyed with them all these frustrating weeks. The Commission demanded to see the President urgently to express shock and indignation at the murder, and to ask for details of the tragedy. Kasavubu replied that the information would be made available when received. But when he was asked why he had transferred Lu-mumba to Katanga, he declined to continue the discussion. He was then asked about Finant and Fataki[2] who had just been transferred to Bakwanga; he replied that it was to ensure their greater security. The next day news came of their brutal exe-cution, and it was followed a few days later by news of the reprisals against the Orientale prisoners, Songolo and his companions. Wachuku felt that there was nothing more for the Commission to do except to pay a farewell call on Kasavubu

[1] See Ch. 12.
[2] Finant and Fataki were prominent Lumumbists captured by the Léopoldville authorities.

and to prepare its report. The Commission read a lecture to Kasavubu on the harmful effects on world public opinion of the recent blood-curdling events and preached a sermon on peace and goodwill among men. In reply, Kasavubu asked for time, when everything would be explained.

The Commission left the Congo on 21 February. Its report, which was issued as a bulky document in three parts, merely endorsed the line that we had been advocating from the beginning, and which Hammarskjold and his Advisory Committee had long ago accepted. Owing to the uncertain leadership of its Chairman the Commission had failed even to attempt to negotiate agreements between opposing parties or to act as a catalyst of conflicting views.

The Commission, on which Hammarskjold and the Advisory Committee had placed such high hopes had come and gone, leaving behind only the stale odour of its fitful and frustrated efforts. The respite that we had longed for from our daily meed of troubles, we had failed to get. In fact, Wachuku's behaviour, both with his colleagues and with ONUC, had added to our problems. The Commission had sat in Léopoldville contenting itself with making disapproving noises while the civil-war situation had become increasingly menacing, the problem of affording protection to threatened individuals and groups became more acute, and the lives of important political personalities were being taken in a savage outburst of personal and political vendetta. What is more, the Congolese had realized the impotence of the sovereign organs of the U.N., the Security Council and General Assembly, to do anything to deflect them from the unbridled pursuit of their personal ambitions. In fact, the situation at the time of the Commission's departure was far worse than it had been on its arrival.

In the provinces, the situation had been deteriorating ominously from day to day. During the anxious months of January and February, when ONUC needed every ounce of its strength to deal with the menacing problems, the U.N. Force was being weakened as contingents from several countries, including the gallant Moroccan Brigade under General Kettani, began the process of pulling out. If the withdrawals were to become effective it would foreclose all possibilities of an increase in the strength of contingents from the remaining countries, thus making very real the risk of the U.N. Force breaking down.

Throughout those two critical months prior to and immediately after the announcement of the death of Lumumba, the Western missions had kept up an incessant barrage of demands for U.N. troops for the protection of European planters, merchants, and missionaries as well as of plantations, industrial enterprises, and mission stations. Hardly a day passed when there was not a deputation of a dozen ambassadors asking for instant action in situations which though serious were often greatly exaggerated, and the U.N. Force Commander was hard put to it to find the troops to meet these influentially backed demands. Among his imperative duties were the prevention of genocidal warfare between tribes, the rescue and protection of U.N. personnel trapped at their posts of duty, the enforcement of neutralized zones between armed groups in angry confrontation, and the task of meeting the direct threats of Mobutu and Tshombe against the U.N. Force itself. My diary and telegrams to New York are full of detailed accounts of meetings with the Western envoys whose sole interest appeared to be the deployment of the entire U.N. Force in rescuing European settlers and in guaranteeing protection to their extensive and far-flung properties.

The U.N. Force Command was strongly opposed to ordering out small patrols—for they did not have the troops for larger formations—a hundred or more miles into disturbed country to rescue a frightened, though not always threatened, planter or family. The Command asked for the concentration of Europeans who wanted protection at a few centres from which they would be escorted to a more protected central place. Our armed convoys sometimes encountered ambushes and determined hostile groups and they often had to fight their way through. What surprised our Force Command and all of us was that despite the troubled conditions, the influx into the disturbed areas of Belgians—even including women and children —continued.

Not content with our efforts to give protection to the fullest extent that our resources would permit, we were asked to assure the free movement of Europeans in the rebellious provinces where our critics were the loudest to proclaim that law and order had broken down. It was difficult to see the logic of asking ONUC to ensure for a small minority group the exercise of a right which the vast majority of the population could not possibly hope to enjoy because of the chaotic conditions. In Kivu, the situation was one of general anarchy which did not distinguish between the colour of its victims. Miller, ONUC's representative in Kivu, with the help of the Nigerian and Indonesian contingents, had arranged an escape route across the river and lake which formed the eastern boundary of Kivu with Uganda and Ruanda-Urundi. Large numbers of refugees found safe refuge by those means while others awaited their turn in the U.N. protected camps.

But complaints continued to be made of the 'passivity' of U.N. troops and the indifference of ONUC's civilian representatives. Newspaper and verbal attacks on the United Nations increased in venom while statements were made by responsible European politicians and diplomats full of false complaints and charges. These inevitably reached the ears of ONUC officials and military contingents and it naturally aroused much indignation among them. I sent Hammarskjold a cable warning of the strong feelings among ONUC personnel which these attacks had generated. I wrote: 'I would make a solemn appeal to you on behalf of all my colleagues, civil and military, to bring to the notice of the Belgian and other representatives the grave consequences of the slanderous charges against U.N. personnel. While we do not ask for praise or recognition for doing what we regard as our sacred duty, we are at least entitled to point to the dangers to the morale of our troops, to the justified resentment among our personnel, and above all, to the dire peril to the Belgian and other foreign nationals, which statements such as Loridan's[1] would only create.'

But the situation, although tense, was not then out of hand. With Lumumba's transfer to Élisabethville, however, we had feared a sudden turn for the worse. I sent several strong official notes to the Stanleyville authorities warning them against acts of violence and reprisal, especially against the Europeans and political prisoners. But on 19 January arrests began, which included twelve Europeans who had been ostentatiously celebrating Lumumba's transfer to Élisabethville. A large number of

---

[1] Walter Loridan was Belgium's Permanent Representative to the United Nations.

Europeans were under the protection of the U.N. Force and others were receiving shelter in a large building near the airport. I repeated my protests to Gizenga and called a meeting of foreign envoys at which General Iyassou gave a detailed account of the action which the U.N. was taking to meet the crisis. A day or so later, Gustavo Duran, who had been placed in charge of the ONUC mission in Stanleyville, reported that the Stanleyville A.N.C. had surrounded U.N. headquarters as well as the camp of the 3rd Ethiopian Battalion, where some one hundred Europeans were being sheltered. With difficulty the Congolese troops were persuaded to withdraw on the personal intervention of General Lundula. A promise was taken from Gizenga to make a radio appeal for calm and to disavow a call to violence made in the local paper *Uhuru*. We asked the foreign missions for lists of their nationals to enable our people to check their safety and to arrange for their repatriation as circumstances permitted. But the view of the foreign missions, which changed radically only after Lumumba's death, was that the Europeans wanting to stay on should be enabled to do so under U.N. protection and saved from harm every time that the A.N.C. ran amok.

Meanwhile, pressures at New York continued as Hammarskjold confirmed:

French Ambassador orally transmitted message from his Government to the following effect: French Government have asked French citizens in Orientale and Kivu to evacuate. They have asked U.N. representative to take all necessary steps to render possible and facilitate such an evacuation, including, of course, protection. They further request U.N. to use its means for prevention of recurring grave violations of human rights. Charpentier seems to have reported that he understood you to feel that you needed fresh instructions from me to carry out what they ask for. I asked if there was not a misunderstanding to the effect that while you had all the instructions and authorizations I could give, such action as Charpentier, and now the French Government ask for, including perhaps military initiative, could not be taken short of new instructions for ONUC generally. I said I consider you as having already adequate instructions but that I would repeat that you could and should take all measures for the stated purpose up to the limit of our mandate as determined by the Security Council and General Assembly. Whether Paris is satisfied with this reply, I do not know, but it is of course the only possible one. I want to recall that in case of emergency, we may, as I stated in General Assembly, stretch our mandate to include what may be considered certain emergency rights in the interpretation of the limits between action in defence of ourselves while fulfilling our duty to protect life and property, on the one side, and so-called military initiative on the other side. It is interesting to see that those who applauded me in the General Assembly for pointing out that I could not take 'necessary illegal action', for example in order to liberate Lumumba, now are those who ask for just that kind of action. Naturally, we do not apply a double standard.

Duran had succeeded in getting *laissez-passer* for all Europeans on the lists provided to him, but he reported that 'by holding them as hostages he [Gizenga] could exert a certain pressure on the other side and it is therefore unlikely that he will agree to free evacuation' (without permits). Duran continued: 'U.N. forces both in Orientale and Kivu are numerically inferior to the A.N.C. and also lack any heavy weapons. Even a minor or local defeat suffered by U.N. would result in reprisals on the European population. In addition, we would be unable to ensure safety of the refugees at approach to airports, of planes taking off or landing; therefore, evacuation must be negotiated and have prior agreement of the authorities.'

Gbenye had issued a decree imposing a tax of 30,000 francs on all Europeans ostensibly to cover the expenses of Belgian prisoners in Stanleyville. I sent a strong protest against this illegal impost; fortunately it proved to be not entirely ineffective. Meanwhile, in the threatened areas, preparations to concentrate the Europeans at or near airports or evacuation centres continued quietly, the authorities being informed only when the refugees were ready for departure. To my reports on the meetings with the Western envoys and the difficulties of the task which had been made more complicated by their unreasonable attitude, Hammarskjold tried to give us what encouragement he could: 'Share your concern but our means to turn the tide of folly are about as effective as yours on the local scene, e.g. in Orientale. Thus for the moment, no other consolation than that consistent efforts tried by principles have a strange way of leading to results! To be less philosophical, we are giving your justified worries very serious consideration. . . .'

On 18 January he cabled: 'There is a growing anxiety among

permanent delegations here about the policies and actions of the Congolese authorities in Orientale and Kivu and other areas, about the right of foreign residents to move freely in the Congo and to obtain exit permits. . . . I feel strongly that if you have sufficient evidence that movement is being restricted and that exit permits are being denied, you should make of this a serious issue of principle and press authorities to observe this fundamental human right. Contents of your [reports] noted with satisfaction, particularly McKeown's trip to Kivu, Orientale, etc.'

This was followed by a visit to me by twelve European envoys with the usual suggestions urging the use of force. I had to warn them that in view of our military weakness, their suggestions were fraught with the greatest danger to the refugees themselves. I had sent General McKeown to the troubled provinces in the hope that the colour of his skin would reassure the envoys that nothing was being left undone that could possibly be done. I sent a detailed reply to Hammarskjold informing him of the measures taken, but expressing doubt about the doctrine of the right of free movement of all foreigners, a right which in the case of the U.N. Force, though guaranteed, could frequently not be exercised. I concluded that the time had come for the mass evacuation of foreigners in view of the unpredictability of the situation in the affected provinces.

Hammarskjold flashed back: 'Your telegrams confirm me in my belief that I need not impress on you the importance of the matter.' And again: 'Fully agree your proposed line of action. Highly desirable send Iyassou and to take any other action which you think helpful as I regard this situation with utmost seriousness.'

The civil-war situation was becoming increasingly menacing. Mobutu had ferried his troops up the Congo River to the border between Équateur and Orientale provinces and sporadic clashes had begun. In Kivu, the Congolese troops were divided among themselves and were maltreating and looting African and European alike. It was the primary responsibility of the U.N. Force to try and stem the drift to generalized fighting and disorder, and we had been planning the setting up of neutral zones between Équateur and Orientale provinces and between Kivu and Ruanda-Urundi. Only with a show of strength combined with energetic diplomatic action could we make ourselves effective. Had we succeeded in calming down the situation, it would have meant greater security for all—for the Congolese whom it was our primary responsibility to serve, for the Europeans and their establishments, for the U.N. technical-assistance personnel, and the government functionaries, who, in Kivu, were themselves living under threats. But that was not to be, as we were forced to bow to pressures and to hypothecate large elements of the U.N. Force to the sole function of locating and escorting the scattered Europeans to safety. This unjust order of priorities caused grumbling among the U.N. contingent commanders and liaison officers at Léopoldville, who protested at the distortion of their functions. General Kettani told me that the Moroccan Brigade was being withdrawn as, apart from his Government's dissatisfaction with the Secretary-General's Congo policies, his own officers, whose views were representative, did not wish to serve under such unacceptable conditions.

In Stanleyville, meanwhile, relations between the Congolese and the European settlers had continued to deteriorate. The blockade had resulted in the economic distress of the local population and had kept the danger of insurrection alive. The position became even more perilous when news of Lumumba's assassination reached the people. It was commonly believed that Belgians were responsible, and one of Tshombe's Belgian officers had been openly boasting that he had administered the *coup de grâce* to the victim. Kasavubu and Mobutu, who had sent Lumumba to his fate, had a string of Belgian advisers around them. To beleaguered Stanleyville, therefore, the savage murder of their idol appeared to be the direct result of Belgian machinations and complicity.

Clashes had been taking place between Belgian troops in Ruanda-Urundi and Congolese troops in Kivu along the border. Eight Belgian soldiers who had 'strayed' across the border were captured at Uvira and carried off in captivity to Stanleyville. Their treatment and release became another of our preoccupations. Thanks largely to Duran's efforts the prisoners fortunately survived their ordeal (which became even more perilous after Lumumba's transfer and death) and were eventually released in fairly good shape.

The situation in North Katanga had been partially pacified

by ONUC which had assumed complete responsibility for order and security in the area. But it suddenly took a turn for the worse early in January when an A.N.C. contingent from Stanley- ville arrived in some thirty trucks in the principal city, Manono. The move over long distances with indifferent communications had been cleverly planned to avoid populated and guarded locations, and took everyone by surprise. The aim of the in- truders was to establish a new province of Lualaba in North Katanga with Manono as its capital and the tribal Chief as its President. Tshombe was indignant at this unexpected incursion, charging a violation of the 17 October 1960 accord signed by him with Brigadier Rikhye on behalf of the U.N. Force, to create a neutral zone in North Katanga. The U.N. Force had undertaken to protect the tin mines and industrial installations in the area, to keep open the railway and other channels of communication, and to prevent any military activity. Tshombe promptly denounced the agreement with the U.N. Force and began making preparations to 'pacify' the area in his own way. He opened a crash programme for the recruitment of foreign mercenaries and building up his army. Manono actually was outside the neutral zone, but it proved difficult to prevent the intruders from Orientale from spreading themselves beyond, as U.N. troops were too thinly scattered over the area.

The Stanleyville troops, on reaching Manono airport, imme- diately launched an attack on the outnumbered U.N. Nigerian troops, causing heavy casualties. Brigadier Ward, the British commander of the Nigerian contingent, called in Moroccan re- inforcements, but the arrival of the first planeload increased the aggressiveness of the intruding force and made further landings impossible. The U.N. Force had reluctantly to abandon the airport and, later, to evacuate Manono itself. One-hour's ex- change of fire had also taken place at Albertville, on Lake Tanganyika, between U.N. Moroccan troops and Stanleyville troops who had advanced there. A cease-fire was arranged with difficulty by Brigadier Ward with Chief Prosper Ilunga. Ward concluded his despatch on the day's events with the words: 'It has been a very, very difficult day.' Ward feared that unless reinforcements reached him by whatever means were available, the U.N. Force would be compelled to pull out of the entire area and to leave Tshombe to carry out 'pacification' by his own methods. I immediately sent General Iyassou to Stanleyville to prevail upon General Lundula to withdraw his troops and, meanwhile, to order them not to attack U.N. contingents or to molest foreigners or the local population. Iyassou was then to fly on to Manono and Albertville to strengthen the dispositions of the scattered U.N. force and to take whatever steps were possible to prevent ONUC troops from being dislodged in the area.

Iyassou's efforts in Stanleyville brought some respite to the hard-pressed U.N. troops in North Katanga, and also in Kivu, where Colonel Ironsi had been badgering the disorderly local authorities. Gizenga and Lundula offered to withdraw their troops from Manono if ONUC gave protection to Prosper Ilunga's Cabinet and Government. This Iyassou rejected outright. But he was able to extract a promise that U.N. troops would not be attacked, and an A.N.C. officer from Stanleyville accompanied him to North Katanga to convey the word to the Congolese troops. In regard to Kivu, Iyassou and Ironsi were more successful. It was agreed that U.N. troops would police the border so as to stop the skirmishing between the Belgian and A.N.C. forces.

About the middle of February, some units of Tshombe's gendarmerie moved into North Katanga, professedly to restore order and to reopen the railway. They followed the traditional Belgian pattern of 'pacification' by setting the torch to thatched villages and shooting indiscriminately at the fleeing inhabitants, all of whom were of the Baluba tribe. The units then fanned out, spreading fire and terror in the countryside, and villages began emptying themselves into the surrounding bush to escape the advancing scourge. U.N. units on the path were warned not to interfere. Soon the objectives were disclosed; they were nothing less than to bring the dissident Baluba to heel, to crush the Stanleyville troops, and to capture Manono and other towns in the area, with a view to establishing Tshombe's hold over North Katanga.

The U.N. Force was about to lose a quarter of its strength by the withdrawal of several contingents and it was difficult to find replacements. Whatever reinforcements could be mustered by road were inevitably delayed in reaching the scene. The best that the U.N. Force could do was to remonstrate with the

Belgian-officered Katanga gendarmerie and with Colonel Crèvecoeur, its chief, to show some regard for civilian life. In ONUC's reports to New York, information was conveyed of the barbarous methods of Katanga's forces so that opinion at the United Nations would be shocked into stopping the horror. At the same time, ONUC officials in Élisabethville carried vigorous protests to Tshombe, whose only reaction was to put the blame on the United Nations for encouraging the Stanleyville régime in its expansionist designs. It was only months later, when the Indian Brigade arrived in the Congo, that Tshombe's gendarmerie was pushed back into South Katanga and relative calm restored in the area. Jason Sendwe, who had been sent to North Katanga by ONUC before the incursion of Tshombe's troops on a mission of pacification, could do little in face of the brutalities of the Belgian-led force. But after its eviction, he again helped to calm down the inflamed population, and especially the fanatical Baluba youth organization.

Troops from Stanleyville made another daring incursion towards the end of February 1961 all the way to Luluabourg where they hoped to win over the local A.N.C. garrison. The sudden appearance of hostile troops in a city believed to be friendly or neutral, coupled with a spate of wild rumours, spread fear and consternation among the Congolese authorities both in Luluabourg and in Léopoldville.

Kasavubu and Ileo were in a state of great alarm and, in their usual manner, blamed ONUC. They hurled an ultimatum that if the incursion was not pushed back by force, they would break off relations with the United Nations. U.N. Force headquarters, lacking any intelligence services, had had absolutely no advance information of the appearance of the intruders. In the vast spaces of the Congo, it was comparatively easy for a well-led force, if it knew the terrain, to move from place to place without detection. ONUC's Military Command urgently despatched staff officers to Luluabourg to investigate the facts.

It appeared that a small column of Stanleyville troops had wound its way along unused tracks through almost 1200 miles of country supposed to be under Léopoldville's control, evading a 400-strong garrison of Mobutu's troops on the way, and presenting itself at Luluabourg A.N.C. headquarters. The

Ghana Brigade, taken aback by this sudden apparition, started parleys with the leaders of the intruders while ONUC officials in Stanleyville immediately called on General Lundula for an explanation. Lundula disclosed that there had been previous approaches to him from the Luluabourg garrison who favoured an alliance with the Stanleyville A.N.C. A column was, therefore, sent to Luluabourg to effect a link-up. But, on arrival, part of the Luluabourg garrison opposed the plan and its Commanding officer, Colonel Ndjoko, took flight and was captured. The North Kasai Government, whose President was absent, scattered in confusion. The U.N. troops rose magnificently to the occasion. Colonel Ankrah of Ghana, by sheer force of personality, persuaded the Stanleyville intruders as well as the local garrison to deposit their arms in custody of the Ghana troops. But the operation was interrupted as the officers of the Luluabourg A.N.C. garrison disappeared from the scene. Colonel Ndjoko was, however, rescued from his captors and despatched to Léopoldville in a United Nations plane. Not a shot was fired by the Stanleyville column which melted away into the bush as suddenly as it had appeared. Aerial reconnaissance a couple of days later by U.N. observers disclosed that the column was well on its way back northwards. The whole episode was like a tropical storm. It passed quickly, but it left a great deal of psychological debris behind.

It was obvious that no progress towards restoring unity and pacifying the country was possible so long as ONUC's efforts were in constant risk of being checkmated by different Congolese armed groups. The policy followed by the Kasavubu–Mobutu–Bomboko triumvirate had only further divided the country as well as the National Army. To bring some kind of order to the A.N.C. was the key to the problem as I had been constantly pressing on the Secretary-General and which I had repeated during his visit to Léopoldville. The question was how it could be done as the Léopoldville authorities had placed the forces under their control in violent opposition to the United Nations Force.

Nevertheless, as the first few weeks of the new year advanced, a new mood of optimism was beginning to be felt. On the international political scene, the differences between the African and Asian states were at last showing some signs of abating.

The Brazzaville group of Francophone African statesmen, who seemed to place Western interests above those of Africa, had been ineffective in their attempts to dislodge the United Nations from the Congo or to build up the strength of Kasavubu and Mobutu.

The Casablanca group of powers as they came to be called, which consisted of Morocco, Ghana, Guinea, Mali, U.A.R., Libya, and Ceylon, had come to adopt a middle line, which was closer to that of India, for example. Avoiding the temptation to back up the Stanleyville régime, they put the United Nations on notice to carry out a series of measures to rectify the situation as the price of their support. These included disarming of Mobutu's troops, release of political prisoners, recall of Parliament, and expulsion of foreign advisers. The fact that all the Casablanca powers had contributed troops to the Congo gave their declaration, made at the level of Heads of State, considerable authority.

Hammarskjold hoped that it would be possible to forge a sufficiently broad consensus among the African and Asian powers to be acceptable to the Kennedy Government which had taken office on 20 January 1961. His talks with officials of the new U.S. administration had given him reason to believe that they would not allow themselves to be tied to the apron-strings of Belgium and their NATO partners, Britain and France, but would pursue an independent line more in consonance with the interests of the United States and the aspirations of the African peoples. The new Kennedy administration had reconciled itself to the possibility of Lumumba's return, provided he could be made to function within the Constitution and in cooperation with the United Nations. Hammarskjold cabled me on 4 February that American papers had carried a story of a 'revised stand in Washington' on the situation in the Congo and that the new administration would support United Nations policies. He concluded: 'This simple victory for realism receives of course comments that Washington has made concession to Soviets.'

If such a line could be developed along a wide common front, Belgian sabotage would be effectively curbed and a stronger policy could be followed with respect to Tshombe and Mobutu. Parallel with this the hostility of the Soviet Union would be held in check by African and Asian support and the Stanley-ville movement contained. Freed from its distractions of maintaining peace between the divided parts of the Congo, ONUC could provide the necessary conditions for the recall of Parliament and the establishment of a coherent central authority.

But could the impending withdrawals of important contingents from the U.N. Force be staved off? Hammarskjold believed that the threats to withdraw had 'had a strong element of wish to exert pressure' on the Security Council to reach a decision regarding the return to the political scene of Lumumba, and to that extent there may have been 'an element of bluff'. Little did he or any of us know that Lumumba's fate had already been sealed.

CHAPTER 12

The Politics of Murder

In the precarious balance between hope and hazard, hazard was soon to triumph over hope. The hope that the spreading violence and hatred would be contained by the political and military restraints imposed by the United Nations, diverting the exuberant energies of the politicians and the military along peaceful channels, was soon shattered. The Congolese, instigated by their foreign advisers, were in open defiance of the United Nations, violating their own promises and commitments. A combination of recklessness and intrigue undermined the work of peace and conciliation. The pent-up passions, freed of all restraints, spread an orgy of violence and bloodshed along their lengthening trail. The politics of murder now superseded the politics of military threats and political polemics.

In New York, the litany was of peace and conciliation. And for a time it seemed that the squabbling nations would join together in common action to save the Congo from itself and the United Nations from total collapse. But the efforts of the United Nations and its representatives in the Congo were almost wrecked by an act of cynical barbarity. Lumumba was treacherously sent to his death. That deed took not only Lumumba's physical life; it also took Hammarskjold's political life. After that event, the United Nations effort in the Congo was called seriously into question, faith in Hammarskjold was shaken, and Soviet demands for his dismissal became insistent.

The failure of the United Nations Force to stem the tide of turbulence had raised doubts in New York about its role and functions. The accent so far had been on the scrupulous avoidance of the use of force, on maintaining the symbolism of a peace force ensuring tranquillity by its very presence. Now the harsh realities of the situation were revealed and it became obvious that more direct and forceful methods were essential. The death of Lumumba was a watershed in the U.N. Operation as it brought about a sharp revision in the concept of the methods to be employed by the United Nations in the fulfilment of its task.

Lumumba behind prison bars had been no less potent a force than Lumumba in freedom. There was no prison in Kasavubu's Congo secure enough to contain him. A mutiny had occurred in Camp Hardy where Lumumba was imprisoned. Congolese officers were assaulted and their wives raped, the mutineers shouting pro-Lumumba slogans and threatening to release him. To the Léopoldville authorities this posed a double danger—that of Lumumba's liberation as well as corrosion of the loyalty of the Congolese army. The mutiny greatly alarmed Kasavubu, Mobutu, and Bomboko, as the Thysville garrison was regarded as the most loyal to the régime. After bribing the mutineers by acceding to their exorbitant demands for more pay and privileges, Kasavubu and his colleagues met Lumumba in captivity and tried to bribe him with an offer of a ministerial post in Ileo's cabinet. Lumumba refused. Returning to Léopoldville, Kasavubu held three days of confabulations with the Commissioners and his Belgian advisers, at the conclusion of which it was decided to deliver Lumumba to his enemies in Katanga.

The actual decision to move Lumumba from Thysville was taken on 14 January, the day following the mutiny, but there was yet uncertainty as to the destination. The choice lay between a prison at Boma in the Bas-Congo area, Élisabethville, or Bakwanga. Boma was almost immediately ruled out as the Provincial Minister refused to accept Lumumba in the Bas-Congo because of the unsettling effect of his presence on the local population. Of the two remaining possibilities, the Belgian advisers favoured Bakwanga, since Kalonji's secessionist régime of South Kasai was less controversial internationally than Katanga where the massive Belgian presence was an incontrovertible fact.[1] Kasavubu and the Commissioners, apparently hoping that with the common enemy in his hands, Tshombe would be more receptive to Léopoldville's approaches for a military alliance and political understanding, rejected the counsel of their Belgian advisers and decided on Élisabethville.

[1] Heinz and Donnay, *Lumumba: The Last Fifty Days*, pp. 77-8.

Moanda was chosen as the airfield of embarkation since there was no U.N. guard there, thus obviating the possibility of any interference. On 17 January, Lumumba and his colleagues, Okito and Mpolo, were secretly taken by ruse from their Thysville prison and flown in a small Air-Brousse[1] plane to the Moanda airstrip. There, the three prisoners were put aboard a DC4 Air Congo plane which flew them to Katanga.

The first reliable information to reach ONUC headquarters about the deportation of Lumumba came in a flash message from Ian Berendsen, the ONUC representative in Élisabethville, who relayed a report from the U.N. Swedish guard posted at the airport. Control over the airport was divided between the Katangan authorities and the United Nations, each of whom patrolled its own area, and, to avoid incidents, both kept out of each other's way. On the evening of 17 January, the curiosity of a small U.N. Swedish guard of six soldiers was aroused by unusual security precautions in the Katangan part of the airport. Peering through their binoculars, the U.N. soldiers saw a plane which had just alighted being ferried to the Katangan area where it was quickly surrounded by a cordon of some 130 Katangan gendarmes who had evidently been awaiting it. Several trucks and jeeps were standing by and an armoured vehicle mounted guard, its cannon pointing towards the door of the aircraft when it came to a stop. Twenty Katangan gendarmes formed a gauntlet between the aircraft and a jeep that had been driven up to receive the prisoners. The first to leave the plane was a smartly dressed African, obviously a high official. He was followed by three blindfolded men whose hands were tied behind their backs. The first had a small beard. As they descended from the aircraft the gendarmes ran up to them, kicked them, and beat them severely with their rifle butts. The three men were thrown into a jeep and four gendarmes jumped into the vehicle. At that point, one of the three prisoners gave a loud cry. The jeep with its cargo led the convoy of vehicles and drove away through an opening made in the fence surrounding the airport. The whole proceedings took only a few minutes, and the U.N. guard, which had not been able to identify the prisoners, did not intervene, as, indeed, it was powerless to do. But, its suspicions aroused, it immediately

[1] Air-Brousse was a Belgian-owned air service in the Congo.

alerted the full Swedish Company and ONUC's representative in Élisabethville.

Ian Berendsen, the ONUC representative, had also heard from another source of the arrival of the prisoners an hour or so after the event. He personally questioned the Swedish guards to ascertain the full facts which he cabled the Secretary-General at New York and ONUC at Léopoldville. The news soon spread in Léopoldville and Élisabethville and was carried by news agencies all over the world.

I asked Berendsen to see Tshombe urgently to demand full information regarding the prisoners—whose identity was no longer in doubt—and to press for humane treatment. Berendsen met Tshombe on 18 January when he questioned him closely about the matter. Tshombe admitted that he had personally seen the prisoners soon after their arrival, adding that they were 'in a sad state' as a result of the savage beatings which they had received in the course of their journey. Berendsen advised Tshombe to send the prisoners back to Léopoldville in his own interest so as to avoid the serious repercussions which their presence in Katanga would inevitably cause. Tshombe explained that for many months the Léopoldville authorities had been making overtures to him to accept the prisoners for confinement in Jadotville prison, but his Government, being fully alive to the political implications, had repeatedly refused. Now the Léopoldville authorities had again pressed their request, and the Katangan Government had reluctantly agreed in principle to consider it. But before a final decision could be reached, a message had come from Léopoldville that the prisoners were on their way. Soon thereafter, Tshombe said he heard of the arrival of the plane carrying them.

Tshombe's protestations about being forced to become a reluctant jailor were, however, belied by the preparations made at the airport and by the communiqué issued by the Katangan Government on 19 January. The communiqué stated that 'at the request of President Kasavubu and with the agreement of the Katangan Government, the traitor Patrice Lumumba has been transferred to Katanga, as the prison of Thysville no longer offers sufficient guarantees'.

The Secretary-General sent an urgent message to Tshombe expressing grave concern at the possible consequences of the transfer and the denial to the prisoners of their right to due process of law. He pointed out that they were being kept under illegal detention as no charges had been preferred nor any trial held. Pressing Tshombe for humane and fair treatment, the Secretary-General said that the Katanga authorities would no doubt consider what steps should be taken to enable the prisoners to have the benefit of full judicial proceedings at a place of competent jurisdiction. Berendsen, in presenting the message, made a personal plea for permission for the International Red Cross to visit the prisoners, which he combined with a protest at their ill-treatment at the airport.

The Secretary-General followed this up with two cables to Kasavubu protesting against the transfer of Lumumba and his companions to a place outside competent jurisdiction without the prisoners' consent, as that would inevitably delay a fair and speedy trial and deprive them of legal advice and facilities. Hammarskjold therefore urged the return of all three prisoners to the jurisdiction of Léopoldville. In his second cable, the Secretary-General conveyed the concern of his Advisory Committee which strongly felt that the incarceration of political leaders was incompatible with the objective of conciliation.

Kasavubu sent no reply to the Secretary-General's telegrams. But Tshombe did. He told the Secretary-General that he considered it necessary completely 'to insulate Mr. Lumumba from any contact with the outside world'.

Rumours about the fate of Lumumba and his companions were not confined to their barbarous treatment; soon stories began to spread that they had been done to death. Berendsen saw Tshombe more than once about these rumours but Tshombe continued to assert that the prisoners were alive and well. In Léopoldville, it was impossible to get an iota of information from the authorities; even the most polite enquiries evoked angry rejoinders about keeping ONUC's nose out of the Congo's internal business.

On 10 February, Godefroid Munongo made a broadcast on Radio Katanga. He announced that Lumumba and his fellow-prisoners had escaped from a farm where they had been held in custody. According to him, they had made a hole in the wall of their room through which they escaped, and after overcoming and gagging their two guards and seizing their rifles, they fled in an automobile which was—conveniently—standing nearby. Munongo announced a reward of 300,000 francs for the capture of Lumumba and 50,000 francs for that of each of his companions, dead or alive. The following day Munongo called a press conference at which he announced that the automobile taken by the fugitives had been found abandoned some distance away and that the search was continuing. It was patent that the story of the 'escape' had been invented to put questioners off the scent, but few were credulous enough to believe it.

Hammarskjold cabled me: 'Insistent rumours here today that Lumumba has been killed. . . . The effect of these rumours in various directions is strongly felt and easily foreseeable in their wider repercussions. In these circumstances, as Conciliation Commission has renewed promise to see Lumumba, it is more imperative than ever that they press ahead with this visit; their personal contact now seems to me best available way of killing rumour which I most sincerely hope is entirely unfounded. Alternative would be that someone from ONUC should try to see him, but that would require a new and special negotiation and be less satisfactory internationally. Both Kasavubu and Tshombe should have the strongest reasons to establish falsity of rumour.' I asked the Commission to proceed immediately to Élisabethville to see Tshombe, or to send a small group there, but it debated the issue for a whole day, the Chairman deciding that any approach to Tshombe would 'upset the Léopoldville authorities'.

Meanwhile, fearing the worst, I issued the following order to all U.N. troops in consultation with the Military Command: 'If the fugitives should turn up and seek asylum, you would be in order in granting it while you seek instructions.'

I later wondered if we could have taken similar action at the time of Lumumba's arrest at Mweka. The circumstances, however, were very different. Then, Lumumba had left ONUC's protection of his own volition and had not sought its help while in flight, nor was his life believed to be in jeopardy. Moreover, there had been no political assassination thus far, although political arrests and beatings and subsequent releases were the order of the day and had, indeed, become part of the Congolese way of political life. Now, not only had a gross illegality been committed in sending Lumumba to an authority not recognized internationally, but what was worse, to a place where his fate was clearly sealed.

Hammarskjold, ever sensitive to the scrupulous observance of legal principles, cabled me: 'We shall again be accused of being soft-hearted to Lumumba as we have been accused of protecting Europeans. In the same way from the opposite side we will be accused of not protecting Lumumba just as we are accused of not giving sufficient protection to Europeans.' He concluded with the fatalistic comment that 'certainly this is an unthankful task but this will not lead you or us to deviate from what is our line'.

On hearing the story of the 'escape' I despatched General Iyassou to Élisabethville, accompanied by Knecht, a former Chief of Police of Geneva serving with ONUC, with instructions to badger Tshombe until the truth was ferreted out. But Tshombe refused to receive Iyassou or Berendsen, and he sent no reply to the persistent requests for information about the prisoners. He had, in acknowledging their arrival earlier, said it was necessary to insulate Mr. Lumumba from any contact with the outside world. Indeed, so complete was the insulation that Lumumba had already been transported to another world.

On 13 February Munongo gave a restricted press conference behind closed doors at which he announced that the 'criminals' had been murdered by the inhabitants of a small village some distance from where their car had been found. The bodies had been buried secretly and the place of burial would not be disclosed so as to prevent 'misguided persons from making it a centre of pilgrimage'. If anyone were to accuse the Katanga authorities of assassination, Munongo said his answer would be: 'Prove it!'

The facts of the crime can now be pieced together. The decision was taken by Kasavubu to spirit away Lumumba and his colleagues, Okito and Mpolo, to Katanga. A ruse was then played to disarm their suspicions in order to lure them away from their prison. A decoy was chosen in the person of a Jonas Mukamba, Assistant Secretary of the Interior, who was known to Lumumba since before Independence. He was sent to inform Lumumba that a revolt in his favour had occurred in Léopold-ville and his return there was being awaited for the formation of a new Government under his leadership.[1] But the prison guards were not so easily persuaded, and Mukamba had to exercise considerable ingenuity in obtaining their agreement to turn the prisoners over. On arriving at the airfield of Moanda, the three prisoners were received by Fernand Kazadi, Commissioner for Defence and a bitter tribal foe of Lumumba's, along with an armed guard. The escort consisted of soldiers of the Baluba tribe, which was fanatically hostile to Lumumba whom they blamed for the massacre of their kin in Kasai. At Moanda, the prisoners were transferred to a DC4 Air Congo plane with a Belgian crew and were accompanied on their long journey by Kazadi and the Baluba guard.

The prisoners were manacled to their seats, but hardly was the plane airborne when they were struck by rifle butts and knocked down by the heavily-shod soldiers, who jumped on their prostrate bodies. So savage were the beatings that the Belgian crew were sickened at the sight. Ultimately, the pilot[2] warned that structural damage would be caused to the aircraft if the frenzy continued. Unable to curb the brutality, the crew locked itself in the cabin in utter disgust.

On arrival in Élisabethville Lumumba and his companions were driven off rapidly to an empty farmhouse belonging to a Belgian settler not far from the airport. It was in this house that Lumumba and his companions are believed to have met their deaths on the night of 17–18 January 1961.

There are at least fifteen accounts of the circumstances of the murder,[3] and all are unanimous in recounting the unspeakable barbarities that accompanied Lumumba's last hours. After Munongo had informed Tshombe of the arrival of the captives, the Katanga Cabinet, attended by several Belgian advisers, met at Tshombe's house to hold a celebration. In the midst of much drinking and junketing, the question of the fate of the prisoners was discussed, and it was eventually agreed that they should be consigned to the custody of the tribal Chief of the Bayeke, a kinsman of Munongo's, in the village of Bunkeya. Munongo

---

[1] Pierre de Vos, *Vie et mort de Lumumba*, p. 281. Also Report of U.N. Commission of Enquiry, Documents A/4964 and S/4976, 11 November 1961.

[2] The pilot was either Commander Pierre van der Meersch or Bauwens.

[3] See Heinz and Donnay, *Lumumba: The Last Fifty Days*, pp. 130-45, for a summary of these accounts.

was commissioned to carry out the decision, and he proceeded to the farmhouse late in the night of 17 January with a couple of his colleagues, all presumably in a state of inebriation. Tshombe had himself earlier seen the prisoners as he informed Berendsen, but it is not clear at what time, or whether he was present during their final moments. On arriving at the farmhouse, Munongo saw Lumumba and it appears that he taunted him, but Lumumba awaited his fate stoically, refusing to ask for mercy. Angered, Munongo took a bayonet from the rifle of a sentry and slowly twisted it deep into Lumumba's side, mocking him awhile with cruel jibes. A Belgian officer who was present fired a shot with his revolver into Lumumba's head to end his agony. A Colonel Huyghes has claimed the distinction for this deed, but he has been challenged by a Captain Gatt for the honour. Gatt was Commander of the guard and he may well have administered the *coup de grâce*.

A particularly revolting piece of information was given me by a newspaper correspondent who claimed that he had heard on good authority that Lumumba's ears had been severed and sent to Kalonji in Bakwanga as proof of his enemy's demise. To remove any witnesses who could subsequently expose the crime, Okito and Mpolo were brought in one after the other and shot in the presence of the body of their chief. Some accounts have it that Okito met his end while on his knees praying beside Lumumba's body.

The question of the disposal of the bodies then had to be decided. It appears from some accounts that the corpses were kept in a refrigerator at the Union Minière's installations or were soaked in formaldehyde to preserve them for a while. Other accounts say that they were hastily buried in the grounds of the farmhouse. Since incriminating evidence of the crime had to be removed, it is doubtful if the bodies were initially buried, and certainly not in the grounds of the farmhouse which lay adjacent to a busy road. It is generally believed that the remains were dissolved in a vat of sulphuric acid at the Jadotville copper plant belonging to Union Minière.

Shortly after the news of his death, the widow of the slain leader came to ask for ONUC's intercession with Tshombe for the body of her husband. It was a moving occasion. When Mme Lumumba had seen me after Lumumba's transfer to

Élisabethville to ask about his welfare, she was well-dressed in European clothes and high-heeled shoes. This time she came bare-breasted and with shaven head, with a cloth around her waist and she sat on the floor in the traditional manner of African mourning. Her young son, carrying marks of beatings received at the hands of Mobutu's soldiers, accompanied her. She was living in a room somewhere in the African quarter and had no money. She was a picture of sorrow and despair. I could do little to comfort her except to arrange for her safety and that of her children by sending them in a U.N. plane to Stanleyville; Kasavubu later protested angrily at ONUC's 'connivance' at taking the lady away from whatever fate he had reserved for her. The families of the other slain leaders were also sent to the safe haven of Stanleyville. Lumumba had himself, sometime earlier, arranged to send his three elder children to Cairo, where they were being well cared for.

I immediately demanded from Tshombe information regarding the remains of the three martyred men, appealing to his humanity and respect for tradition. His reply was that any revelation of the place of burial would 'fan the flames of passions which, in the interests of the world, should be allowed to subside'. I renewed my request, this time quoting Bantu custom and Christian tradition. Tshombe, lamenting my ignorance of Bantu custom which, he said, proved conclusively ONUC's inability to deal with the affairs of an African country, replied that to uncover the bodies would be a serious violation of Bantu custom as the souls of the deceased would haunt the survivors!

The reactions to the murders began like an African thunderstorm with low rolling reverberations steadily gaining in intensity till they became deafening. Léopoldville had remained strangely quiet. But soon an attack was made on members of the Abako tribe (Kasavubu's), several of whom were badly injured and some mutilated. In Luluabourg, the eerie calm was broken by attacks on some Europeans, one of whom was killed. From Stanleyville, Duran reported that the public had been too stunned to express any emotion and that an unreal atmosphere prevailed in the city which was completely deserted during the period of official mourning. General Lundula had made appeals for calm which had been largely heeded. But a segment of the A.N.C. marched into the European quarter on hearing of a convivial party to celebrate the murders and attacked three Europeans, one of them fatally. Shops and schools were closed in many towns all over the country and spontaneous absences from work became common. Our main worry was about Stanleyville where the brooding suspense continued, but Duran was full of praise for Gizenga and Lundula who had shown unexpected restraint. An enormous requiem mass, attended by 25,000 people, dispersed peacefully after exhortations from the authorities to remain calm.

In Léopoldville, where the Chief of Security, Nendaka, and his colleague, Kazadi, were supreme, a new wave of terror was unleashed. Arbitrary arrests began and there was an agitated flow of politicians to 'Le Royal', fearful of deportation and execution. The U.N. Force was clearly unable to provide individual protection to the host of scared politicians. A protected camp was quickly set up to which threatened persons began to flock with their families. Kasavubu complained bitterly that the camp had been opened without his permission, and the Western embassies complained that its creation would give the Léopoldville authorities a bad name. But there was no question of dismantling it, as its capacity had soon been filled to overflowing and none of the refugees was prepared to leave.

At this point, it would be appropriate to turn to New York, where the Security Council had been in session frequently during January and February. Hammarskjold wanted the Security Council to give urgent attention to the civil-war situation, the plight of the European refugees and the misdeeds of the A.N.C. He had also been working on a plan to break the Katanga stalemate, where the genocidal activities of Tshombe's Belgian-led gendarmerie had coincided with a large-scale recruitment of foreign mercenaries and the arrival of military aircraft and other warlike supplies. I had sent New York detailed reports on these matters which had been circulated to members of the Council. General McKeown had been clamouring about the weakness of his military position which would become intolerable after the departure of various units at the end of February. I had pressed Hammarskjold to take up these matters with the Security Council and also to seek its endorsement of an operational directive issued to the U.N. Force with which Hammarskjold said he was in 'absolute agreement'—specifying the situations where intervention was essential. At the same time, I had asked for the Council's authority to take measures, if necessary by means of force, for the removal of mercenaries and other undesirable foreigners. McKeown had made an assessment of his military needs which amounted to at least twenty battalions as against the fifteen that would remain with the Force at the end of the month. Four of these he wanted for Léopoldville city where the U.N. Force was out-numbered and out-gunned by Mobutu's A.N.C. As the Force was everywhere thin on the ground, it had lost control of surface routes and had to rely heavily on aircraft for movement. But here again, there were serious deficiencies as many of the odd assortment of thirty-two aircraft were in need of spare parts and repair while some had been badly shot-up. The air staff wanted another thirty-two aircraft, including a dozen modern transport planes. We felt that to compensate for our weakness in numbers, our efficiency should be improved by giving the Force additional powers and initiatives, particularly of a pre-ventive nature. I had issued a new directive to the U.N. Force requiring it to prevent armed conflict by every means other than the use of armed force; to protect unarmed groups; to accord maximum protection to refugees; to assure the safety of political leaders seeking it; to ensure the security of hostages; and to counter any outside force, including paratroopers, by armed force if necessary.

It was imperative to take effective measures to stem the tide of turbulence wherever we could, and to the limit of our capa-city. The horrors being wreaked on the tribal population in North Katanga by Tshombe's Belgian-led gendarmerie were particularly revolting. Tshombe was rapidly building up his military strength, and streams of foreign adventurers were pouring into Katanga drawn by lust for loot and adventure. They came from Belgium, South Africa, Rhodesia, Britain, and France, and included members of the former French Foreign Legion, and remnants of the 'Algérie Française' group. Unless the United Nations acted quickly to push Tshombe's murderous minions out of North Katanga, it would be immeasurably more difficult to do so later.

I wired Hammarskjold that the situation in Katanga had

developed into virtual genocide against the Baluba and Basonge tribes by the Katanga gendarmerie led by Colonel Crèvecoeur which had brought into focus the question of the responsibility of the United Nations. I had sent repeated warnings to Tshombe, the latest of which had been conveyed personally through General Iyassou. But our written and verbal protests had proved to be entirely ineffective. It was high time for forceful steps to be taken by ONUC to put a stop to the massacres, and I asked the Secretary-General's concurrence to extend our powers to include protection of the innocent by force.

Hammarskjold was quick to wire back: 'I am going to stage long-planned approach to Tshombe in short initial statement in Security Council tomorrow, combining Tshombe's attitude on our investigation[1] with Kalonji's "offensive", arms import, mercenaries, uncooperative attitude on reconciliation, etc., with its obvious outside support. Unavoidable that my comments will get concentrated on Tshombe's case. Risk of this approach is dual: it may be overshadowed by storm over Lumumba, and may create extreme tension between U.N. and Tshombe. But we will have to go straight on in interest of U.N. itself and therefore have to face these risks.' The Secretary-General then offered his comments on the proposals made by us. While he did not necessarily accept the theory that Katanga's military moves had been coordinated with Kalonji and Mobutu, he did not exclude the possibility of concerted military action—'which certainly has not been worked out by Congolese brains'—but for the moment he thought that we should concentrate on Katanga as the most immediate question. He therefore endorsed the phrase 'to prevent the burning of villages and the killing of civilians with force if necessary' on the ground that the Katanga attack had strong elements of genocide. He added: 'Katanga has no excuse for its action and we have no excuse to stand passive. The same action should be taken against Kalonji's forces.' But in case of confrontation between Gizenga and Mobutu troops, the Secretary-General drew a distinction, as the two armed groups were opposing each other without involving civilians. But even there, the Secretary-General said, the United Nations should continue with its efforts at pacification by interposing itself between the

[1] Into the circumstances of Lumumba's death.

forces to bring about cease-fires and to set up neutral zones supervised by U.N. troops.

In the Security Council, instead of two members from Africa and Asia—Tunisia and Ceylon—there were now three: Liberia, the U.A.R., and Ceylon. The African and Asian delegations had been in contact with the Secretary-General with a view to evolving the highest common denominator of agreement. While the delegates were still negotiating among themselves, the Soviet delegation jumped the gun by calling for a meeting to discuss Belgian violation of the Trusteeship Agreement in the trust territory of Ruanda-Urundi by its connivance in the abortive Kivu expedition[1] of 1 January 1971.

The Security Council met on 1 February when the Secretary-General drew the Council's urgent attention to the tasks of the U.N. Force in the light of the demands from different quarters that it use military initiatives to end the Katangan secession, to suppress the Stanleyville régime, to rescue political prisoners, and to protect Europeans, and this at a time when the Council and Assembly would have seriously to consider whether the Force should continue or be liquidated in view of its serious weakening through withdrawals. However, if the A.N.C. could be returned to its proper role and subjected to reorganization, Hammarskjold felt that the U.N. Force could yet carry out its tasks. Its liquidation, as the Soviet Union had proposed, would only expose the Congo to catastrophe. The Secretary-General therefore sought from the Council its approval of the far-reaching measures that the situation required.

At this time, the new U.S. administration was reviewing its foreign policy and President Kennedy had said in his inaugural address: 'Let both sides explore what problems unite us instead of belabouring those problems that divide us.' The President and his advisers were agreed on the imperative need both to give the Secretary-General more positive support and to show greater receptivity to the African and Asian view. The new United States policy for the Congo therefore included support for the Secretary-General, the exclusion of foreign—particularly Belgian—interference, a new federal Government embracing the leaders of all factions (including Lumumba), and, as an

[1] See pp. 162-3.

essential condition, the neutralization of all Congolese military forces.

Belgium reacted in alarm to these developments. She felt slighted at not having been first consulted by the Kennedy administration. The U.S. plan would severely undermine the authority of President Kasavubu, it was argued, as legitimate Head of State and open the way for 'Communist penetration'. The neutralization of Congolese troops would enable the United Nations to set up a 'shadow government' under its authority and create a virtual trusteeship in violation of Congolese sovereignty. The line was taken in Brussels, Paris, and London that in trying to persuade the United States to adopt a new policy, the Secretary-General was hoping to overcome Soviet hostility to himself by advocating the release of Lumumba as a price for African and Asian support.

Hammarskjold's appeal to the Security Council evoked a sympathetic response from the African and Asian delegates, but many felt it did not go far enough. Some asked for the release of all political prisoners, the withdrawal of foreign military personnel, and the reopening of Parliament as parallel measures to neutralizing the Congolese armed forces.

During the search for a consensus, the Katanga authorities announced that Lumumba and his colleagues had 'escaped', followed by another announcement three days later that they had been killed. The situation suddenly changed radically and the Security Council was called hurriedly into session.

The Council met on 13 February in an atmosphere of gloom and acrimony. After a brief statement by Hammarskjold confirming the tragic news, Stevenson, the new U.S. delegate to the United Nations, took the floor. Describing the news as 'depressing and deplorable', he emphasized the need more than ever to accelerate the quest for a consensus, and, in a number of detailed proposals, he appealed to members to avoid any steps that might further inflame the situation. He was answered by Zorin, who found Stevenson's proposals inadequate and re-engaged in a savage attack on the Belgians and the Secretary-General. Prophetically, he said that 'the Congolese people will some day erect a majestic monument' to Lumumba.[1] He

[1] Mobutu, as President of the Democratic Republic of Zaïre, as it is now called, has erected a statue and monument to Lumumba costing several million dollars.

concluded by presenting a draft resolution incorporating the demands made in the Soviet Government's statement, including the dismissal of Dag Hammarskjold 'as a participant in and organizer of the crime'.

The Secretary-General, after expressing deep regret for the assassinations, said in reply to Zorin that it was 'vain to argue against those for whom truth is a function of party convenience and justice a function of party interest'. He went on to describe events in connection with Lumumba's arrest leading to his death. Quoting Lumumba's appreciation of the United Nations in the Congo as 'the guardian of democracy', Hammarskjold said that Lumumba had often written to him expressing full confidence in him, and had endorsed his statements as being fully 'in keeping with truth and reality'.

Explaining why the United Nations could not have used force to prevent Lumumba's arrest, Hammarskjold said that the responsibility rested with the Council which had established the mandate which prohibited initiatives by the U.N. Force. He added pointedly that 'a single voice does not change the decision of a major organ'. In blackening the Organization and discrediting its representatives, he said, the real victim was the future. It was ironic that those who were guided solely by the interests of the Congo should be attacked by those who pursued entirely different aims. The Secretary-General deplored the fact that the Soviet Union had personalized an issue which in reality concerned an institution. To be a road-block to those from all sides who sought to make of the Congo a happy hunting-ground for their national interests was to make oneself the target for attack by all those whose plans were thwarted. 'From both sides the main accusation was a lack of.objectivity,' he said, 'but the historian would find in this balance of accusations conclusive evidence of impartiality.' Returning to the demand for his dismissal, Hammarskjold said it was clear that there would be no agreement on a successor and the Soviet view of a triumvirate would prevail, thus endangering the Organization at a time of great international tension when it was most needed. In other circumstances he would have bowed to the opposition of a great power, but he could not do so now unless it were the wish of the uncommitted nations. Hammarskjold then suggested an investigation into Lumumba's death

and he outlined, for the Council's approval, the strengthened
directive given to the U.N. Force. He did not ask for an additional legal mandate, but only for the Council's confirmation
of the extension of the powers which the U.N. Force already
possessed for use in certain specified emergencies.

The three African and Asian members of the Security Council had been holding continuous discussions regarding the out-
lines of a draft resolution which would substantially strengthen
the capacity of the U.N. Force to take effective action to meet
the emergency. It would have to be so balanced as to obtain
the agreement of the United States without, at the same time,
attracting a Soviet veto. But while these efforts were being
made in New York, the macabre drama of torture and murder
was continuing in the Congo.

On 16 February I reported to Hammarskjold a rumour that
Finant, Fataki, and a number of others kept prisoner in Léopoldville, had been flown to Bakwanga where they were believed
to have been killed. Hammarskjold wired back urgently: 'In
appropriate way you should get across to Tshombe and Kalonji
my very strong concern regarding this matter and my firm
demand for protective steps so that no harm to lives of people
concerned occurs. Were the lives of the persons to be endangered
or lost, I would denounce the acts to the Security Council
in the most categorical terms. Although it is now popular to
regard such actions of mine as those of Pontius Pilate, you
know as well as I that this is maximum that we can manage. . . .
I fail to believe that information concerning the fate of Finant,
etc., can be right. You should track it down by all means, and
if it is verified, how can I do otherwise than denounce the
Kasavubu régime?' Referring to the previous day's bitter attack
on him by Zorin, Hammarskjold added: 'Here the battle goes
on and there have never been any hands more covered with
blood than mine according to those who, for reasons of their
own, remember that this is Easter time.'

I was greatly saddened by this message, for apart from my
anxieties about the fate of another batch of innocent victims,
Hammarskjold had, for the first time, given expression to a
sense of resignation and despair. The pressures on us at Léopoldville were equally intense, and both to relieve my own
feelings and to offer what solace I could, I wired back: 'You

refer to the effects of Easter on our critics there; here the agony of Gethsemane is prolonged and we daily bear our cross in patience.'

The resolution sponsored by the three African and Asian members of the Council urged the United Nations to take all appropriate measures to prevent the occurrence of civil war, including the use of force in the last resort. It enjoined on the U.N. Force to take positive measures to create the necessary conditions in which the Congolese leaders would be able to take political initiatives to restore the equilibrium of their country.

The fate of the three-power resolution of 21 February remained in considerable doubt. Although Stevenson was veering round to the view that more drastic action was necessary, the hard-liners in the State Department and the Pentagon were still tugging hard to restrain him. Hammarskjold was worried about the fate of the resolution but even more about its implementation, as he wired me: 'Situation as regards resolution very confused. Thorough talk with sponsors shows that, as usual, their high-mindedness as regards aims is just as high as their ideas about how to achieve them remain low. It is very uncertain whether Afro-Asian resolution can be adopted, but it is certain that if it is, with all its laudable but perfectly acceptable aims, I shall be accused of sabotage within two weeks because it does not provide for any new means to achieve the aims; their point regarding withdrawal of Belgian personnel was fully covered already by my *démarche* of 8 October, the results of which remain of blessed memory.' But, referring to the latter question, he added more hopefully: 'Story from so-called "reliable sources" is that Belgians tonight have got instructions to withdraw "progressively" all Belgian nationals in the military ranks and also allegedly on the political side. In substance it is not good enough, but it interests me because it indicates that they could have already done it long ago.' The United States had been bringing pressure to bear on Belgium and had been given certain assurances, but unfortunately, as so often before, they proved to be false.

While the Council was in brief recess, the Léopoldville authorities had taken another step in the politics of murder. On 9 February a group of pro-Lumumba personalities including

Finant, who had been President of Orientale province and was arrested by Mobutu's troops, had been deported to Bakwanga. When I heard the news I immediately wrote to Ileo as Head of Government, demanding the fullest information and warning that responsibility for the fate of the prisoners could not be evaded on the pretext that some other authority was now responsible for their custody. The Secretary-General in turn warned Kasavubu in the severest possible terms of his responsibility. No replies to our letters or to our persistent verbal enquiries were received from Kasavubu or Ileo. Perhaps Kasavubu, as a former seminarian, felt that 'where no law is, there is no transgression'.[1] In the event, we were informed by Kalonji that the prisoners had been 'tried' by a customary court of tribal chiefs and executed the same day.

News of these cold-blooded murders electrified the delegates in New York and shocked the Security Council into taking up the matter with renewed urgency. On 21 February the three African and Asian members introduced a second draft resolution dealing specifically with the question of political assassinations. It called for a condemnation of political violence and assassinations, asked the Léopoldville authorities to put an immediate stop to such crimes which had shocked the conscience of the world, demanded active measures by the United Nations to prevent such outrages, if necessary by the use of force, and called for an investigation into the crimes and punishment of their perpetrators.

The debate centred on the proposal to condemn political assassinations in the Congo and on the call to the United Nations to take all possible measures for the prevention of outrages, including the use of force as a last resort. The Nationalist Chinese representative, in pressing for a separate vote on the phrase 'including the use of force', which was eliminated by his veto as well as the abstention of the five Western powers and their friends, drew the teeth out of the resolution. The next vote was on the substitution of the words 'in various parts of the Congo', in place of the specific reference to Léopoldville, Katanga, and South Kasai. This proposal too was vetoed, and the resolution was not adopted. In quibbling over the terms and in failing to condemn the barbarities being committed in

[1] Romans 4:15.

the Congo, the Security Council had administered to itself a great moral blow, as members seemed more concerned about which authorities committed the crimes than about the crimes themselves. It was only a couple of days later that news of the reprisal executions in Stanleyville came to light. Perhaps the Council could have deferred a decision, so as to have included Stanleyville as well in the condemnation, had it not been so concerned with the form of the resolution at the expense of its substance.

The Secretary-General, while deploring the failure of the second resolution, welcomed the adoption of the first three-power resolution of 21 February as it gave a stronger and clearer framework for United Nations actions. Hammarskjold's comments on the debate were cabled to me soon after:

I have sent in clear, resolution as it finally emerged; noble aims and no new means or legal rights! However, I squeezed in my final intervention on the main resolution to one advantage, saying that I was sure that member nations realize that this would make necessary new troop contributions. The same matter will be taken up this afternoon in Advisory Committee as background of requests to select number of countries which this time, I think, may succeed better than before; maybe we can even break Morocco. I shall cable you conclusions from Advisory Committee meeting. The opinion of the Committee is essential on practically every point, vague as the text is and keen as a certain party is to demonstrate ill-will and colonialism on our side. . . . We have heavy work ahead regarding all measures of implementation and must establish even closer cooperation than usual. Regarding specifically investigation, Zorin holds that we cannot have a part in it as it should cover also our 'crimes'.

At ONUC headquarters, we 'who against hope believed in hope',[1] were elated that despite the disappointments and frustrations of the past, the Security Council had at last united in adopting a resolution which was more in context with the realities of the situation. I wired back to the Secretary-General: 'Sincere congratulations on splendid result achieved in the Security Council. Your efforts stand fully vindicated.' Hammarskjold and we had begun studying the resolutions and considering measures to give practical effect to them. Hammarskjold had sent urgent messages in the most peremptory

[1] Romans 4:18.

terms to Kasavubu, Tshombe, and Kalonji containing stern warnings regarding their personal responsibility for any future threats to life, reminding them of the norms of civilized behaviour and informing them of the sense of horror which had been universally felt over the grim events. He asked me to send a similar message to Gizenga in case the frenzy had already spread there.

I was soon informed by Duran that it had. He reported, 'The die seems to have been cast. I have just been informed by a most reliable authority that this morning shortly before noon, Lokoso[1] and his four military colleagues, Songolo and the nine other parliamentarians were executed at Camp Osio. According to the source, the execution was witnessed by members of Gizenga's entourage and the Provincial Government, by Louis Lumumba and by General Lundula himself. I have called Lundula to check the news; he was so vague and hesitant that I am afraid the news is true.' All Duran's efforts and our protests and warnings had been in vain and Stanleyville had also followed the slimy trail of political murder. But the Belgian soldiers taken prisoner were alive, and we redoubled our efforts to ensure their continued safety and eventual release.[2]

The Secretary-General had been having prolonged discussions with his Advisory Committee regarding the scope of the resolution of 21 February and measures for its implementation. His comments followed:

After four discussions in Advisory Committee I have a feeling of going backwards, not forwards. Members are getting more and more anxious not to commit themselves on any points of real significance 'because they are controversial'. So we have again the absurd situation where the Security Council has passed the buck, both as to initiative and to interpretation, to Secretary-General, being itself in a difficult position if the questions are turned back, while, on the other hand, the Secretary-General is refused the advice of most interested member countries who, at the same time, as amply shown in the past, reserve their full right to criticize afterwards.

After this unpromising preface, the Secretary-General offered his own interpretation 'since the Advisory Committee refuses

---

[1] One of Mobutu's A.N.C. officers arrested in Stanleyville.
[2] They were released in April 1961.

to interpret the Security Council resolution', although he added that 'it may give you some guidance but I am fully aware that it is on the meagre side'. He expressed the hope that the question would not arise in an acute form before he 'managed to face those really responsible to some form of clarification—if that is at all possible.' With reference to the civil-war threat, I had pointed to the difficulty of controlling military movements of Congolese armed units, since ONUC's control over road and river transport was largely ineffective and over air movements, precarious. I had suggested that we would be on safer ground in using dissuasion and argument rather than an empty show of force—as U.N. troops were so thinly scattered on the ground—to which Hammarskjold agreed, especially in view of Ghana's decision not to allow the involvement of its troops in any conflict between Kalonji's forces and Stanleyville. Hammarskjold added: 'I am afraid that in the circumstances, with the political gale blowing here and everything we do being held against us, this is all I can say, as Afro-Asians lie low.'

The 21 February resolution had demanded, in categorical terms, the immediate withdrawal and exclusion from the Congo of Belgian and other foreign personnel of certain prohibited categories. President Kasavubu reacted sharply to the resolution. He informed the President of the Security Council that the Congo would never permit the implementation of the resolution as his Government regarded it as an infringement of its sovereignty which the Congolese people would defend 'with all the resources at their command'. He affirmed the right of the Congolese authorities to take such measures as they thought fit for the reorganization of the army and the employment of foreign instructors. In commenting on Kasavubu's letter, Hammarskjold reminded me of his letter of 8 October to Brussels asking for the withdrawal from Katanga of Belgian military and para-military personnel, etc., adding, 'put together, these two documents clash beautifully'.

The problem of Belgians engaged in legitimate activity, whether as employees of the Congolese authorities or in trade and commerce, had been a constant preoccupation with ONUC, as the United Nations could not possibly provide the thousands of teachers, magistrates, technicians, and similar personnel required for work in non-political and non-military fields. Linner and I and ONUC's civilian consultants had discussed the question at length with the Secretary-General during his visit to Léopoldville in January. In particular, we had asked him whether the possibility of recruiting Belgians as U.N. experts, even from among those willing to cooperate, should be ruled out. Hammarskjold said there was no *a priori* objection to Belgians working for the Republic of the Congo and that at an early stage of the Operation there had been a possibility of recruiting competent U.N. technicians familiar with the country and its languages from among Belgians who had divorced themselves from colonial attitudes. But the Belgian reflux and its accompanying circumstances had made the question of Belgian withdrawal 'a hot political issue'. The Belgian Government had gone on the defensive on shifting grounds: on the one hand it said that Belgians still, or again, in the Congo were there in an individual capacity; on the other hand, it had asserted its right to make bilateral technical assistance arrangements with the Congolese authorities. Unfortunately, the Belgians had misunderstood the Secretary-General's request that all types of Belgian assistance should be channelled through the United Nations as implying an intention to evict all Belgians, root and branch. The idea of the Secretary-General was really to establish a base line, reconstructing Belgian assistance from the bottom upwards and not from the top downwards, within a United Nations framework. The Belgians, for their part, felt that they could not mortgage their bilateral approach. But at the moment, recruiting Belgians as U.N. technicians would invite strongly adverse reactions on the international scene. The Secretary-General concluded: 'There is no conflict of principles. There is a time, however, and there is a way.' Hammarskjold declined to issue any instructions on the question of the employment by the U.N. of Belgians, as he felt it would be unwise 'to codify an attitude which should remain rather fluid'. His instinct was right, for had anything issued in writing, it would have provided his critics with just the evidence they were looking for to confirm their charge that he was 'a henchman and agent of the Belgian colonialists'.

The Belgian Government of Prime Minister Eyskens was bitterly hostile to the 21 February resolution unless it was redefined out of all semblance to its real meaning. But when Paul-Henri Spaak became Foreign Minister a few weeks later on the coming to office of a Socialist-orientated Government, he tried to alter Belgian policy towards Katanga and the rest of the Congo. His success, in face of the opposition of the Union Minière and other strongly entrenched Belgian commercial and political interests, was, however, negligible. In Britain, support for Katanga continued unabated. It became clear that although it had voted for the resolution, the British Government had no interest in its implementation.

The Léopoldville authorities rebounded to the resolution as to the sting of a viper. Kasavubu had isolated himself from all Congolese nationalist influences as well as from the envoys of African and Asian countries who still remained in Léopoldville, and he was under the exclusive influence of his Belgian advisers and Western missions. He broadcast a statement in unusually vehement language sounding a call to arms against the United Nations. Stating that the country was being betrayed by the United Nations which threatened to put it under its trusteeship after forcibly disarming the national army, he announced the mobilization of all national resources to oppose the United Nations. He made an impassioned appeal to Tshombe to join forces with him to face the common 'mortal danger'. He concluded: 'Congolese men and women, soldiers of the A.N.C., arise and go forward; let the leopard, symbol of the Congo, show his claws, make his mighty voice resound and leap forward towards the foe.'

Meanwhile, the Military Bulletin of A.N.C. headquarters at Léopoldville published a statement that by disarming the A.N.C., the United Nations would take away from the country its sole means of ensuring law and order, and the world would think that the Congolese people were incapable of defending themselves. It continued: 'A military man without arms is not a soldier. The United Nations considers the Congolese as children, for if a child possesses arms, they must be taken away from him.' Then with the country disarmed, it would become easy for the United Nations to impose a trusteeship and the next step would be to make it again into a colony. But that would never be permitted to happen, continued the Bulletin The military, who were the élite of the nation, would form a

Patrice Lumumba

Antagonists converse: Stevenson and Gromyko

Two generals: McKeown and Mobutu

solid bloc to prevent the United Nations from arrogating any power to itself. The Bulletin concluded: 'It is better to die than again to fall under foreign domination.'

Tshombe announced a 'total mobilization' to oppose the United Nations which he said had made a declaration of war against Katanga and the whole of the Congo with the express purpose of ending their sovereignty. To prevent any action being taken against his Belgian advisers and employees, he declared the grant of Katangan nationality to all, white or black, who asked for it. Tshombe concluded with an appeal to the people to rally around his Government in that crucial hour for the defence of their homeland. Albert Kalonji in South Kasai declared the resolution null and void. For their part, the Stanleyville authorities did not express any public reactions although the resolution applied equally to the territories under their control.

The threats hurled against the United Nations and the open incitement to violence had an instantaneous effect. Instead of the increased powers given to the United Nations being put to use to curb violence between opposing Congolese factions, they had to be invoked by the U.N. Force to defend itself in the Lower Congo area and in Katanga from the frenzy of hatred and violence that had been deliberately aroused. A press campaign against the United Nations was also launched, and charges levelled that it was trying to bring about the establishment of Communism in the country, and I and some of my colleagues became the targets of particularly scurrilous attacks. When I reported to Hammarskjold on the malevolent cacophony that had been let loose accompanied by a monstrous wave of outrages against United Nations personnel, he wired back:

Every day brings too much for appropriate comments. I note that *Courrier d'Afrique* carries reactions even more preposterous than those for which I have been a target. As I said yesterday to one of the Soviet people, 'Kasavubu has again broken with Dayal and your Government has broken with me; are there any relations left but those between Dayal and me!' . . . I fully grasp the problem. We all have to work with imperfect means and human frailties, but the outcome is in the long run determined more by steadfast adherence to principles and endurance than by the current shifts in the situation.

In this new 'Battle of Britain' those who try in the deeper sense to be the friends of all are bound to be treated as the enemies of all. This you know as well as we do, and therefore things I believe somehow will work out right.

CHAPTER 13

Embittered Intransigence

The Léopoldville authorities reacted to the 21 February resolution in a mood of fear and defiance. The United Nations
tried to reassure Kasavubu and his colleagues about the real
import of the 21 February resolution. The Secretary-General
explained that the world community was more concerned with
the future than with the past; with pacification, not with
punishment; with cooperation, not with condemnation. But
it was difficult to exorcise the spectre of retribution which
haunted the minds of those of whom it could be said that 'there
is no sin but ignorance'.

Kasavubu and Mobutu had convinced themselves that their
troops would be forcibly disarmed, exposing them to the retri-
butive justice of the United Nations. An investigation into
Lumumba's assassination, they feared, would reveal their culpability, while the recall of Parliament would restore the pre-
ponderance of the Lumumbists. They frantically opposed any
suggestion even to discuss the measures which could be taken
towards the implementation of the resolution. To pre-empt
the U.N. Force from taking any initiatives of its own, they
embarked on a campaign of defiance and slander against it.

The Secretary-General addressed a series of letters to President Kasavubu, explaining in practical terms the precise meaning of the decisions taken by the Security Council. In his first
message, he pointed out that the work of the United Nations
to assist the Congo had been reduced to a holding operation,
whereas, with loyalty and cooperation, it could have brought
peace and progress to the country long ago. The deterioration
had continued up to, and indeed beyond, the point of political
assassination. This had placed the United Nations, whose
warnings had been consistently ignored, in serious jeopardy.

The Secretary-General stressed that the 'utter seriousness' of the 21 February resolution was derived from the background of past events. The resolution represented an attempt to cut through all that had hampered the U.N.'s efforts and it was the strongest and most decisive expression of the concern of the Council to maintain certain standards without which harmonious political development would be impossible. It also emphasized the Council's intention to put an end to conditions which not only threatened the world community but were of mortal danger to the Congo itself. The Council had emphasized the imperative need for reconciliation on a nation-wide scale. Those were the objectives. But it was 'shocking', the Secretary-General complained, to hear repeated allegations by the President and his colleagues that the United Nations was bent upon establishing 'trusteeship' over the Congo.

Pointing to the looming danger of civil war, the Secretary-General said that the question was one of taking pacifying and preventive measures, and not of coercion. But, at the same time, the United Nations would not allow itself to be forcibly deterred from carrying out the necessary measures. The Council's decision regarding the expulsion of specified classes of foreign personnel was intended to eliminate elements which had frustrated the goals of the United Nations and had fostered secessionist tendencies. Explaining the inter-linking of the two parts of the resolution, the Secretary-General said the purpose was to create the objective conditions which would facilitate the convening of Parliament. The provisions of the Loi Fondamentale imposed certain obligations on the Congolese authorities which they must respect if the Congo were to emerge as a democratic nation. The reorganizing and disciplining of the Congolese armed units in order to eliminate any possibility of interference by them in the political process was a logical corollary. The Secretary-General added that it was intolerable from the point of view of the country's internal and external security that its armed forces should behave as principal agents in its political life, especially since different units frequently acted on their own initiative. In conclusion, the Secretary-General requested President Kasavubu's support and cooperation in the implementation of the provisions of the Security Council's resolution.

In a second letter, the Secretary-General referred to the draft resolution by the African and Asian powers condemning the assassinations, and he emphasized that although the resolution had not been adopted for reasons that were purely technical, its substance had received unanimous approval. He said that the President would surely understand the extreme seriousness of the sentiments of profound shock and revulsion with which the Council had reacted to the assassinations. The attitude of the Council, which the Secretary-General said he shared with the strongest conviction, implied a decision that such acts must be considered as serious international crimes. Hammarskjold conveyed a solemn warning that any repetition of such crimes would entail the gravest consequences for their perpetrators. Finally, the Secretary-General exhorted the President to fulfil his manifest duty to observe proper standards of conduct.

In a third letter on the subject, the Secretary-General asked President Kasavubu to inform him of the steps he intended to take for the repatriation of undesirable foreign personnel. The Secretary-General also addressed a stern letter to Tshombe, explaining the mandatory nature of the Security Council's decisions, and demanding full information about the mercenaries and other foreign personnel operating in Katanga.

The Secretary-General followed up his *démarches* to the Congolese leaders with a communication to the Belgian delegation regarding the mandatory character of the Security Council's decisions on the immediate withdrawal of all Belgian and other foreign military and para-military personnel, political advisers, and mercenaries. Drawing attention to the legal obligations which the resolution imposed on all member states, the Secretary-General requested the Belgian Government to take prompt remedial measures in conformity with the terms of the resolution. He emphasized once again the critical importance of the effective implementation of the relevant parts of the resolution which were the particular responsibility of the Belgian Government.

The Secretary-General's messages to the Belgian Government and Congolese authorities were in language of the utmost urgency and conviction. Yet the Belgian Government continued to quibble about taking concrete action, although it had proclaimed its willingness to comply with the requirements of the resolution. To avoid any further delay, particularly on the ground of Belgium's professed inability to understand the scope of the resolution, the Secretary-General agreed to send a representative to Brussels to examine the ways and means of applying the resolution.

President Kasavubu, for his part, seemed to have been rather overwhelmed by the Secretary-General's succession of letters. He replied that while he had read them, it was not possible for him to reply to all the points which had been raised. Confining himself to the question of reorganizing the army, he complained that irresponsible talk of 'disarming' by responsible United Nations officials had created the greatest animosity among the Congolese soldiers against the United Nations and its personnel, provoking them to commit acts of hostility towards anything connected with United Nations services. The President regarded as impossible and completely Utopian the simple expulsion of Belgian personnel, whose number was not a hundred or so as 'incorrectly' reported by the Special Representative, but only fourteen. But President Kasavubu did not explain why the task was so Herculean if the number involved was indeed minuscule. So far as the question of reorganization of the Congolese army was concerned, the President insisted that his person, which was above party politics, was best able to insulate the army from politics. Furthermore, the reorganization must embrace the entire country, including Orientale, Kivu, South Kasai, and Katanga. A National Defence Council should be established under the Chairmanship of a 'neutral' personality responsible to the President, comprising representatives of the Congolese and United Nations forces. But the Congolese Government would reserve the right to accept or reject technicians recruited by the United Nations for training the army. The President preferred to keep silent about the inflammatory broadcast that he had made or the equally incendiary statements made by his Prime Minister and others against the United Nations Force. But, louder than words, the actions of the Léopoldville authorities during the coming days were to provide the answer to the Secretary-General's questions.

On 26 February the A.N.C. suddenly put up road-blocks on the outskirts of the city, detaining United Nations soldiers,

including five Tunisians who were forcibly disarmed by forty
Congolese. The same evening, a car carrying United Nations
personnel in the city was detained and its occupants forced to
run at bayonet point for two and a half miles to a military
camp where they found nine other international personnel, one
of them an Italian Colonel bleeding from a facial cut, lying on
the floor. Further outrages were committed to the accompani-
ment of threats that all United Nations personnel would be
killed before they could disarm the Congolese troops. That
same night a British woman secretary working with the United
Nations was arrested and raped twice.[1]

The U.N. Force Command was indignant at these outrages,
but it restrained itself, responding at first only with missives.
General McKeown addressed a strong protest to the A.N.C.
Commander against 'the brutal attack, arbitrary arrests and
bestial acts' to which United Nations personnel had been subjected. He said that he was enquiring into this sudden outburst
of revolting violence against U.N. personnel to ascertain if it
was part of a general plan or an example of a complete lack
of discipline in the A.N.C. But he warned that the U.N. Force
would oppose such acts 'with the maximum of force'. I also
protested vigorously to Prime Minister Ileo, who blamed the
U.N. Force for harbouring the intention of disarming Congolese soldiers and charged it with provocation, quoting the testi-
mony of a Western diplomat in support of his allegation. The
A.N.C.'s reply to McKeown's protests was to continue its
threats and isolated attacks on U.N. personnel.

It was evident that energetic action was imperative to put
a stop to these outrages which were infuriating the U.N. troops
and demoralizing its civilian personnel. One-sided restraint
only made the lawless elements of the A.N.C. bolder. Indeed,
some U.N. units had been so impressed by their peaceful role
that they hesitated to use their arms even in self-defence. But

[1] Sir Ian Scott, British Ambassador to the Congo at the time, has questioned
the veracity of this occurrence in his book, *Tumbled House*, which recounts his
experiences in the country. Why a woman should have made a false report so
damaging to herself, to her immediate superior, ONUC's Chief of Personnel, and
to have confirmed it by going to hospital for treatment, passes one's comprehension. The Sudanese officer who was with her at the time also made a full report
about the affair. It was on the basis of the statements of the two persons concerned
that the Force Commander, General McKeown, made his own report. One cannot
imagine that so conscientious and down-to-earth a soldier as General McKeown
would have collaborated in a fanciful flight of the imagination.

those that showed a disposition to fight back fared better. In consultation with the U.N. Command, I issued orders putting the Operation in high gear in the light of its enhanced powers and functions under the 21 February resolution. A new directive called for a more active role on the part of U.N. troops in preventing lawlessness and disorder. Further detailed instructions were issued explaining the situations when force could legitimately be used, and U.N. troops were strictly forbidden from surrendering their arms without resistance.

In informing Hammarskjold of these directives, I commented .sourly: 'Ours is truly a peace force as some military units seem to have imbibed the spirit of absolute non-violence. . . . No army in the world would tamely surrender its arms, not even the Salvation Army!' Hammarskjold, while fully endorsing these orders, replied: 'You have been absolutely right when you have gone ahead on the strength of the impact of the resolution. . . . The resolution is in itself to be regarded as instruction.'

Léopoldville was in the grip of panic and insecurity as Nendaka and Kazadi, the 'Security' chiefs, pursued their lawless activities. No politician or official was safe from arbitrary arrest and maltreatment. Personal vendettas and tribal animosities were given full rein. A refugee camp with barbed wire and armed guards which had been quickly organized by the U.N. Military Command filled to capacity with Congolese families within a couple of days. The list of refugees read like the capital's social register.

Kasavubu and Ileo made angry protests to ONUC for opening the camp without their permission. Some of the Western envoys shared their view that the refugee camp and the security measures taken by General McKeown were a provocation to the Congolese. But it would have been sheer folly to have let down our guard and inhuman to have dismantled the refugee camp. The U.N. patrols were welcomed by the public as they alone gave a sense of security to the citizens as well as by the foreign missions on whom they kept a vigilant and protective eye. The Belgian residents, too, greatly welcomed the blue helmets, for no one, African or European, trusted the Congolese troops. So far as the protected camps were concerned, ONUC had been compelled, as a humanitarian act, to organize them not only in Léopoldville, but also in Stanleyville, Bunia, Bukavu, Goma, and Kindu, all in areas controlled by the Stanleyville régime. In Luluabourg, some 1,200 persons had been admitted to a protected camp when local A.N.C. troops had killed some civilian inhabitants for tribal reasons. In Katanga, extensive protection had been provided at Luena and subsequently in Élisabethville, where Baluba tribesmen were being persecuted and arrested in large numbers.

The violent A.N.C. reactions in Léopoldville were clearly not spontaneous but had been deliberately incited by supposedly responsible leaders. The Secretary-General's closely reasoned letters explaining the import of the February resolution, supplemented by ONUC's efforts to reassure the Congolese leaders that reorganization of the A.N.C. under mutually agreed arrangements was very different from disarming it, produced no effect. The latent antagonism against the United Nations, fanned by foreign intrigue, reached the point of combustion and all restraints went up in flames. By way of example of the type of propaganda being carried on against U.N. personnel, a rumour had been spread that there had been a secret agreement between Lumumba and Nehru for the immigration of two million Indians into the Congo as a price for India's support of the Congolese nationalist leaders. The story even appeared in one of the local (foreign-owned) newspapers and Kasavubu's representative at New York, Loliki, had the audacity to repeat it in the Security Council on 7 February. The Indian representative indignantly repudiated the malicious fabrication. When we at ONUC made enquiries about the origin of the rumour, we discovered that at a party at which some U.N. personnel were present, a British woman consular officer was heard to spread the fable into the ear of a Congolese journalist. Having tracked down the story to its source, I confronted the British Ambassador with it. He first denied it and then promised to make enquiries. The next day he came to inform me that the lady in question had been recalled home. She was, I was told, due for repatriation in any case, and had been apparently regarded as a convenient means to spread a slander against a sister Commonwealth country. I am convinced that the British Government had nothing to do with this deplorable affair and that it was a piece of purely local enterprise.

The objectives of the 21 February resolution had been spelt out as respect for human rights, restoration of democratic institutions, exercise of the free will of the Congolese people on a basis of conciliation, and elimination of interference by Congolese armed units in the political process. Far from being shamed by the revulsion felt in the Security Council and all over the world at the recent frenzy of political murders, Kasavubu began systematically to flout every principle underlying the February resolution and, indeed, all previous United Nations resolutions. As a first step, Kasavubu, unmindful of his high office, made abject overtures to the rebel régimes of Katanga and South Kasai on a basis of sovereign equality. The aim was to forge a military alliance between Léopoldville, Élisabethville, and Bakwanga, with the unproclaimed but evident objective of opposing United Nations troops by force everywhere. The pact, which was signed on 28 February, stated that in view of the 'menace of Communist tyranny and the passivity of the United Nations', the three signatory parties had decided to put their military forces together to combat the common danger, and to establish permanent contacts between them on an economic and military plane to coordinate their actions. The President, by entering into an alliance with the rebel régimes, greatly strengthened their hands and weakened those of the United Nations in dealing with them.

A decision was then taken by the axis to hold a summit conference to discuss the political situation. The choice of venue fell on Tananarive in the Malagasy Republic, a country that strongly supported Tshombe. At Tananarive, the axis partners, Tshombe, Kasavubu, and Kalonji were accompanied by a number of foreign advisers and Congolese supporters. Tshombe, in his key speech, expounded the thesis that the Congo faced three dangers. The first was trusteeship by the United Nations; he said it was clear that the United Nations wanted to treat the Congo as conquered territory and to impose colonial domination over it. The second mortal danger was of Communist penetration which was facilitated by a lack of understanding on the part of the Western bloc. The third was that of a new Korean type of war which would engulf the whole country. To meet these perils, the leaders of 'ex-Belgian Congo', as he described it, must adopt a common front before the forthcoming meeting of the General Assembly to prevent the implementation of the 21 February resolution and to demand the withdrawal of the U.N. Force. The second step should be to divide the country into a number of separate States, linked together by a form of Common Market, and presided over by a Coordination Committee. After the complete pacification of the country, the question of constitutional structure could be reviewed.

Five resolutions were adopted by the Conference which decreed that the Congo would become a 'Confederation of States' with Kasavubu as its President. Each State would be sovereign but a joint Committee of Coordination would be established. The military alliance of 28 February was confirmed. While the new Confederation would be prepared, on certain conditions, to cooperate with the United Nations, the Conference declared the 21 February resolution to be totally unacceptable as it violated Charter principles. Ileo's Central Government, which was described as 'provisional', would come to an end with the establishment of the Coordination Committee. The final documents were signed by the participants on the basis of their tribal or regional affiliations.

In Léopoldville, the reactions to the Tananarive resolutions were generally hostile. On his return, Kasavubu, and his associates too, began to have second thoughts. How could so many small states be economically viable, and would not Katanga, with its wealth, dominate the confederation? Also, the furthest that Tshombe was prepared to go was to have a broad economic union. All that Kasavubu had achieved was to obtain an acknowledgment of his Presidency over a nebulous confederation.

Stanleyville's reactions were of unmitigated hostility. It denounced the Tananarive decisions as a betrayal of the Congolese people by a group of eighteen individuals who participated at the meeting and who represented nobody but themselves. It particularly criticized Kasavubu for agreeing to the division of the country in violation of the constitution. As by now over twenty countries had recognized the Stanleyville régime as the 'legal' Central Government of the Congo, the danger of foreign support to Stanleyville was likely to increase if the alliance between Léopoldville and Élisabethville were to present a threat to Gizenga.

The General Assembly was due to recommence in March and the Léopoldville authorities feared that it would adopt an even stronger resolution than that passed by the Security Council on 21 February. They felt that the Tananarive decisions, despite their defects, provided them with an argument that the Congolese could take their own decisions without interference by the United Nations. Along with their new understandings with Élisabethville and Bakwanga, a weakening of the United Nations operations in the field was necessary to demonstrate their ability to handle the situation themselves. Attempts had previously been made to impose a stranglehold over the movements of U.N. troops, but now a much more determined attempt was made to sever their lifeline. At the same time, a propaganda attack was launched on the Special Representative accompanied by insistent demands for his recall.

On 1 March, the Léopoldville authorities peremptorily demanded that the U.N. Force relinquish control of Ndjili airfield, the nerve-centre for its movements of troops and supplies. They also demanded the evacuation of the United Nations military camp at Parc Hembise, and forbade entry of U.N. troops into Congolese military camps. While energetic correspondence was going on between the Secretary-General and President Kasavubu who were trading charges against each other's forces, the Congolese decided to act. They first began shelling a small Sudanese contingent at the naval base of Banana for no apparent reason. The base was temporarily evacuated, and a company of Indonesian troops was hurriedly flown into Kitona to hold it against attack and later to retake Banana.

Banana commanded entry to the port of Matadi and its seizure would prevent U.N. troop arrivals by sea and also stop supplies. The next targets could be the military base at Kitona and airfields in Léopoldville and the Lower Congo region. Throttling the United Nations at the port of entry would open the way for the arrival of foreign arms which, as we learnt, an emissary from Léopoldville had already been sent abroad to seek.

That our fears were very real was confirmed by a telegram

from Hammarskjold which said that 'United States channels
have informed us that they have received a warning from Léopoldville indicating that concerted action against U.N. Force
in Léopoldville is not unlikely. . . . Taking this general warning,
which apparently has been given more than normal credence
in Washington, together with information which you yourself
have transmitted to us in course of last two days regarding military situation, we can only urge you to take all possible precautions. I of course sincerely trust that all of this is false alarm.'

The alarm was far from being false as the U.N. Force was
soon to suffer a military defeat at the hands of those whom it
had come to help. The Lower Congo region had been patrolled
by a battalion of seasoned Moroccan troops who had just been
pulled out following their Government's decision to withdraw
them from United Nations service. It was replaced by a contingent of one third its size, consisting of only some 350 Sudanese,
first, because more troops were not available, and secondly,
because the area had been generally quiet.

On 3 March, the Sudanese Colonel commanding the detachment, accompanied by an escort, was stopped by A.N.C. troops
as he was about to board a plane at Moanda en route to Léopoldville. An argument followed and in the mêlée some shots
were fired. It was not established who fired the first shot, but
the outcome was that the Congolese troops fled, leaving two
of their number behind. The Colonel proceeded on his way,
while his second-in-command with his escort went to Banana
to deliver the two disarmed Congolese soldiers to their unit.
On arrival at the camp, a discussion was in progress when the
Sudanese were suddenly fired upon from the rear by a Congolese soldier. In return, they fired at and killed their assailant,
whereupon the A.N.C. troops opened up with their weapons,
forcing the Sudanese to withdraw.

The next morning, the streets of Matadi appeared deserted
and there was an air of excitement among the inhabitants while
suspicious A.N.C. troop movements were observed. The U.N.
communications centre which was manned by Canadians was
fired upon without warning by Congolese troops. A small Sudanese guard, which had been sent there earlier as a precautionary
measure, returned the fire. At the same time, the Sudanese
camp, situated some distance away, was fired upon from the

direction of the A.N.C. camp situated on a hill overlooking their camp. The Sudanese, in self-defence, returned the fire. Repeated attempts were made by the Canadian and Sudanese officers to bring about a cease-fire. Several Sudanese were wounded at the radio centre which was soon overrun and the personnel taken prisoner. As soon as news of the outbreak reached Léopoldville, the U.N. Force Commander contacted A.N.C. headquarters and arranged to send his representatives along with the Acting Prime Minister, Delvaux, to Matadi, to put a stop to the fighting. But while the discussions for a cease-fire were going on, the A.N.C. troops resumed their attack with small arms, mortars, and anti-tank guns against the lightly armed Sudanese. The Sudanese fought back gallantly to defend themselves, but they were heavily outnumbered and outgunned. With ammunition running out, they had no option but to accept, under duress, the harsh terms imposed by Delvaux. These were that the Sudanese evacuate Matadi the same day with their arms and remaining ammunition and equipment. But when the Sudanese left their positions, they were immediately disarmed, stripped of their equipment including their helmets, and placed under armed guard. The contingent returned to Léopoldville humiliated and bitter. The Sudanese Government, shocked by the outrage, insisted on the withdrawal of all its troops from the Congo.

The loss of Matadi was a heavy blow at a time when the U.N. Force needed all the moral and material strength that it could muster. General McKeown and we feared that it might increase the intoxication of the Congolese troops and invite the criticism of states which had contributed troops to the U.N. Force. We were equally concerned about the large quantities of stores which no longer had U.N. protection and had to be abandoned to the Congolese authorities. But our greatest worry was about future shipments, as during the next three weeks no less than thirty-three ships with U.N. supplies were expected to berth at Matadi.

While the Léopoldville régime was trying to cut ONUC's jugular vein, the French Ambassador came to inform me that the six European Common Market partners had agreed between themselves to make a grant of six million dollars worth of aid to the Congo. Charpentier asked for a meeting to be arranged between the Congolese authorities and U.N. experts to discuss how the aid could best be applied. I was wary about the offer, and even more about the timing. To present so generous a bounty to the Congolese at that time would increase their truculence and would be seriously misunderstood by many delegations at New York, especially those with troops in the Congo. I recalled the suspicions aroused at the expenditure, a few months earlier, of one million dollars to pay and feed the A.N.C. which many delegations regarded as baksheesh to encourage Mobutu's takeover. I therefore decided to refer the matter to the Secretary-General for instructions. These came promptly. Hammarskjold said the whole proposal was misconceived both in regard to its motivations and timing. I was asked to shelve it, which I did as politely as I could. Understandably, it did not endear ONUC either to the prospective donors or the eager donee.

We resumed our negotiations with the Congolese authorities on the Matadi affair. Kasavubu was away at Tananarive and Bomboko, his Minister of Foreign Affairs, was unwell. I called several times on Bomboko at his hospital, accompanied by General McKeown and Vladimir Fabry, our legal adviser, to seek his help in straightening things out. Bomboko, looking weak and more boyish than ever, said the Sudanese were to blame for the outbreak and the U.N. Force must make amends. After much discussion, it was agreed that both sides should carry out independent investigations into the affair.

By this time news had arrived that the services of an Indian Brigade consisting of some 4,700 troops had been requested by the Secretary-General for the U.N. Force. This significant addition to the U.N.'s depleted strength would decisively tip the military scales against the A.N.C. This thought began to worry the Léopoldville authorities as they could no longer hope to dislodge the U.N. Force by sheer weight of numbers. The Cabinet held a three-and-a-half-hour meeting at which it decided to make seven demands. These were: suspension of all relations with the United Nations if the Special Representative were not recalled; public retraction by him of the accusation of Congolese responsibility for the Matadi outbreak; control by Congolese authorities of all United Nations air traffic; refusal of pilot facilities to ships carrying United Nations supplies and personnel; surrender by the United Nations Force to the A.N.C. of all strategic points; ban on circulation of U.N. troops with arms in Léopoldville; appointment of an 'honest and impartial' Special Representative in the Congo. It was evident that these 'demands' were at least partially aimed at dissuading the Government of India from sending its troops to join the U.N. Force.

Since the replacement of the Special Representative had never before been pressed as an urgent issue, it would be appropriate to trace the matter to its origin. On 14 January 1961 I received a request from President Kasavubu's office to transmit an urgent message to the Secretary-General, which when received was found to contain a demand for my recall. I was a little surprised because a few days earlier at a function at the President's house, Kasavubu had asked my wife and me for a date for a party in our honour! The letter said that the United Nations had failed to provide protection to President Miruho of Kivu province from abduction from his capital by Stanleyville troops, and that his Minister of Education, who had been seized at the same time, had died of torture. United Nations representatives could not escape their responsibility for 'complicity in the murder' and President Kasavubu was therefore asking for the recall of the Special Representative whose 'irresponsibility and partiality had shocked Congolese opinion'. Furthermore, the letter insisted that the United Nations take immediate measures to help the President of the Republic and the central authorities to 'disarm the rebel bands' of Gizenga and Lundula and to put 'a stop to their mischief, once and for all'. Only on this condition could cooperation be maintained between the United Nations and the authorities of the Republic.

Hammarskjold replied the very next day to the effect that he regretted the President had not raised the matter with him personally when he was in Léopoldville a few days earlier. Regarding the two concrete instances for which the United Nations, and particularly the Special Representative, were being held accountable, he had pleasure in informing the President that the Kivu Minister of Education was alive and well and that, having been exonerated of all charges against him, he was free to return home. As regards the Bukavu incident when

Miruho was abducted, the President had been misinformed about the facts and particularly about the responsibility of U.N. troops in the area. As for the Special Representative's part in the affair, he happened to be away from Léopoldville when the incident occurred and heard about it only on his return. As to the request for military action against the Stanleyville régime, in view of the question of principle involved, it could not be initiated by the Secretary-General or the U.N. Force, short of new instructions from the Security Council. But in no circumstances could any blame be attached to the U.N. Force or the Special Representative who had acted strictly in accordance with the general rules laid down for them. The Secretary-General went on to explain that the Special Representative was not a diplomatic official accredited to the Congolese Government and was therefore not subject to recall at the request of that Government. He was a senior United Nations official under the special authority of the Secretary-General under Article 101 of the Charter which entrusted the Secretary-General with the sole authority to appoint or remove international civil servants. Furthermore, under Article 100, the Secretary-General was precluded from receiving any instructions from any member state in regard to the discharge of his responsibilities. He personally shouldered full responsibility for the actions undertaken on his behalf by his Representative. The Secretary-General concluded that in view of the importance of the issue, he was releasing the correspondence to the Security Council for such action as the Council might consider fit to take.

The Security Council took no action. But some ten days later, President Kasavubu returned to the charge. He argued that some person must be held responsible for every situation and it was not for him to determine whether Mr. Dayal was or was not personally responsible! Raising a new point, he said that his Government was not bound to accept contingents in the U.N. Force from whichever countries were decided upon by the international organization. Similarly, it must be able to make its views heard about United Nations officials serving in the country. Therefore, in asking for the replacement of the Special Representative, the President said he was suggesting the creation of a climate which would promote better collaboration with the United Nations.

To Kasavubu's second letter, the Secretary-General sent a formal reply to the effect that he had already covered the ground in his first letter and that his Special Representative had been 'carrying out faithfully and flawlessly' the policy defined for the Congo by the main organs of the United Nations. But on 1 February, Kasavubu repeated his request on the ground that the Special Representative 'had lost the confidence of the Congolese people', and should be replaced by a 'neutral personality'. To this the Secretary-General sent an even firmer reply. He said that the United Nations had gone to the Congo to help the country at great sacrifice to itself, without any other interests to defend than those of the Congo itself. In view of the facts, one would not have expected a renewed complaint to be made which was devoid of any solid or objective basis. If United Nations representatives were to feel that at any moment they could be attacked for their official activities without proper cause and for doubtful motives, it would be impossible to recruit capable officials to perform such important functions. As Kasavubu knew, the Secretary-General went on to say, he had very closely followed Mr. Dayal's activities as Special Representative and he was convinced that he had fulfilled his duties faithfully and scrupulously according to his instructions, the mandate, and the Charter. His Special Representative therefore enjoyed his fullest confidence. Voicing surprise that the same accusations had been repeated which had already been refuted, Hammarskjold said that Kasavubu was inconsistent in expressing his confidence in the Secretary-General while denying it to his Special Representative. Any criticism of the Special Representative must be considered, in fact as well as in law, as criticism of the Secretary-General himself. Concluding, the Secretary-General said that he attached particular importance to the question as he could not, in all objectivity, recognize any justification for the complaints, and that he would be doing the greatest harm to the Operation of the United Nations and to the Congo itself, were he to recall Mr. Dayal.

When Kasavubu found that the Secretary-General was unyielding on a problem which he had himself created, he tried another tack. One day I received a telephone call from the President's official Secretary, Emmanuel Kini, that he wanted to see me urgently, insisting that the appointment be at my residence. I was a little suspicious as most official visitors saw me in my office where I was available all through the day. However, I hurried home a little earlier than usual to find my visitor already awaiting my arrival. After some miscellaneous talk, Kini said he wanted me to know how much the President regretted that he had not been able to receive me; the President found himself in a difficult position but, with my help, matters could be smoothed over. I said that I was always available to the President, but he had refused to see me since the time he asked for my recall. I reminded Kini about the President's request to me when I last met him, about a party for my wife and myself, yet, the very next day, the President had asked for my recall. Kini said that I should understand that the President's hand had been forced and he hinted at various foreign influences working on the President. Kini then returned to the subject of the President's position. He said that Kasavubu had always wanted to avoid violence and he was anxious to cooperate with the United Nations. The President was quite prepared to drop his demand for my recall as he had nothing against me personally, provided that the U.N. Force would cooperate with him. Everything could change if the U.N. Force were used to end the Stanleyville rebellion. If only I would give the word, all the frictions would disappear and harmonious relations would be established between the United Nations and President Kasavubu.

I replied that the U.N. Force was bound by the mandate and by the instructions of the Secretary-General, whose agent I was. The Force could not be used to influence the outcome of a political conflict, and under the mandate it could not intervene against Orientale just as it could not against Katanga. Kini argued that the two situations were different and a liberal interpretation of the mandate would be in order to restore the Stanleyville situation. I then had to tell Kini firmly that I could not be party to any violation of my mandate and instructions, and if that was the price demanded for better working relations, I was not prepared to pay it.

One of my political advisers was a very capable and earnest U.N. official, Jean-Pierre Martin, a Frenchman. Kasavubu often used to telephone Martin direct whenever he had anything to convey to ONUC. One day in the course of a particularly long conversation, Martin asked the President to be good enough to receive the Special Representative, as it would be more convenient if he were personally to answer his questions. Kasavubu replied that it would be 'suicidal' for him to receive the Special Representative so long as his attitude did not change. When Martin enquired in what respects a change was desired, Kasavubu referred to Stanleyville and Bukavu. Martin tried to explain why the U.N. Force could not intervene in the manner desired by the President, but Kasavubu remained unconvinced.

But although President Kasavubu resisted receiving me after 12 January 1961, I was in constant personal contact with the new Ileo Government which came into being on 9 February. It was certainly awkward to be denied direct access to the President although official meetings with him, as experience had shown, seldom produced any tangible results. Neither the Secretary-General nor I and my colleagues at ONUC at first felt undue concern over Kasavubu's letters for my recall as it seemed to be the Congolese habit to break off relations only to restore them soon thereafter.

The Congolese authorities were determined to extract the last ounce of advantage from ONUC's discomfiture at Matadi. Hammarskjold informed me that of the four possible alternatives, viz. acceptance of the impossible conditions; their refusal followed by military action; general withdrawal of the entire U.N. Force; and playing for time by exercising full political pressure while building up ONUC's military strength, only the last was acceptable. Hammarskjold added: 'We have come to a point where I consider it impossible to accept any longer that responsibility for choices of this enormous general significance should be pushed into the lap of the Secretary-General because of the impossibility of any of the major organs to agree on a line of action. I have so far taken up this hopeless but vitally essential role; it seems now that we have gone over the brink, and therefore must seriously consider putting the problem to the Security Council. . . . Even a gain of twenty-four hours here may mean something in this situation.'

Hammarskjold wanted time to think over the problem in the context of the wider issues involved, and he promised to send me his evaluation of the political situation. But he added, 'at two in the morning I do not believe it is the right time to start writing such a paper'. However, in his next cable he said that though he owed us his comments on the political situation, he did 'not feel much up to it without getting more of a perspective'. His report on his meeting with Kwame Nkrumah was, however, in somewhat more hopeful vein. He said: 'Had three hours today with Nkrumah, when back of some unrealistic suggestion of Accra type, I sensed new awareness of possible intentions of certain big power, and therefore, also a greater understanding of what the U.N. has achieved over eight months; he seems to know what might have happened and what may still happen. This new realism is of course counteracted by unavoidable deep suspicion against certain other elements. I was struck by his attitude in one respect; he treated Lumumba's fate as "an episode" and was very careful to avoid all that might reflect on Kasavubu. (I leave the interpretation to you.)'

Hammarskjold had sought the advice of his Advisory Committee regarding the dilemma in which Matadi had placed the Operation. He put the issues bluntly to the members but he looked in vain for guidance, commenting to me: 'All speakers obviously wanted to avoid the issue, and with the single exception of India which did not accept our being "pushed around", they shared in varying degrees great reluctance to accept co-responsibility in instructions which would entitle you to organize the military recapture of Matadi. I held the line that short of unanimity, I could not give such instructions without the support of the Security Council.' The Secretary-General therefore concluded that ONUC must continue to make all efforts to bring the negotiations with the Léopoldville authorities to a successful and peaceful conclusion. But it was out of the question to accept the Congolese conditions which would jeopardize the whole Operation necessitating the reconsideration and discontinuance of both the military and civilian operations. The members of the Advisory Council wished to consider the matter further if negotiations failed. In conclusion, Hammarskjold sent us a message of exhortation combined with a word of caution: 'Thus exercise all your patience and understanding, show all your tenacity and stick to principles both as regards

legal stand and substance of conditions and our need to be in
Matadi, etc., and "be kind" while keeping your Security Coun-
cil powder dry (remembering that even the Security Council
cannot change reluctance of, at present, all contributing African
Governments to register any casualties in the service of the
United Nations).'

We patiently continued our discussions with the Congolese
politicians, McKeown with Delvaux, and I with Bomboko.
Delvaux was willing to concede that the United Nations could
not be kept out of Matadi, but Bomboko said that the local
population would first have to be appeased. Slowly, the temperature began to lower, although there was a false alarm of
an outbreak in the middle of the night which led the U.S.
embassy to alert its nationals. The next day the discussions
were resumed with the whole Cabinet, this time led by Acting
Prime Minister Jacques Massa whom I met for the first time
in that capacity. I was anxious to force a quick settlement of
the Matadi affair as I was soon due to leave for London and
New York for consultations.

Mekki Abbas, a senior Sudanese official, had arrived to join
the U.N. mission as my deputy, and he accompanied me to
the meeting. To our surprise, the Acting Prime Minister himself
came to escort us to his office where we were met by a well-
turned-out guard of honour, complete with fanfare. I reported
to Hammarskjold that 'wonders never cease' as Delvaux stood
up solemnly at the commencement of the meeting to read a
speech thanking 'dear Mr. Dayal', wishing him 'bon voyage,
a pleasant trip to New York, and a quick return'. There were
also warm words of welcome for Abbas, and promises of full
cooperation and forgetting past difficulties, etc. Thereafter we
all went to Bomboko's hospital room where the discussions
continued for two hours. The upshot was that it was essential
in the Government's view to pacify the Bakongo population
before the return of U.N. troops to Matadi could be effected.
The principle of a peaceful return was not disputed and Bomboko specifically stated that no conditions whatsoever would
be attached to it. But he cautioned that only Kasavubu could
influence his people and that talks should be resumed with him
on his return. I suggested the despatch of a peace mission to
the area, but a decision on that matter was also left over till

Kasavubu's agreement was obtained. A base had at least been established for a peaceful solution to a difficult problem by securing the Cabinet's withdrawal of the impossible conditions which it had tried to impose.

Hammarskjold had asked me over to New York to be present for the meetings of the resumed session of the General Assembly and of his Advisory Committee, but I had been forced to defer my departure because of the Matadi situation. The Secretary-General also wanted me to stop over in London to meet the Heads of State and Prime Ministers who had assembled for the Commonwealth Conference, to explain the Congo situation and to gather their support.

Hammarskjold had chosen the Sudanese Mekki Abbas to act as Special Representative during my absence. It was a skilful choice as regards nationality, as the Congolese were somewhat repentant over their treatment of the Sudanese troops, especially as Sudan had been scrupulously correct in keeping aloof from the intricacies of Congolese politics. The Secretary-General had passed over Linner, the next ranking civilian official in Léopoldville, as he had done in November during my earlier visit to New York because he felt that an African would be more acceptable. I had been asking for months for a senior African deputy and a very capable delegate had in fact been selected some months earlier. His Government, however, had refused to release him. I hoped that Abbas would now fill that role. At the Cabinet meeting I introduced Abbas to the Congolese Ministers and functionaries and felt that I could leave with an easy mind, as the worst of the crisis now seemed to be over. Before setting out from 'Le Royal', I wired Hammarskjold: 'I leave here in an hour with the tension palpably reduced and perspectives opening up for the peaceful settlement of the Matadi–Banana affair, and possibilities for the development of some measure of cooperation. I also have the great satisfaction of leaving affairs in Abbas's competent and forceful hands.' That was to be my last message from the Congo.

CHAPTER 14

Vicarious Stewardship

My wife and I had hardly slumped into our seats in the Air France jet at Brazzaville airport after a day of hectic activity when we heard the heavy tread of armed men clambering up the stairway into the plane. The stewardess came over to say that the Brazzaville Chief of Police wanted to see me. The said gentleman with his bodyguard soon appeared and he asked me brusquely if Gizenga was on the plane. Surprised, I replied that I did not know. Thereupon the Chief of Police asked some more questions about Gizenga and I referred him to the Captain of the aircraft. He and his men stamped up and down the aisle; and for a moment we feared that we might be arrested or deplaned. But after some talk with the aircraft's crew, the intruders departed. Great was our relief when the plane took off. We wondered about the strange incursion and what could have occasioned it.

On reaching Orly airport in the small hours of the morning, we were met by Marc Schreiber, the United Nations Resident Representative in France, and a host of newspapermen and photographers. Schreiber hurriedly took me aside and said the unusual commotion was due to a Reuter report received during the night that I had brought Gizenga away with me! I briefly questioned Schreiber about the origin of the *canard* but he was as puzzled as I was. He then held hurried consultations with the throng of correspondents and returned to tell me that French television would like to interview me on the situation in the Congo. I gladly agreed to the interview and to a press conference thereafter. No one asked me about Gizenga.

Changing planes at Orly, we flew on to London. At the airport we were received by Gibson Parker of the U.N. and a representative from the Indian High Commission with a message from Prime Minister Nehru asking us to drive over immediately to see him. When we arrived at Mr. Nehru's residence, he asked us to accompany him to the country seat of Lord Mountbatten for the evening.

An hour or two later as we drove through the rolling grounds of Mountbatten's estate, we saw fields of yellow daffodils, numbers of horses frolicking in the pastures, and herds of cattle in the meadows. We were ushered into a drawing-room opening on lawns stretching down to a stream that meandered through the grounds, with a view of leafy woods beyond. Mountbatten and his daughter, Pamela, Nehru and his sister, Vijaya Lakshmi Pandit, then Indian High Commissioner in London, were at tea. Our host invited us to join them and then, at Nehru's bidding, I recounted the United Nations' problems in the Congo, while Nehru provided a lively running commentary.

Tea over, Nehru asked me to take a walk with him when we could continue the conversation as he had many questions to ask. Donning our raincoats, we tramped up and down the sodden lawns in the drizzling rain. Nehru questioned me closely about Hammarskjold's policy, what we were trying to do in the Congo and why we were not being more effective. I told him of the difficulties with the Congolese, the problem of inadequate political support and the tendency to personalize issues at the expense of principles. Nehru was convinced that Hammarskjold must be supported but asked me to persuade him to use the U.N. Force in a more purposeful manner. He mentioned Hammarskjold's request for Indian troops and asked for my opinion. I replied that it was imperative for India to come to the assistance of the United Nations, for if the Operation failed, it would have disastrous consequences. Nehru replied that the Operation must not be allowed to fail as it would destroy the United Nations and threaten peace in Africa. If he were to send Indian troops to the Congo, he would not allow them to be insulted or pushed around. He was worried about the fact that U.N. troops were more lightly armed than the Congolese and felt that their weakness invited attacks against them. However, on balance he would accede to Hammarskjold's request, with the caveat that he would insist on their effective use.

Nehru then asked how long I expected to be away from my

post in Pakistan and reminded me that the six-months period for which he had lent my services was already over. I said it all depended upon him and Hammarskjold, but they would perhaps wish to balance the needs of the Congo with those of Pakistan before taking a decision.

My appointment next morning was with Mrs. Sirimavo Bandaranaike, Prime Minister of Ceylon, who questioned me about the Congo horror stories that had figured for months in the world's newspapers. She particularly asked about reports of cannibalism in the Congo. I had to admit that this did, in fact, exist among certain tribes in some parts of the country, and that investigations had proved that several of our own U.N. soldiers, Irish and Nigerian among others, had met their end in this manner.

I next called on Sir Abu Bakr Tafawa Balewa, Prime Minister of Nigeria. Sir Abu Bakr said he had been worried by incidents involving the Nigerian forces in the Congo and he had, at one time, thought of withdrawing his contingent. I gave the Prime Minister the necessary explanations, emphasizing that we were keeping in as close touch as possible with the Congolese authorities and were certainly not trying to bypass them or dictate to them.

The same evening I called on Mr. John Diefenbaker, Prime Minister of Canada, at his hotel suite at Claridge's. He asked why there had been so much criticism of the conduct of ONUC. I gave him the reasons, and added that those who were trying to undermine the Operation were playing into the hands of those who wished to paralyse the United Nations. The Prime Minister asked what further help Canada could give and made a note of our transport difficulties and need for additional aircraft. He said he was convinced that the U.N. effort must succeed and assured me of his support.

My next call was on Edward Heath, then Lord Privy Seal in Harold Macmillan's Cabinet. Mr. Heath admitted that his Government had misgivings about various parts of the 21 February resolution, which they thought went too far. The British position appeared to be that after having voted for the resolution they did not want to see its implementation. About the Belgian presence, Mr. Heath said that he felt the problem had been taken care of, at which I expressed both surprise and satisfaction. It was clear that Mr. Heath's information was based upon the reports of his envoy in Léopoldville, Ian Scott. Mr. Heath then expressed his approval of the decisions reached at the Tananarive Conference, and singled out Tshombe as a commendable politician for his part in preserving order in the Congo. I was rather disturbed by Mr. Heath's information and views, of which I informed some of the Commonwealth Prime Ministers.

My next call was on the President of Ghana, Dr. Kwame Nkrumah. The Osogyefo had just been to New York and Washington and was optimistic that the Operation would now receive sufficient political and material support to enable it to continue. Nkrumah pooh-poohed the Tananarive decisions which he was certain would amount to nothing. He added that Kasavubu had practically abdicated at Tananarive, and in view of the resolutions adopted there, he was no longer entitled to be considered as President of the Republic. The conversation left no doubt in my mind that Nkrumah was prepared to back ONUC despite his critical opinions. The name of Lumumba was, surprisingly, not mentioned at all, nor was there any interest shown in Gizenga or other Stanleyville politicians.

My meeting with Tunku Abdul Rahman, Prime Minister of Malaysia, was friendly, informal, and spontaneous. The Tunku felt that the weight of the African and Asian members should be brought to bear on the United Kingdom to persuade her to modify her pro-Belgian policies. Malaysia was a small country with a diminutive army, said the Tunku, but it would be prepared to denude itself to the last soldier in support of the United Nations.

The last Commonwealth leader on whom I called was President Ayub Khan of Pakistan. President Ayub said he was glad I had survived the perils of life in the Congo, but he was full of reproach at my having deserted my post in Pakistan. He reminded me that he had warned against my leaving Pakistan at that juncture, adding, 'You see what has happened to our relations.' I had been kept only partially informed of the state of Indo-Pakistani relations, but what I had heard was far from reassuring.

Field-Marshal Ayub Khan's views on the Congo were

soldierly, direct, and forceful. According to him, the United Nations had been toying with a situation which needed drastic measures. The Congolese were obviously quite incapable of governing themselves and the United Nations must assume responsibility for running the country for a period of ten years. He added that Pakistan would consider supplying combat troops, if requested.

My round of interviews had given me a better perspective of the attitudes of Commonwealth countries towards the involvement of the United Nations in the Congo. I had the assurance that the seven countries with troops in the Congo would maintain and strengthen their support. The African states, despite their misgivings, would remain firm. Canada's unconditional assistance could be relied upon. And India had made up her mind to respond to the Secretary-General's request for a brigade. If more troops were needed, there was now a definite offer from Pakistan. But of crucial importance was the attitude of the British Government, which was unfortunately most equivocal.

At New York, the pace of activity on the 38th floor at United Nations Headquarters had remained undiminished. Hammarskjold was as alert and exacting as ever, but there seemed to be a trace of weariness about his eyes. He said he was delighted to find me looking well and asked how I managed to keep so fit and calm. I replied that I did not have to apologize for my good health as he knew, far better than I did, the therapeutic effect of hard work.

Discussions with the 'Congo Club', presided over by the Secretary-General, went on day after day, weekends included. The evening meetings began after six, and continued during dinner and well towards midnight.

One of my earliest interviews in New York was with Adlai Stevenson. When I was ushered in, Stevenson first asked me about my health. I thanked him and said I felt as well as I believed I looked. He then asked whether I was not finding the strain of the assignment too great. I was a little surprised at this continuing solicitude for my health and replied in all modesty that although it was no doubt a heavy burden, it was not unbearable. Stevenson then asked if I did not feel like taking a holiday. I replied that I would certainly welcome

one, but it would be irresponsible on my part to ask for leave
at a time when the Secretary-General needed my services.
Stevenson then observed that perhaps my long absence from
my post in Pakistan was not good for Indo-Pakistani relations
and asked when I thought I would return to Karachi. I said
I was a civil servant and did not regard myself as indispensable
in any post; as regarded my return to Pakistan, the matter was
one between Mr. Hammarskjold and Mr. Nehru. Stevenson continued to conduct our meeting on this strange level; throughout the interview he did not ask a single question about the
Congo or the problems besetting the Operation. I now got
the measure of the extent to which some great states and statesmen had been infected by the propensity of the Congolese to
personalize issues at the expense of principles. There was more
interest in the figures of Kasavubu and Lumumba, Tshombe
and Mobutu, Gizenga and Bomboko, than in what they stood
for. And in the United Nations context, there seemed to be
more concern about the personality and nationality of international officials than about the problems which they were
tackling.

I discussed the phenomenon with Hammarskjold who was
in the double grip of a direct attack on him by the Soviet Union
and vicarious attacks on me, his Special Representative, and
on other U.N. officials and military contingents serving in the
Congo. Hammarskjold's reply was that not a single decision
or action taken by ONUC had been validly questioned on
grounds of inconsistency with his instructions, the mandate, or
the Charter. He said that he would firmly refuse to make any
sacrificial offering of any member of the Operation as an act
either of appeasement or of atonement.

As the date for the resumed session of the General Assembly
approached, delegations began to align their sights. Some of
the West European powers hoped that the Tananarive decisions
could be invoked to bypass the 21 February resolution, but
the United States, along with the majority of African and Asian
powers, were aware that Kasavubu himself was having second
thoughts about what Tananarive had, in fact, achieved.

The question of the despatch of an Indian Brigade was still
pending as, despite agreement in principle, the Government
of India insisted on assurances that the troops would be actively

used. An Indian military delegation arrived in New York to discuss the matter with the Secretary-General and me. I urged the early despatch of the Brigade as any delay would make the task of restoration of order and legality all the more difficult. The delegation, satisfied with the assurances received, sent a favourable recommendation to Delhi. A few weeks later, the Brigade arrived in the Congo and was quickly deployed in the most sensitive areas, greatly strengthening the U.N. Force which had been seriously weakened by the withdrawal of the Moroccan Brigade, and of battalions from the U.A.R., Sudan, and Indonesia. The Indians served in the Congo with distinction and intrepidity and took a leading part in bringing about the eventual end of Katanga's secession.

The efforts of the Asian and African powers at the United Nations to hammer out a joint resolution failed to produce an acceptable draft. The impasse was finally resolved by twenty African and Asian countries along with Yugoslavia presenting one draft and seventeen other countries, another.

The twenty-one-power resolution[1] called upon Belgium to conform fully and promptly with the will of the United Nations. It urged that Belgian and other foreign military personnel and political advisers be completely withdrawn within a period of twenty-one days, failing which, sanctions would be applied. The seventeen-power resolution[2] referred to the report of the Conciliation Commission and urged release of all political prisoners and recall of Parliament, and decided to appoint a new Conciliation Commission of seven members. The Secretary-General was asked to take the necessary measures of implementation. Significantly, the Brazzaville group of African states, which was committed to support Kasavubu, had opposed the 21 February resolution, and did not co-sponsor either resolution.

The resumed Fifteenth Session of the General Assembly met on 21 March to continue its debate on the Congo. Andrei Gromyko, Foreign Minister of the Soviet Union, was the first speaker. He advocated the establishment of a supervisory Committee of African states to guide the activities of the United Nations mission in the Congo. He urged the convening of

[1] A/L. 339.
[2] A/L. 340.

Parliament and expulsion of the Belgians. He concluded with a scathing attack on the Secretary-General personally and on his policies. Stevenson devoted his speech mostly to answering Gromyko's arguments and accusations. He said there were two Congo problems, one in Africa and one in New York. The unprecedented difficulty of the Secretary-General's task could be lightened only by avoiding persistent recrimination. Stevenson concluded that it was necessary to reconcile the aspirations of the Congolese leaders with the Security Council's resolutions.

The delegate of the Congo in his turn lashed out at delegations which had introduced draft resolutions and accused them of interference in the affairs of the Congo. He claimed that the Congolese people were perfectly capable of looking after their own affairs and lauded the achievements of Tananarive. He blamed the United Nations mission in the Congo for the continuing disorders, which could have been settled if the Special Representative had not confined himself to his 'ivory tower in "Le Royal"'.

The Secretary-General repeatedly intervened in the debate to refute the accusations made against him by representatives of the Soviet Union and East European states. Quoting from Gromyko's statement that the Secretary-General had 'sullied himself' with Lumumba's murder and that 'it is not only he who wields the knife or revolver that is the murderer', Hammarskjold placed the facts before the Assembly for its judgement. He countered another of Gromyko's charges that he was behaving as though he was 'the Prime Minister of a World Government'. He said he could have presented the Assembly with a *fait accompli* by resigning at the behest of a great power. But he regarded the will of the General Assembly as his law and the Assembly could consider itself seized of a standing offer of resignation. He warned, however, against weakening the executive by empowering a big power to break the term of office of a Secretary-General by withholding its cooperation from him for reasons of a partisan nature, contrary to the principles of the Organization. For then the office of Secretary-General would lose its impartial and independent character.

The twenty-one-power resolution, which was the first to be tabled, was put to the vote. In separate votes on the operative paragraphs, references to a time limit for withdrawal of Belgian mercenaries and to the imposition of sanctions in case of non-compliance, were defeated. The resolution was then adopted by sixty-one votes to five, with thirty-three abstentions.

The seventeen-power resolution was then taken up. A number of delegations demanded a separate vote on the deletion of the reference to the Secretary-General in the resolution. The result was a massive vote of confidence in the Secretary-General as the Assembly decided to retain the phrase by eighty-five votes in favour, eleven against, and five abstentions. The resolution as a whole was finally adopted by sixty votes to sixteen with twenty-three abstentions.

There remained the question of financing the Operation, on which prolonged discussions had taken place in the Fifth (Administrative and Budgetary) Committee. The Secretary-General had asked for authorization to incur expenditure to the extent of $135 million till the end of October 1961. But many delegations had objected to the extraordinary expenditure on the mission—which amounted to almost twice the annual budget of the Organization—being considered as part of the regular expenses of the Organization under Article 17 of the Charter. The Fifth Committee felt that since the Operation had been repeatedly authorized both by the Security Council and the General Assembly, it could not be allowed to collapse for lack of funds. The Committee therefore adopted a resolution, admittedly of an interim character, which permitted the expenditure requested by the Secretary-General without prejudging the questions of principle raised in the discussions.

When the Assembly took up the resolution regarding the financing of the Operation on 21 April 1961, some Latin American delegations opposed the method of financing proposed in the first resolution as they felt that the permanent members of the Security Council, on whom fell primary responsibility for the maintenance of peace and security under the Charter, and Belgium, because of 'its unfulfilled obligations as a colonial power' in the Congo, should bear the brunt of the expenditure. Some delegations had also proposed that twenty-five per cent of the expenditure should be borne by states which had economic interests in the Congo. The draft resolution proposed a rebate of seventy-five per cent in the rate of assessment of developing countries. The United States representative offered a

U.N. land reclamation project for the unemployed

Hostile greeting: Baluba tribesmen and A.N.C. rebels await arrival of U.N. representatives in Albertville

The U.N. overcomes Tshombe: Katangan Fouga fighter shot down

voluntary contribution of $15 million in addition to the $32·5 million which would be the United States' assessment under the resolution. He added a proviso that the voluntary contribution would be conditional on the adoption of the resolution. But when the vote was taken at midnight, the resolution was lost. In the absence of authorization there would now be no funds for the Operation to continue past the hour. Mongi Slim of Tunisia rose to the rescue on a point of order. He pointed to the 'regrettable situation' which the United Nations faced when a mission, four times authorized by specific resolutions of the Security Council, was now denied funds by the Assembly. He therefore proposed that the debate on the item of financing the Operation be kept open and that the session of the Assembly—which was to have terminated at midnight—should continue until the question was settled. C. S. Jha of India then proposed that the Secretary-General be authorized to incur commitments on the Operation for another month, by which time the question of financing should be settled. At length, the Assembly decided to return to the matter later that night.

The Secretary-General and his staff set to work to contact various delegations, to try to bring about a change of heart. When finally the Assembly reassembled, it adopted the resolution, after increasing the rebate to eighty per cent. On this note, the stormy and fateful Fifteenth Session of the General Assembly came to a close at six o'clock in the morning.

CHAPTER 15

Reluctant Release

In Léopoldville, meanwhile, a situation of total immobility prevailed. To every constructive suggestion the Léopoldville authorities countered with a barrage of irrelevancies. Mekki Abbas's reports presented a picture of gloom and frustration. To add to the Secretary-General's problems, Abbas was having difficulties with his own staff, which further reduced his effectiveness.

Abbas's first task with the Congolese was to bring about the peaceful return of U.N. troops to the seaport of Matadi, about which promises had been made to Abbas and me by the Congolese Government before my departure. When Abbas took up the matter and asked for a firm date, he was told that as Matadi was in the Bas-Congo area, a decision must await Kasavubu's return from Tananarive. When Kasavubu arrived in Léopoldville, he wanted time to study the situation. He then said that public opinion in the area was inflamed and time was needed for tempers to cool. When pressed, he said that the Congolese would themselves assure security for U.N. civilian personnel and stores at Matadi, and no U.N. troops were required.

Hammarskjold continued to press Abbas to take energetic steps to restore the U.N. presence in Matadi, not merely as a symbolic act to repair its loss of prestige, but to ensure that ONUC's lifeline was not abandoned to Congolese hands. Since Abbas had not been able to make much impression on Kasavubu, Hammarskjold invited the American, British, and French representatives at New York to use their influence to secure a decision from Léopoldville. The Secretary-General's view was that unless negotiations made appreciable progress, the Léopoldville authorities must tacitly accept the *de facto* return of U.N. troops to Matadi without resistance. Hammarskjold told

Abbas in a message of his talks with the three ambassadors at which he 'gave them a very disillusioned picture of motives, tactics, understanding and integrity' of the Léopoldville authorities, 'pointing out squarely that present anti-U.N. tactics . . . are suicidal, because, if successfully maintained, they will throw us into alternative of disintegration of U.N. Operation with continued loss of prestige and of positions, or a switch over to use of force which would give U.N. Force entirely changed character.' He continued: 'With these consequences of attitudes of Kasavubu, Ileo, Mobutu and others, it must be major duty of those who wish stability and progress in and around Congo to talk irresponsible leaders into entirely new attitude of co-operation with U.N., or at least avoidance of harassment, dropping effort at control and strangulation. Matadi is case in point and return there peacefully, preferably through negotiation, of reasonable guard force within next few days essential.' Hammarskjold added that he believed 'this strip-tease approach made an impression' on the three ambassadors.

The alternative was for the matter to be taken to the Security Council, where the Secretary-General said he would be forced to expose 'the poverty and pettiness' of the Léopoldville politicians. That would include the intemperate anti-U.N. statements made by Kasavubu and Mobutu, and Ileo's threat to take over the Kitona base by force. But, said the Secretary-General, he would prefer to avoid this course and he hoped Congolese resistance would be softened because of their 'healthy . . . and not unfounded fear of our potentialities. Alternatively, with the volatile and excitable temper of the Congolese, it may lead to renewed harassments.' Hammarskjold further instructed Abbas to make daily efforts with Kasavubu and others and to keep him closely informed of their reactions. He added the caution that although his talks with the three ambassadors were held in secret, there was risk of a 'vulgarized and exaggerated version' appearing in the press.

A week passed, yet there were no results. Kasavubu and others continued to raise unconnected matters while evading the crucial issue of Matadi. In irritation, Hammarskjold wired Abbas that 'the recital of old wrongs cannot be any excuse for any delay in a clean stand on our *aide mémoire* and its question of principle. . . . Needless for us to recite all that they have done wrong. Let us instead try to put them straight.' Hope of diplomatic support from Western missions in Léopoldville had begun to evaporate, and Hammarskjold added: 'Believe that you should make this stand of mine very clear to Timberlake and Scott as I fear that—I would hope out of incomprehension—they have so far been working against us and that they may again give Congolese false hopes unless it is made crystal clear where we stand.'

The Secretary-General's *aide-mémoire* to Kasavubu was a strongly worded document which began by a reference to statements by the President and other leading personalities to the effect that the presence of the U.N. Force was no longer necessary. These statements had given the impression that the intention of the Congolese authorities was to make it impossible for the United Nations to perform its task. If the President were to make a request for withdrawal of the U.N. Force, the Secretary-General would have to approach the Security Council. But if that was not the intention, it would be essential for the President to clarify the position by a formal agreement regarding the status and rights of the U.N. Force. This would obviate all future friction and misunderstandings. Abbas was directed to ask the President to take a clear public stand to remove any impression that the U.N. was in the Congo 'in its own interest and against the will of the authorities'. Hammarskjold pointed out that the contradiction between the tacit acceptance by the Congolese of the United Nations and their public utterances opposing it gave them the advantage of playing on both sides.

It was now difficult for Kasavubu to evade a reply. In his letter to the Secretary-General he made various counterproposals. Hammarskjold commented to Abbas: 'Kasavubu's letter is completely unsatisfactory although it might have been worse. Now he opens the door enough to make it unwise for me to carry matters straight on to the Security Council.' He again called in the three Western ambassadors and told them that it was essential for the Matadi problem to be settled as elements of the Indian Brigade would soon be arriving by sea while the Indonesian Battalion was about to depart. He could certainly not accept Kasavubu's counter-suggestion that the Belgian firm of Otraco should handle all supplies and movements of

U.N. troops at and from Matadi. The Secretary-General instructed Abbas, at the same time, to press on with the status agreement, explaining to Kasavubu that its signature by him on behalf of his country would be a manifestation of his recognition as Head of State of the whole of the Congo. But, Hammarskjold added, despairing of Kasavubu's good sense: 'If we had to deal with a more experienced and mature opposite number, I would regard their counter-proposal as brazen. Who can believe that they could not control reactions in Bas-Congo? And how can they believe that this staggered arrangement— with first two officers and then, after a week, ten and then still a delay depending on their judgement on psychological situation —would provide a solution?'

Before meeting Kasavubu, Abbas, as instructed, met Timberlake and Scott, who made their own counter-proposals. To these, Hammarskjold reacted: 'Timberlake's and Scott's observations strike me as singularly unconvincing. Two questions: is a small number of Nigerian police better protected against incidents than a somewhat larger number, and, further, when and why did the population turn hostile to U.N. troops . . . as that incident [Matadi] was provoked and run solely by A.N.C.? . . . However, stand of two ambassadors . . . means that we will not have necessary support for our line.'

The meeting with Kasavubu was, not unexpectedly, equally unpromising, and aroused the Secretary-General's 'serious misgivings'. He took note of the 'distortions of fact' adding that Kasavubu was 'guilty of schoolboyish contriving when he alleges that the Congolese have been seeing the U.N. Operation as an attempted parallel central authority'. He was astonished at Kasavubu's reference to the 'States of the Confederation' of the Congo, based on the still-born Tananarive formula, and even more at the suggestion that the U.N. should not communicate direct with Tshombe, Gizenga, or any of the provincial authorities. But what particularly disturbed the Secretary-General was Abbas's reticence in rebutting the distortions of United Nations policies and actions, on the flimsy excuse that he did not wish 'to annoy' Kasavubu and his advisers. Hammarskjold sent Abbas a sharp rebuke: 'I am frankly disturbed that all of these distortions and specious arguments were put on the record by Kasavubu and Bomboko apparently without challenge or effective rejoinder by the U.N. representatives present.' Referring to some of these distortions, the Secretary-General exclaimed: 'There must somewhere be drawn a line of distinction between illusion and fact.'

Abbas wired back further excuses, saying that he did not wish to start a debate. But Hammarskjold told him that 'our worry is that we have seen time and again how our Congolese friends succumb to the common weakness of propagandists, that is to convince themselves unless contradicted.' Pointing to the inconsistencies which were 'the latest development of their imagination', Hammarskjold commented: 'What we fear is that what you regard as natural courtesy . . . will be interpreted by Bomboko as tacit acceptance.' He added that 'the fairy-tale presentation of the situation . . . is one which either is countered at once or better forgotten', and what had caused him 'serious misgivings' was that on the next occasion the pattern would be repeated of their 'talking themselves into an imagined position, giving them a fiction of a justification for feelings of outrage and self-righteousness'.

The Léopoldville authorities fired another salvo at the United Nations when Delvaux made a virulent attack on the Organization and some of its officials in the Congo. Hammarskjold told Abbas: 'I have rarely seen a worse and more consistent misrepresentation of U.N. role, a more slanderous misrepresentation of facts or more vicious attempts at character assassination.' He asked Abbas to present a 'formal and serious protest' adding that 'if we are to believe in good faith of the President, we must expect him publicly to disown these attacks' and to tender an apology. The United Nations, added Hammarskjold, 'would also be entitled to ask for apologies for attacks on various persons, like Dayal and Duran', based on 'utter falsehoods'.

Hammarskjold again had 'a most serious talk' with the U.K. and U.S. delegates regarding what Scott and Timberlake had told Abbas at which he expressed his 'deep disappointment' that the two ambassadors had done nothing regarding Matadi or freedom of movement. He warned that if the Matadi question was not settled soon, the U.N. would be forced to direct its supplies through the port of Pointe Noire (in Congo-Brazzaville) adding that he hoped 'their Governments now will use their chance to mend their ways and to get Scott and Timberlake going in proper direction'.

A week passed and pressure on ONUC's supply situation was reaching breaking point. The Congolese continued to pose new conditions to which Hammarskjold reacted: 'We are most shocked at this new show of bad faith on Congo side. . . . They cannot link up Matadi with Ndjili;[1] they cannot start the old story of popular reactions all over again; they cannot refuse Nigerians access to arms necessary for their own minimum protection! . . . Americans and British will be informed for what it is worth. . . . We wish to act on trust in Kasavubu, but we cannot continue to do so if he, before the whole world, shows lack of faith putting us in the position of innocent fools.'

Meanwhile, in Léopoldville, the U.N. officials Francis Nwokedi and Robert Gardiner had negotiated a draft agreement regarding the 21 February resolution, which the Congolese authorities declared their intention to accept subject to a number of provisos. The Secretary-General commented that 'it appears that the attempt of Kasavubu and Bomboko in accordance with their usual tactics is to delete anything imposing obligations on them.' The Secretary-General objected to the phrase that acceptance was subject to respect for Charter obligations since it cast a reflection on the Security Council. Also, the resolution called for the elimination of all deleterious foreign influences—which placed the discretion with ONUC—while Kasavubu insisted that he alone would decide on the foreign personnel to be excluded. As regards reorganization of the A.N.C., the President said the programme would be framed by him without reference to the U.N., although it was the U.N. Command's responsibility to carry it out. Hammarskjold concluded that Kasavubu was trying to draw out the U.N. emissaries while conceding little or nothing. But it proved to be too late to make any changes, as commitments by ONUC negotiators had already been made to the draft. Many members of the Advisory Committee shared Hammarskjold's reservations regarding the extorted concessions but on balance they were prepared to go along with the agreement in the hope that it would help in a settlement of the problem of Matadi. After a few weeks' further delay, a small U.N. force was allowed to

[1] The airport serving Léopoldville, closed by the U.N. to Congolese politicians. See pp. 34, 39, etc.

return to Matadi, and the port again became available to U.N. supply ships.

On the political plane, the capitulation at Tananarive was weighing heavily on Kasavubu who was anxious to wriggle out of his unequal undertakings. Feelings against Tshombe were rising in Léopoldville as, in violation of the Tananarive accords, he was still conducting an independent foreign policy. He had recently paid an official visit to Brazzaville where he had promised financial assistance for building a dam. He was also continuing his repression of the North Katanga dissidents and denying them the right to form their own government. Kasavubu began secret *pourparlers* with the Stanleyville authorities who had strongly opposed Tananarive, and indications were received from Gizenga that he was willing to negotiate with Léopoldville on the basis of a return to legality and the reopening of Parliament. At the same time, Léopoldville and Stanleyville troops facing each other along the Orientale border entered into friendly contact with each other. At the end of April, the Stanleyville blockade was lifted.

The scene now shifted to Coquilhatville, capital of the province of Équateur, which had been agreed on after much negotiation as the venue of a conference to discuss implementation of the Tananarive resolutions. To this conference both Tshombe and Gizenga were invited, but Gizenga, despite earlier indications, refused to attend as he was unsure of his security. However, he sent a military delegation. Tshombe arrived, accompanied by a large entourage, including half a dozen European advisers.

Some two hundred delegates from all parts of the country attended, including a Balubakat delegation led by Jason Sendwe. The presence of Sendwe angered Tshombe who had come in a mood of supreme confidence, hoping by intimidation to dominate the Conference and to wreck Léopoldville's agreement with ONUC. Kasavubu, in his opening speech, asked for the revision of the Tananarive decisions on matters of substance. Tshombe reacted with an ultimatum demanding the abrogation of the agreement with ONUC and the expulsion of Sendwe's delegation as the price for Katanga's participation. The Conference side-stepped Tshombe's threats and set up two Committees, one to discuss the agenda and the other, questions of procedure, including the seating of delegations.

When the Conference resumed the following day, Tshombe repeated his ultimatum and, not receiving satisfaction, walked out of the hall. Jason Sendwe's delegation was thereupon admitted by the unanimous vote of all members present. Next morning at a press conference, Tshombe attacked the Léopoldville leaders for going back on the Tananarive accords, and he and his 'Foreign Minister', Évariste Kimba, made for their waiting plane to return to Élisabethville. But A.N.C. soldiers on guard refused to allow the plane to depart, and Tshombe and his friends spent the night under surveillance at the airport. Attempts were made by Adoula, Bomboko, and Ileo to persuade Tshombe to change his mind, but he stubbornly refused. The following day another effort was made but Tshombe insisted on being allowed to depart, failing which, he challenged arrest. The A.N.C. soldiers had, however, already taken their decision, and Tshombe spent a second uncomfortable night in the waiting-room. The Conference had been in session, meanwhile, and it gave its approval to the 17 April agreement with ONUC. As a first step in its implementation it decided on the arrest of Tshombe's European advisers; it then decided to place Tshombe himself under house arrest.

Tshombe's detention caused a sensation. In the Western countries which had strongly taken the line that the United Nations had no authority to protect Lumumba, there were loud cries for United Nations intervention to free Tshombe. The African and Asian countries which had called for U.N. action to liberate Lumumba now kept silent. Tshombe's ally, the Abbé Fulbert Youlou of Congo-Brazzaville, declared the arrest 'an act of piracy', a sentiment strongly echoed by the Belgian press. The Léopoldville authorities announced that Tshombe was charged with crimes against the state and he would be tried for high treason.

With the discomfiture of Tshombe, the Conference set about reversing the Tananarive decisions, largely under the inspiration of Bomboko and Adoula who bitterly opposed confederation. It decided to establish a federal structure and to call an early meeting of Parliament with a view to restoring constitutional government. The Conference also decided to set up a number of new States, twenty in all, by breaking up existing provinces.

There would be a President of the Federation and each State would have its own President. The Federal Congress would have an equal number of deputies elected by State legislatures and there would be a Council of Presidents, presided over by the Federal President. The centre would be responsible for foreign affairs, defence, security, customs, communications, planning, etc., while residuary powers would rest with the states. During the period of transition, existing parliamentary institutions would be allowed to complete their four-year term. A mixed U.N.-Congolese commission would be set up to draft a new constitution on the basis of the twenty-one resolutions adopted by the Conference.

ONUC representatives played an unobtrusive but significant part in guiding the discussions to workable conclusions. Hammarskjold had instructed them to try 'to find ways to introduce, with all due subtlety, the idea of meeting of Parliament, under U.N. protection of participants. . . . The sooner the stamp of constitutionality in that way is put on Central Government, we could get under way with various urgent steps. . . . Such development, formally if possible always on government initiative, would of course also change fundamentally character of military presence, switching it back to police service.' The Secretary-General went on to say that once Parliament was convened, ONUC would start phasing out its troops to the extent that the Congolese army could take over its functions on behalf of a unified government, leaving enough troops required to support U.N. civilian operations and to prevent a recurrence of tribal warfare. He concluded: 'Of course this is still a dream but sometimes dreams may be used to give a proper sense of direction and in informal "chats" even U.N. officials should be permitted to dream—if it serves a good U.N. purpose.'

But Hammarskjold fully realized that the 'dream' could become reality only if Katanga were reintegrated into the Congo. Tshombe had met his first serious reverse, and if he could be deprived of his Belgian underpinning, Katangan secession would collapse. The Secretary-General spelt out his ideas in a communication to ONUC in which he said that United Nations political strength was 'mainly a function of what we show ourselves capable of doing in North Katanga'. He therefore asked for more active use of Indian troops in North Katanga to re-impose a neutral zone, before Kasavubu, 'with his peculiar sense of political timing', asked for U.N. initiatives to end both the Katanga and Orientale secessions.

Tshombe's arrest without protest by ONUC was becoming politically embarrassing as United Nations doctrine had now been established to oppose all political arrests. Abbas had neither protested nor asked for due process of law, which the Secretary-General noted with regret, as being 'due to a misunderstanding that Tshombe should not count on any intervention in his favour unless he asked us for it'. The Secretary-General explained that U.N. policy was to grant physical protection only when specifically asked for, but it should act promptly and unilaterally in maintenance of United Nations principles regarding fair treatment and proper legal process. Hammarskjold sent a letter to Kasavubu reminding him of the decisions of the General Assembly and Security Council which called for observance of basic human rights and fundamental freedoms in the Congo, and he insisted that Tshombe and his associates be given humane treatment and necessary legal facilities.

Fortunately for Tshombe, the era of political assassination in the Congo was over. He was transferred to Léopoldville and kept in detention while continued efforts were made to persuade him and his followers in Katanga to cooperate in making the Coquilhatville decisions effective by sending Conakat deputies to the projected meeting of Parliament. Tshombe's arrest was due to the initiative of the A.N.C. troops in Coquilhatville which had been fraternizing with the Stanleyville A.N.C. delegation, and they were determined to force the politicians to come to some agreement to end the political stalemate.

In Élisabethville, Tshombe's arrest came like a bolt from the blue. But his followers remained loyal to him and set up a triumvirate under Munongo to carry on the government in his enforced absence. Munongo declared that his primary objective was to secure Tshombe's release, but he was not prepared to pay the price of submission to Léopoldville's demands. In Belgium, a new Government had been formed with the Socialist Paul-Henri Spaak as the new Foreign Minister, a strong advocate for revision of Belgian policy towards Katanga and the United Nations. It was agreed by the moderates in Élisabeth-ville that if Katanga stayed away from Parliament, a government dominated by Stanleyville could well follow, further reducing Katanga's chances of independent survival.

But Munongo and his group, backed by Belgian 'ultras', opposed any concessions as it would destroy all that Katanga had fought for. They were convinced that Katanga was strong enough, both militarily and financially, to withstand any attack by the Léopoldville A.N.C. As for the United Nations, they relied on the Western position that the U.N. Force could not be used to impose a political solution. The Katanga triumvirate, therefore, prevaricated while Léopoldville set about making preparations for reactivating Parliament.

President Kasavubu approached the United Nations for assistance in reconvening Parliament, and the Secretary-General asked me to prepare a plan. The most suitable venue was the University of Lovanium with its extensive campus and its ample conference and housing facilities. Situated some twenty-five kilometres from Léopoldville, it was removed from local pressures and possible interference by the Congolese army, making the physical protection of deputies easier. ONUC was instructed to lend its good offices to persuade Gizenga and Munongo to participate under guarantees of personal safety, the aim being to make the session, for the first time, fully representative of all six provinces.

The security and immunity of the precincts was to be enforced by strong U.N. detachments posted around the neutral parliamentary zone. The security of parliamentarians was to be assured by housing them in the neutral area or in well protected buildings. For the protection of families of deputies, U.N. mobile patrols were to be provided. ONUC would assist with road travel arrangements from the interior and make available U.N. air transport. Security precautions in Léopold-ville would include prohibiting large gatherings, restricting the sale of liquor, and confining A.N.C. troops to their barracks. Foreign political advisers would be excluded from the neutral area. Abbas was asked to discuss the suggestions with the central authorities and to make necessary preparations after obtaining their general approval. On the Secretary-General's instructions

I sounded a cross-section of delegations regarding the proposals and found their reactions generally favourable.

Early in May I received an invitation from Senator Albert Gore of Tennessee, Chairman of the African Affairs Sub-Committee of the Senate, asking my wife and me to luncheon to meet him and other members of the Sub-Committee in Washington for a discussion on the Congo. Hammarskjold thought it would be useful to explain to the Senators what the United Nations was trying to accomplish and to enlist their sympathy, particularly for the plan to recall Parliament. I would combine the visit to the Senate with calls on officials at the State Department and with meetings with the influential Washington press.

The luncheon meeting in the Senate's private dining-room brought thirteen Senators, with Senator Gore as the host, and included Senators Hubert Humphrey, George Aiken, Stuart Symington, John Sparkman, Mike Mansfield, Frank Church, and Paul Douglas. The atmosphere was extremely friendly. The Chairman, in introducing us, paid a warm tribute to my wife and me, thanking me for my work for peace. I explained the U.N. mandate in the Congo and plans for the future. Then followed a spate of questions, the Senators fully agreeing to the need for reactivating constitutional processes. Some wanted to know if Gizenga was a Communist and the extent of Soviet influence in the Congo. The importance of the technical-assistance programme met with unanimous approval as well as the indispensability of the United Nations presence in the country. A number of Senators asked who would be the most suitable politician to head a new constitutional government. I gave them the name of Cyrille Adoula which many Senators noted down. The meeting concluded with generous remarks from Senators Humphrey, Symington, and Church regarding ONUC's work.

My call next day on the Secretary of State, Dean Rusk, was less encouraging. Rusk observed that the situation was much changed since our last talk in November before he took office, and asked about recent events and future perspectives. He had received reports that Stanleyville had become stronger and enquired about the reliability of United Nations troops, mentioning the Ghana Brigade in particular. Rusk was a good listener but he gave no assurance of U.S. support for U.N. policies.

The U.S. and British delegations had again renewed their request to Hammarskjold for a change in the direction of the U.N. mission. To meet their pressures, Hammarskjold had prepared a note outlining his plans for reorganizing Léopoldville ONUC headquarters. The note said that to relieve the Special Representative of his heavy burden of responsibility in view of the scope, diversity, and character of the tasks devolving on him, it was proposed to establish a group of three members of equal status. One of the members would act as Chairman, and each member would be assigned a specific responsibility. The post of Special Representative would be abolished, but I would return to the Congo for a short period till the group was ready to take over full responsibility.

Chester Bowles, Under-Secretary of State, to whom I gave a copy of the note, expressed no opinion on the proposed reorganization nor did Rusk. Bowles said that the problem with the Congolese was mostly psychological owing to their lack of historical background. As a friend, he advised that I should not return to the Congo, as any further deterioration in the situation would be attributed to me. 'The task is a thankless one and no man could have done it better', he added by way of encouragement. Both Rusk and Bowles were then much preoccupied by the Cuban Bay of Pigs fiasco, and they had little time for the Congo. But to some extent they felt relieved that the United Nations, for all its inadequacies, had managed to insulate the situation and to prevent it from threatening international peace.

I had hoped to return to Léopoldville on the conclusion of the debate in the General Assembly. But Hammarskjold first suggested that I should await a settlement of the Matadi affair and Kasavubu's acceptance of the 21 February resolution. He then wanted me to draw up plans for reconvening the Congolese Parliament and to return to implement them personally. That would provide a convenient watershed in the Operation, after which I would be free to leave the assignment. A provisional date for my departure to Léopoldville was fixed and Hammarskjold asked Abbas to inform President Kasavubu and his colleagues who were then in Coquilhatville.

Abbas reported that the President's reaction was very negative, and Mobutu's was violent. Threats of physical harm were made and of complete non-cooperation with ONUC. There-upon Hammarskjold sent Rikhye to Léopoldville to try and pacify Mobutu, and to explain to him the temporary nature of my return. Rikhye reported that the threats should not be taken too seriously, as it was a Congolese habit to exaggerate their intentions. I therefore made preparations to leave in the last week of May for a stay of a few weeks, hoping to set arrangements for the meeting of Parliament in train.

The Western campaign against my return had been gaining momentum and Ian Scott had been flown over from Léopold-ville to see the Secretary-General, to add his voice to the chorus. The main criticism was that I did not get on well with President Kasavubu and General Mobutu, and, overlooking the fact that it was during my stewardship of the Operation that Lumumba had met his end, I was accused of being pro-Lumumba. There was no specific criticism of any of my actions or decisions, only vague innuendoes about my being pro-nationalist and even pro-Communist.[1] No amount of probing at ONUC headquarters by my detractors was able to reveal anything disparaging about the conduct of affairs, the entire U.N. staff at Léopoldville loyally and staunchly supporting the impartiality of the decisions taken.

Sections of the Western press joined vociferously in the orchestrated campaign and some sent special correspondents to the Congo on muck-raking expeditions. But their despatches contained only inconsequential accusations, the gravamen of which was that I had failed to support President Kasavubu, Mobutu, and the Commissioners against Stanleyville and had opposed Tshombe's secession. The press, which a few months earlier had hailed my 'monumental' patience and impartiality, now regarded me as 'arrogant', 'abrasive', and favouring the nationalists. Nothing was substantiated, the criticisms being based on hearsay and, more often, on sheer prejudice.

But there was opposing pressure for my return from other quarters. The African and Asian countries were insisting on my resuming my assignment in order to speed up work for the recall of Parliament. They told the Secretary-General that if

---

[1] The *Washington Post* came out with a cartoon by Herblock showing me in a jeep, blazing the trail for Khrushchev in the Congo who was following in a bull-dozer.

he gave in to Western pressures, they would regard it as favouring the Western political line which they were convinced was
opposed to implementation of the 21 February resolution. They
had given unqualified approval to my reports and my handling
of the situation and they insisted on my return to bring about a
restoration of legality. The Soviet Union pointedly kept out of
the controversy, for, as Zorin told me, it held Hammarskjold,
the principal, and not his agent, Dayal, accountable.

In India, the course of the mission had been followed with
deep interest, and newspapers carried daily accounts of the
campaign against me which greatly angered Indian public
opinion. The Indian Parliament had frequently discussed the
Congo and my work had received praise from different sides of
the House. There was a stormy interlude in the Lok Sabha on
3 April 1961 occasioned by reports of Western attacks on me.
Mr. Nehru rose to condemn the campaign, which he found
'distressing'. He said that while India's 'best men' could not
be sent on deputation for indefinite periods, my withdrawal
from the Congo at that stage would create a new balance of
forces against implementation of the Security Council's resolutions, which would 'affect the situation very much'.[1] There
were demands for withdrawal of the Indian contingent as the
attacks on me were regarded by the legislators as an insult to
the country.

I was taken aback by the virulence of the controversy. It was
the last thing I had expected when I undertook the assignment.
While I did not ask for praise for doing my duty, I felt deeply
hurt at imputations against my impartiality. The problems with
Kasavubu and Mobutu were not of my making. They were the
result of their own actions. Yet the blame was being put on
ONUC and not on the Congolese leaders. That was the measure
of impartiality of the critics who charged ONUC with partiality.

I often told Hammarskjold of my distress at finding myself
involved in controversy and repeatedly offered to return to my
interrupted work in Pakistan. I said that he had only to give the
word and I would leave with a clear conscience, having done
my duty to the best of my lights and capacity. But Hammarskjold would not hear of it. He insisted that my departure at
that stage would seriously weaken his own political position

[1] 1961 Lok Sabha Reports.

and adversely reflect on his conduct of the Operation. The attacks on me, he said, were, in reality, aimed vicariously at him. In any case, he regarded them as unwarranted and unjustified, and he could not, in all fairness, abandon me to the wolves. He had repeatedly told critics that I had carried out my duties faithfully and loyally and with his complete approval. He said he would not bow to any pressures which would undermine his prerogative to choose his own representatives and sap the morale of the international civil service.

I had no option but reluctantly to overcome my own resentment and distress at the unjust persecution and to defer to the Secretary-General's wishes. But Hammarskjold had not taken into account the capacity for continued obstruction on the part of Kasavubu and Mobutu. Abbas had not stood up well to the demands of the mission and Hammarskjold decided to relieve him. Abbas was instructed, when he paid his farewell call on Kasavubu and Mobutu, to present to the President the Secretary-General's letter informing them of my date of arrival. Their outburst was hysterical and violent in the extreme. Kasavubu said he would abrogate every single agreement with the United Nations and would actively obstruct its functioning. Mobutu said he would turn his soldiers on all United Nations personnel and there would be a state of war with the Organization. Both uttered threats and imprecations and said they would stop at nothing to prevent my setting foot in the Congo, Mobutu even threatening assassination.

Abbas's telegram came late at night and I was hurriedly summoned from a dinner party to a midnight conference with the Secretary-General and his principal advisers. There was a long minute of silence while I read the message and took my decision. I said it was no longer a question of political pressures in New York, but of basic considerations of physical survival of the Operation and the safety of its personnel. While I understood the Secretary-General's reluctance to release me in face of political manoeuvring motivated by cold-war considerations, the situation now was one of jeopardizing the lives and honour of ONUC officials in the Congo. I could never forgive myself for killings or outrages against U.N. personnel as the price others would have to pay for my return. Nor could I regard with equanimity the collapse of the Operation to which the

Secretary-General and his colleagues, including myself, had dedicated so much anxious toil. I was thankful to the Secretary-General for firmly upholding me against political attack, thereby standing up for a principle in which all of us so strongly believed. But I was sure that he would not wish to endanger the future of the Operation and the safety of its personnel.

Hammarskjold could not but agree although he did so with much reluctance. It now remained to work out the modalities. The Secretary-General himself drafted a withering letter to Kasavubu with a message to Abbas asking him to deliver it personally. Hammarskjold told Abbas that he should make it clear to Kasavubu that the United Nations has 'found it practically impossible to work with people who for over four months take such stands as those demonstrated'. He continued: 'Kasavubu and company gladly talk about breaking agreements and relations based on agreements. Have they realized that we are the giving party and that we may take their word seriously and break ourselves?'

In his letter to Kasavubu, Hammarskjold said: 'I must note with the deepest disappointment that your confidence in the United Nations and myself does not enable you to accept as a United Nations official in Léopoldville a man who enjoys my own full confidence. I am disappointed that you still lend credence to accusations and allegations for which I have found no basis and on which I have repeatedly tried to give you clarifications.' He continued that in the circumstances Mr. Dayal no longer saw any possibility of making a constructive contribution to the U.N. assistance Operation in the Congo and that he did not wish to continue with the assignment. He concluded with the words: 'It is with reluctance and great regret that I have to accept his conclusion, for it is my firm conviction that he has carried out his United Nations responsibilities with an ability matched by his loyalty and integrity.'

I suggested to the Secretary-General that it was important to inform Mr. Nehru before the story was leaked to the press by the Léopoldville authorities. The Indian Ambassador, C. S. Jha, was thereupon called in, and he and I drafted a personal message to Mr. Nehru. I told the Prime Minister that the Secretary-General had stoutly withstood Western pressures, and had tried to overcome the virulent animosity of the Léopoldville authorities and was in no way to blame for his failure. The decision to withdraw was the only possible one, which I had now taken. I urged that it should not influence the attitude of the Government of India towards the Operation which should receive its full political and military support. Everything depended on the Indian Brigade which was holding key positions in the Congo, and its withdrawal would sap the U.N. Force of its strength. In his reply received next day Mr. Nehru accepted the recommendation about the Indian troops and acquiesced in my decision, although he deeply regretted the circumstances.

Hammarskjold issued a press communiqué in which he stated that as emphasis in the work of ONUC was now shifting from the diplomatic to the administrative field, the work of coordination would now be largely undertaken at U.N. Headquarters in New York. No new Special Representative would be appointed and activities in Léopoldville would be coordinated by the senior U.N. official in the capacity of Officer-in-Charge. The Secretary-General expressed his 'full gratitude' for my services which he said had been 'marked by the highest ability and level of performance, equalled by loyalty to the purposes of the U.N. and unfailing integrity'.

News of my resignation created a sensation and made headline news the world over. In many African and Asian countries the Western powers were blamed for imposing their will on the Secretary-General. In India there was an outburst of anger and a sense of outrage; a torrent of indignant questions was asked in Parliament. Mr. Nehru tried to pacify members by explaining the circumstances, and he accused the Western powers, especially the United States and British envoys, of obstructing the United Nations. Commenting on my work he said: 'So far as Shri Rajeshwar Dayal is concerned, he left his mark wherever he worked as a very able person and he is respected in the U.N. and in the Congo in spite of many people criticizing him there, and he came away with great dignity.'[1]

My last official appearance as a member of the international civil service was at a meeting of the Congo Advisory Committee at which the Secretary-General took members into confidence in explaining the circumstances of my resignation and made

[1] Lok Sabha debates, June 1961.

fulsome references to my work. Many joined in the tribute while expressing regret at my departure. The Secretary-General had asked me to continue in the Secretariat as one of his principal advisers, but I declined as I was anxious to resume my work in Pakistan.

My decision to leave was received with relief not only by my political opponents, but also by our personal friends. Many of them had been genuinely worried about our physical safety as they had no illusions about the capacity of the Congolese to carry out their threats. They were indignant about the attacks on me and I shall ever be grateful to those American and European friends for the great efforts they made with press and politicians on my behalf. They tried to dissuade us from continuing with a thankless—and dangerous—task and to recognize that there were limits to human endurance. Most touching was Hammarskjold's solicitude; he told me he had been greatly worried about our personal safety—as my wife had insisted on remaining with me throughout these difficult months—and he would have carried a heavy burden of guilt if anything had happened to us. That was the only occasion on which I had known Hammarskjold reacting to a threat of physical danger either to himself or to anyone associated with him.

On 27 May 1961 ended my mission for Hammarskjold in the Congo.

Some two weeks after my departure, when the moral issue raised by it was still being feverishly debated, Hammarskjold in his *Markings* (London, 1964, p. 174) inscribed a poem carrying the date of 18 June 1961. The role of two great powers in the affair was widely known, and there was anxiety regarding the impact of the circumstances on the position of the Secretary-General. Many have wondered what inspired the graphic imagery employed in the poem:

> He will come out
> Between two warders,
> Lean and sunburnt,
> A little bent,
> As if apologizing
> For his strength,

His features tense,
But looking quite calm.

He will take off his jacket
And, with shirt torn open,
Stand up against the wall
To be executed.

He has not betrayed us.
He will meet his end
Without weakness.
When I feel anxious,
It is not for him.
Do I fear a compulsion in me
To be so destroyed?
Or is there someone
In the depths of my being,
Waiting for permission
To pull the trigger?

It was not someone's hand and no compulsion on Dag Hammarskjold's part, but the hand of destiny that, on 17 September 1961, pulled the trigger in an African jungle.

CHAPTER 16

'A Catastrophe which is a Triumph'[1]

My mission to the Congo had ended, but its aftermath had not. The stress and turbulence that had encompassed us during the preceding months was to continue and to take as its levy the life of the Secretary-General himself.

It is not within the scope of this book to make a climactic analysis of the events that covered the four months following my departure from Léopoldville. In June 1961 Antoine Gizenga agreed with Kasavubu to join a new Government under U.N. protection. Tshombe, while still under arrest in Léopoldville, undertook to cooperate with the Central Government, and was accordingly allowed to return to Katanga. Once there, Tshombe, true to type, declared that he had no intention of abrogating the independence of Katanga to any central power.

In the first week of August, Cyrille Adoula was appointed premier of the Federal Government, and Gizenga's Stanleyville régime was dissolved. The United Nations gave its full backing to these events, the Secretary-General assuring Adoula that the member states now recognized his Government to be the only legitimate one in the Congo. By September, however, pressure for immediate action against Katanga had increased in Léopoldville, making a confrontation inevitable.

After my departure as Special Representative, the Secretary-General had decided that no new appointment would be made at that level, and that Sture Linner, who had been in charge of the civilian operation of ONUC, would have his general responsibilities extended to become 'Officer-in-Charge', with

[1] Dag Hammarskjold, *Markings,* p. 169.

Mahmoud Khiari taking over the civilian operation and the political contact work.

The Secretary-General's representative in Katanga was at this time Conor Cruise O'Brien, an Irishman. Under the code name of 'Rumpunch' he, together with Khiari, organized the expulsion from Katanga on 28 August 1961 of foreign officers in the gendarmerie as specified in the February 21 resolution. Although the operation met with no initial resistance, it was inconclusive. The representatives of ONUC then decided to take urgent action to ensure the reintegration of Katanga, by force if necessary. The Central Government in Léopoldville had, under Adoula, issued warrants for the arrest, as a last resort, of Tshombe and some of his key politicians. The objective of Operation 'Morthor',[1] to give it its code name, was to secure the cooperation of Tshombe and to forestall any armed resistance by a show of strength by the U.N. Force in Katanga. On 13 September, and without having referred the plan back to the Secretary-General for authorization, the U.N. troops in Élisabethville were mobilized against the Katangan forces. A series of fierce clashes followed, with casualties on both sides. It soon became clear that the small contingents of U.N. troops were not equal to the sheer superiority in numbers of the Katangan soldiers and Belgian mercenaries.

Hammarskjold had already decided some time before these events to mediate personally between the politicians in the hope that they would agree on a meeting to discuss a way out of the impasse. At the time of the launching of 'Morthor' the Secretary-General was already bound for Léopoldville.

Hammarskjold was unaware during his flight from New York that ONUC had launched a military operation, using methods which he had forbidden, to achieve an objective which was unauthorized. The only indication he received that something was afoot was when his plane made a refuelling stop in Nigeria and press correspondents asked for his comments on the events of the last few hours. Hammarskjold truthfully replied that that was the first he had heard of them.

At the Léopoldville airport the Secretary-General was received by Adoula, members of his Cabinet, and by Mobutu and Linner. He looked calm and unruffled as usual, but

[1] Hindi for 'smash'.

impatiently awaited the conclusion of the airport ceremonies to get down to work.

On the drive into town Hammarskjold closely questioned Linner about developments. All that Linner could tell him was that the action was a continuation of 'Rumpunch'. But something had gone very wrong, as U.N. troops were locked in unequal combat without accomplishing any of their objectives. Hammarskjold's immediate anxiety was to stop the bloodshed and to extricate the United Nations from the military and political confusion into which it had been so suddenly plunged.

It was clear that the scope and character of the action had greatly overstepped the Secretary-General's express instructions and stringent reservations. ONUC did not have the right to make arrests of Congolese politicians, a task which it had repeatedly declined in the past as in the case of Lumumba. Moreover, it was not wholly consistent with its policy of the renunciation of force for the attainment of political objectives. Its role was limited to the expulsion of foreign military personnel with a minimum degree of force and to ensuring its own freedom of movement. It was certainly not its purpose to end secession by the explicit use of force. The Secretary-General had not been consulted about the wide sweep of Operation Morthor or informed of its scope and objectives.

The question of responsibility immediately arose. Khiari purported to have acted on Linner's authority, but Linner denied having given any. The chain of command ran from the Secretary-General to the Officer-in-Charge and from the latter, through his emissary, Khiari—to whom he had delegated considerable powers—to ONUC's local representatives in Élisabethville. Linner surely must have authorized the long flight by his immediate advisers, Khiari and Fabry, to Élisabethville, and he had presumably given them some instructions, written or oral. What those instructions were and what action was taken to ensure that they were correctly conveyed and scrupulously implemented have not been disclosed. The troops under General McKeown's overall command were to be engaged in an action of unquestioned danger and his views were obviously of crucial importance. But McKeown was at no time taken into confidence regarding the operation. O'Brien has repeatedly affirmed that he acted under instructions and he presumed that before they were passed down to him, his senior officers had taken all the necessary steps to secure proper authorization. There was clearly a lamentable lack of communication and coordination—if not of understanding—at the highest levels of ONUC. This could be accounted for only by the fact that the normal procedures had, for reasons which have not been explained, been disregarded. Perhaps it was hoped that a swift and sudden action would produce the desired results which would then be presented to the Secretary-General as a *fait accompli.*

If the expected collapse of Katangan resistance had occurred, the political repercussions would not have been unmanageable, as it could have been argued that the results had justified the means. But ONUC had made a series of tragic misjudgements. Katanga's fighting capacity had been grossly underestimated while the relative strength of the U.N. Force had been exaggerated. The legal difficulties had been largely ignored, as well as Hammarskjold's warnings against a head-on clash.

International reactions were swift and strident. The Western press was in full cry, accusing U.N. troops of atrocities against unarmed civilians and prisoners. *Libre Belgique* described the events as 'a premeditated crime' and the *Dernière Heure* likened ONUC's actions to those of the Nazis. Even some of the more liberal newspapers, traditionally sympathetic to the United Nations, expressed concern at the involvement of a peace-keeping force in battle. Hammarskjold's comment to his aides about the press attacks was that they were 'a nuisance, but of no lasting significance. The general public was like any street mob, spontaneously taking the side of the bum against the policeman.'

In the Governments in Brussels and London there was bitter criticism of Hammarskjold. Roy Welensky in Salisbury alerted his troops and manned the border. The new British Ambassador to the Congo, Derek Riches, under instruction from Whitehall, asked the Secretary-General if he had changed his mind since giving assurances to the British Government that the U.N. would settle the Katanga problem only by peaceful means, and if so, the reasons for the change. Riches warned that if ONUC had taken offensive action to achieve a political result contrary to its mandate, his Government would withdraw all support from the Operation. Hammarskjold replied that the action was a continuation of the interrupted efforts made on 28 August as the Consuls had not fulfilled their undertakings to O'Brien to round up the foreign mercenaries. There had been no change of policy, but the United Nations had to carry out its task to evict undesirable foreign military and other personnel and it had been compelled to use force in self-defence. He emphasized that the immediate need was for a cease-fire as fighting was continuing and costing lives; for his part he would try his best to achieve one and he asked for cooperation in his efforts. As events were to prove, Whitehall was not satisfied with the explanation.

The United States, in contrast to its Western allies, publicly backed the U.N. action although privately it conveyed to Hammarskjold, through its Ambassador in Léopoldville, a thinly veiled warning. In a statement it declared that the unity of the Congo was essential to its progress and stability, and the U.N. had been acting in support of the Central Government to suppress separatist movements and the threat of civil war. But it regarded the hostilities as unfortunate and hoped that they would soon end. The countries of Asia and Africa welcomed the renewed military pressure on Katanga, India considering the action to be fully within the rights of the Organization. But they insisted that the trial of strength be carried to a decisive conclusion. The Central Government of the Congo, pleased that the U.N. Force had gone into action, hoped that Tshombe would at last be brought to his knees.

Hammarskjold knew that Tshombe would not agree to a cease-fire until his advantage over the U.N. troops had been effectively neutralized. He wired Bunche to approach the Ethiopian delegation for two or three jet planes for service in Katanga to be used to ground Tshombe's Fouga fighter. Some of his advisers were eager to fly reinforcements to Élisabethville to crush the gendarmerie but Hammarskjold firmly overruled them. The Secretary-General instructed O'Brien that U.N. troops should not fire except in self-defence and that any new military action must first be cleared with him. His aim was to call a draw, with neither side winning or losing the round as that would offer the best hope of negotiations. It would also give time to pause and think, as it was clear that the struggle, if it continued, would be protracted and bloody, with damaging political repercussions.

Meanwhile, the Katangans aggressively continued their offensive, forcing their opponents to fight on defensively with their backs to the wall. The U.N. troops were chafing at the restraints which the Secretary-General had imposed and were eager to force a decision to end their defensive role. O'Brien joined them in pressing for a vigorous retort. In Kamina a Baluba chief defected to Tshombe and his mercenary-led troops attacked the base, parts of which had to be evacuated by the U.N. In Jadotville, an Irish company was surrounded by an overwhelmingly superior force led by whites. The Irish had been sent as protectors of the large European population in response to the pleas of their Consuls, but when they arrived, the would-be protectors were greeted with jeers and insults and set upon treacherously by the Katangan troops. Attempts to relieve them were foiled by the destruction of road bridges and murderous opposition by the white-led gendarmerie. A Fouga fighter jet had shot up one U.N. transport plane in the air and three on the ground and had been harassing O'Brien at his residence and U.N. personnel in their quarters.

Hammarskjold, in spite of Katangan excesses and O'Brien's importunity, refused to countenance a military riposte so as not to exacerbate the situation further. He hated bloodshed and was not prepared to engage a peace force in offensive tactics even to extricate itself from danger. He had decided to stake his full authority and prestige to force a cease-fire. He was furious at statements issuing from U.N. sources in Élisabethville that the United Nations was resolutely pursuing the operation to end Katanga's secession, and sternly reprimanded O'Brien for breach of instructions. O'Brien, for his part, felt that he had been faithfully carrying out Linner's and Khiari's instructions at great personal danger and he could not understand what he saw as a change of mood in Léopoldville. His Irish blood seemed to rebel at having to turn the other cheek to Tshombe's aggressiveness. The British Ambassador had been pressing for a public disclaimer of O'Brien, but Hammarskjold, who admired O'Brien's courage and ability though not his judgement, refused and tried, instead, to find a diplomatic way out of the tragic situation.

News arrived that Lord Lansdowne, Under-Secretary of State at the Foreign Office, was arriving in Léopoldville on behalf of the British Government, and Hammarskjold prolonged his stay in Léopoldville to meet him. O'Brien had been attempting, with the intermediary of British Consul Dunnett, to arrange a meeting with Tshombe armed with a letter from the Secretary-General proposing a cease-fire without conditions. But Dunnett, contrary to his promise, failed to produce Tshombe. Meanwhile the fighting continued with renewed intensity, U.N. troops barely managing to hold their own in Élisabethville while they were heavily beleaguered in Kamina. The plight of the Irish company was now perilous but it gallantly fought back and refused repeated demands for surrender.

Lansdowne met Hammarskjold on the morning of 16 September, both attended by their respective advisers. Lansdowne expressed the shock of his Government and people at the action of the U.N. troops which appeared to be engaged in a punitive war against Katanga. He demanded an explanation as to why U.N. policy had changed and if it was now the intention to bring about a political solution by force. He was very critical of O'Brien's actions and public statements and demanded his immediate dismissal. Hammarskjold explained the origins of the conflict and the role of foreign elements, emphasizing the defensive nature of the action and its limited aim of completing the work begun on 28 August. Lansdowne drew attention to the inconsistencies between what the Secretary-General had told him and the reports which he had received from the British Consul in Élisabethville.

The advisers then withdrew and what transpired thereafter between the two men is not known and can only be deduced. But from Lansdowne's subsequent statement in Parliament, it is clear that the Secretary-General told him of his unhappiness at the fighting and his intention to bring about an unconditional cease-fire. There are accounts that Lansdowne took the Secretary-General severely to task and threatened to denounce him publicly if the fighting did not immediately stop. There was also an implication that Tshombe would be supported militarily from Northern Rhodesia and the United Nations would get bogged down in a war of attrition which would effectively destroy the Organization.

Whatever the facts, there can be no doubt that the conversation between the two men was tough, and for Hammarskjold extremely unpleasant. After the meeting, the U.N. officials found Hammarskjold anxious and preoccupied. Heinz Wieschhoff, normally indomitably cheerful, was dejected, and he exclaimed to one of his U.N. colleagues after the meeting, flinging up his hands: 'All is finished; all is finished.'

The Secretary-General had prepared a cold but conciliatory letter to Tshombe which he had showed Lansdowne. In it he reminded Tshombe of the latter's commitment to the objectives of the United Nations to maintain law and order, to prevent civil war, and to evacuate certain categories of foreigners. Tshombe had also accepted the idea of reconciliation and had agreed in principle to a cease-fire. There was therefore no evident conflict of views in regard to basic principles. The Secretary-General offered to meet Tshombe personally to find peaceful methods of resolving the present conflict and asked him to issue urgent orders for a cease-fire which the U.N. troops, on their side, were immediately enforcing. He suggested Ndola in Northern Rhodesia as the place of meeting. Lansdowne approved of the tone and contents of the letter, which the Secretary-General also showed to the Prime Minister, Adoula, who, likewise, offered no objection.

On 16 September the Secretary-General received a visit from the U.S. Ambassador about which he informed Bunche in characteristic vein with a mixture of irony and political perspicacity:

American Ambassador made today on behalf of Kennedy, Rusk and Lord Hume *démarche* requesting me to remain in the Congo as long as the hostilities in Katanga continue. They believe 'that this is extremely desirable to demonstrate the seriousness with which the responsibilities of the Secretary-General under U.N. resolutions are being carried out'. I assume that the same seriousness thus supposedly demonstrated is considered by the distinguished Foreign Ministers and the President to apply to the terms of the resolutions themselves.

My reply to the American Ambassador was that I have to judge from day to day. As follows from messages to Tshombe I must at least wait for outcome of this effort and thus cannot leave tomorrow. As message should be published at least Monday morning, reason for my absence from General Assembly will be obvious without special explanation.

Have also received special message from Dean Rusk expressing 'dismay that U.N. should have taken such a serious step, jeopardizing what it sought to accomplish in Katanga and in the Congo'. He continues: 'While we recognize that the U.N. had warned us that energetic action might be required in Katanga, we consider the timing most unfortunate and would have counselled at least against it at this time.' I replied that impact of the Katanga problem on reconciliation of the rest of the Congo and on the balance between leading personalities in the Cabinet was such that what we did was indeed the minimum necessary in order not, repeat not, 'to jeopardize what it sought to accomplish'. The timing was imposed on us by events and this could not have been influenced by considerations which we otherwise might have shared. . . .

I am certain that just as every paper believes that I went to Léopoldville for the Katanga problem, every paper will take for granted, if and when the approach to Tshombe is made known, that this is result of 'constructive proposals' made by Lansdowne for Western powers. Both groups of governments would rather like this interpretation. (For the record it may be said that the approach was decided upon and message written before I received Lansdowne.)

From aesthetical viewpoint, we should be satisfied to note that suspicions and even language from various sides start to show beautiful balance.[1]

Bunche replied: 'The pieces all fit well and dirtily together. I love your last sentence for its balanced irony.'

The position of U.N. troops in Katanga declined catastrophically during the day. The beleaguered Irish had suffered grievous casualties and news came of their surrender. Two of Tshombe's Ministers had gone to meet Welensky in Salisbury and Tshombe had threatened 'total war' against the United Nations unless it vacated Katanga forthwith. The Ethiopian fighter planes had been held up for want of flight clearance over Uganda, still a colony, from the British Government; and the Katangan Fouga pirate had the freedom of the air for its murderous sorties. Flushed with his victory over the Irish, Tshombe proposed to O'Brien, through Dennett, a meeting at Bancroft in Northern Rhodesia where he hoped to dictate his terms as to a vanquished enemy. O'Brien, stunned by Tshombe's impudence, strongly advised the Secretary-General against acceptance of the demand. Mr. Frank Aiken, Foreign Minister

---

[1] The reference is to the Eastern and Western blocs.

of Ireland, arrived to enquire into the fate of the Irish Company, along with the assurance of his Government's continued support for the United Nations. That was the only ray of sunshine in an otherwise dismal day.

Tshombe's reply to the Secretary-General arrived at noon on 17 September accepting the principle of a cease-fire but on condition that all U.N. troop movements cease, including the despatch of reinforcements. Hammarskjold showed annoyance with the reply and he instructed O'Brien to inform Tshombe that the Secretary-General found it impossible to accept any conditions for a meeting and by introducing them, Tshombe was only delaying the necessary measures for the protection of human life. He wished to assure Tshombe that the cease-fire, when effected, would not alter the *status quo*. The message was, however, not delivered by Dennett, who informed O'Brien that Tshombe was not available, and that he and his entourage had already made plans to travel to Ndola.

The Secretary-General, without awaiting Tshombe's response, went ahead with his preparations to meet him at Ndola. According to O'Brien, the choice of venue was not the Secretary-General's but had been forced upon him. Lansdowne, however, has said that the Secretary-General himself proposed Ndola and he was both surprised and pleased at the choice and offered to make the necessary arrangements. O'Brien was opposed to Ndola as it would have implied that the meeting would be under the mediation and patronage of Welensky, Tshombe's avowed friend and ally, and would have every appearance of surrender. The African and Asian countries were shocked at the venue because of its political implications. Kamina would have been preferable but the U.N. garrison was under siege and exposed to the depredations of Tshombe's lone-ranger plane. In the midst of these developments, Hammarskjold had, momentarily, hoped that things might conceivably take a turn for the better as there was a report on 16 September that the gendarmerie at Jadotville had 'kicked out their white officers to fraternize with the Irish', but this information unfortunately turned out to be false. Hammarskjold felt that if the Ethiopian jets arrived in time, Tshombe would lose his military advantage and would be in a less bellicose mood. The Secretary-General therefore entertained the furtive hope, as he told Bunche in a message, that he might succeed in persuading Tshombe to return with him to Léopold-ville to continue the discussions. That explained his anxiety to have the Ethiopian jets with all possible speed, for every hour in that desperate situation counted.

Hammarskjold asked McKeown to fly immediately to Élisa-bethville to make a personal assessment of the military hazards and fast dwindling alternatives. The threatening presence of Lord Lansdowne meanwhile hung like a cloud over Léopold-ville. By now, Hammarskjold had few options open to him; the U.N.'s key card, the Ethiopian jets, which would rob Tshombe of his devastating advantage, was in British hands, but London continued to prevaricate. After his talk with Riches on 16 September, at which he requested permission for overflight and refuelling, Hammarskjold wired Bunche: 'I trust they will react promptly although I have some doubts.' Next day, 17 September, after his morning meeting with Lansdowne, Ham-marskjold again cabled Bunche that 'it is rather doubtful that permission for refuelling in Uganda will be granted, therefore you should immediately explore possibility of flying over Sudan with stop at Juba where presume high octane available'. That was Hammarskjold's last message.

The fateful meeting at Ndola had been set for 17 September. In the morning, the Secretary-General received Lord Lans-downe who had promised to make the necessary arrangements, but word had still not been received from London about the place of meeting. Lansdowne offered to accompany Hammar-skjold himself to ensure that there were no unforeseen compli-cations, but Hammarskjold would not hear of it as it would have been politically embarrassing to have gone on his delicate mission in the company of one whose country was so deeply involved in the Katanga affair. Instead, he suggested that Lansdowne travel independently in a U.N. plane and, after supervising the conference arrangements at Ndola, leave for Salisbury before Hammarskjold's arrival.

The next question with Lansdowne concerned clearance for the flight of the Ethiopian jets. Lansdowne tried to dissuade Hammarskjold from starting what he described as aerial war-fare at the very moment when he was negotiating a truce. Ham-marskjold insisted the jets were essential for the protection of

U.N. troops as they would be employed strictly for defensive purposes. Lansdowne made the offer that the British authorities would try to persuade Tshombe to ground his Fouga, leaving Hammarskjold to wonder why they had not done so earlier. Did they fear that without mastery of the air, the Katangan forces would be at the mercy of U.N. troops? Seeing that Hammarskjold was adamant, Lansdowne recommended to London that clearance be granted. The U.N. jets arrived five days later, but it was five days too late, as during the critical period, the military situation remained heavily in Katanga's favour. The Secretary-General proceeded to his assignment with destiny with his hands tied down in his negotiations and even his personal safety in jeopardy.

In the afternoon, London's consent to the Ndola meeting arrived but Lansdowne, with Hammarskjold's approval, had decided to go anyway. The Secretary-General's time for departure was approaching and many preliminary arrangements had to be made. Because of the danger from the Fouga, the flight plans were not disclosed and a decoy plan was deposited with the air-control tower. The accent was on secrecy as the Secretary-General wished to avoid speculation or publicity about the visit, his main concern being with the results. The Albertina, the DC-6B four-engined turbo-jet which was to convey Hammarskjold, had taken General McKeown the previous day to Élisabethville and had encountered Katangan anti-aircraft gunfire which had caused some superficial damage. Necessary repairs had been carried out by Sweden's Transair engineers and the plane, which was on charter with ONUC, was pronounced airworthy. U.N. air control had been given the frequency of the plane's radio but with the caution that it was only to receive messages from it and was, on no account, to establish contact with it. This precaution was intended to avoid revealing the location of the plane in flight. Only on approaching Ndola would the plane establish ground contact and seek permission to land.

The Secretary-General's party consisted of Heinz Wieschhoff who had accompanied him from New York, and Vladimir Fabry, who was included because of his close personal knowledge of the situation as ONUC's legal adviser. Bill Ranallo, the Secretary-General's personal bodyguard from New York, was joined by a colleague from ONUC's security services, Sergeant Harry Julien. Alice Lalande, a Canadian secretary who had worked with ONUC from the beginning of the Operation, was to look after secretarial work. The rest of the party included two Swedish guards, a U.N. French security guard, and an Irish investigator. The Captain of the aircraft, Hallonquist, was assisted by a crew of five Swedes.

Hammarskjold's plane left Ndjili airport at 3.51 in the afternoon on its seven-hour flight over the trackless forests of the Congo. It made due east to avoid Katanga, taking a southerly turn at the Congo's eastern frontier, flying over Lake Tanganyika. At about two hours' flying distance from Ndola, it made its first contact—with Salisbury. At ten minutes past ten it flashed past the Ndola airport in the pale light of a dying moon after having received clearance to land. Lord Alport, the British High Commissioner to the Central African Federation, had arrived in the afternoon from Salisbury to attend to arrangements for the conference. He had earlier received Lord Lansdowne who, as arranged, made ready to depart when the Albertina appeared in the skies. The Albertina was making the usual turn in preparation for landing when radio communication with it was suddenly lost. Alport, who had been conversing with Tshombe in the office of the Airport Manager, Williams, conjectured that 'something must have caused Mr. Hammarskjold to change his mind and to decide not to land at Ndola as previously intended'. But Lansdowne had categorically told Alport and the Rhodesian authorities that Hammarskjold was definitely coming and he himself 'was absolutely convinced' of it.

When the Albertina vanished carrying on board its messenger of peace, the Ndola airport officials began to speculate on the political reasons for its failure to land, ignoring the steps which, as technicians, they were enjoined to take. The 'Uncertainty Phase' must be declared thirty minutes after an incoming plane fails to land, yet this was delayed by another fifty-two minutes. The 'Alert Phase' comes into operation five minutes after landing clearance has been given and a plane unaccountably fails to land. This phase was not declared at all. The final warning, the 'Distress Phase', should immediately follow the 'Alert Phase' when the absence of news spells danger of a probable crash. This was issued only six hours later. These facts are clear from the reports both of the Rhodesian and United Nations investigation Commissions. In other respects, however, there were important differences of opinion in the reports of the two Commissions.

The wreck, although it lay only some nine miles from the airport, was not located until fifteen hours later. All but one of the sixteen passengers were dead and most of the bodies and the fuselage were badly burnt. The plane had struck the tree tops and then cut a long swathe in the jungle before it crashed and went up in flames. The Secretary-General had been thrown out of the plane with grievous injuries, but his body was not scorched. The Rhodesian Commission said that his death was instantaneous, but a Swedish Commission was of the opinion that it was not and timely medical help would have briefly prolonged his life, although the injuries were fatal. The only survivor was Sergeant Julien who had a broken ankle and fifty five-degree burns. He lingered on for a few days. His life could have been saved if he had not lain exposed to the African sun for so many hours.

The glow caused by the explosion of the aircraft on impact had not gone unnoticed. A European assistant inspector of the Rhodesian police saw it and reported it to the Ndola police station, but he associated it with a bush fire or a flash of lightning. Later that night, however, another European police officer thought the matter was of sufficient importance, as the flash had been seen not far from the airport, to report it to the airport authorities. The Airport Manager, Williams, who had been vainly calling the Albertina and had checked up with Salisbury and Lusaka, asked Salisbury to contact Léopoldville. Not receiving any word, he closed the airport at 1.15 in the morning and left for his hotel. When he was later awakened to be informed by the police officers of what they had seen, he thought that nothing could be done at that hour. When he returned to work at 7 a.m. on 18 September, he found that Salisbury had already issued a Distress signal at 4.45 that morning.

There was a good part of a squadron of Rhodesian Air Force planes on the runway at Ndola and also three American planes. Yet Salisbury had not given the order for an aerial search although first light was at 4 a.m. ONUC officials at Léopoldville were distraught when they heard of the disappearance of the Albertina and they approached the American Ambassador for help. He immediately sent his air attaché to Ndola who arrived there at 10 a.m. and insisted on an immediate aerial search. It was then that a Rhodesian pilot went up in the air and located the wreckage at about 1 p.m. The American air attaché, Colonel Ben Matlick, was the first to reach the scene by vehicle.

There was intense suspicion the world over that Hammarskjold had fallen victim to foul play for there were many who would have welcomed his disappearance. But the Rhodesian Commission came to the conclusion that the crash was the result of pilot error. The U.N. Commission, however, left open several possibilities, although there was no conclusive evidence about any. It did not rule out the suggestion of sabotage as the Albertina had been left unguarded at Ndjili airport for several hours. True, the cabin had been inspected by U.N. security officers before the plane took off, but the possibility of a time bomb being inserted into the undercarriage, or of tampering with the braking system or controls could not be overruled. No tape recordings were kept of the conversation between the Ndola control tower and the Albertina and the U.N. Commission felt that the possibility of incomplete landing instructions could not be excluded.

There were statements by some African witnesses that they had seen a smaller plane attack the Albertina. The U.N. Commission found the denial of the Belgian pilot of the Fouga not entirely conclusive, and was of the opinion that the possibility of an unknown aircraft having been in the air could not be ignored. But there was no concrete evidence to prove that the Albertina had in fact been shot down, either from the air or from land. As for pilot error, the U.N. team again did not rule it out, but it found no indication that it was the probable cause. In its view, without specific proof to the contrary, none of the possibilities could be excluded and they attached equal weight to all of them. They were very critical of the lack of initiative and timely action on the part of the Ndola airport authorities. If the latter had acted according to the accepted rules, Sergeant Julien at least would have been saved and the mystery of the tragedy would have been unravelled.

The cause of the disaster will never be definitely known. But the tragedy shows how vulnerable to the hand of man and to shafts of fortune was the foremost servant of the world community. Unprotected and under relentless pressure, he was carried almost inexorably to his death while on a mission of peace. He who had consorted with presidents and kings met his end in a lonely jungle, clutching leaves and grass in his dead hands.

Hammarskjold's decision to embark on his last desperate venture was forced on him by the pressure of political circumstances. He was determined to bring the bloodshed in Katanga to an end. He would have done it in his own way without appearing in sackcloth and ashes to meet a perfidious politician for whom he had both contempt and pity. But the forces working against him were vast and inscrutable. He was haunted by the ultimatum of the British Government and the warnings of the United States. He had no choice but to throw himself as a pawn into the desperate gamble.

Hammarskjold was to have left for New York on 16 September, leaving categorical instructions to ONUC to end the fighting by means of every device of conciliation. But Lansdowne's visit forced him to defer his departure. He wanted to meet Tshombe hoping against hope to bring him over with him to Léopoldville. Instead, he agreed to meet on doubtful terrain to negotiate a truce, practically on Tshombe's terms. He needed time, but time was denied him. Instead of keeping himself in reserve, leaving it to his subordinates to bring about a truce, he was himself forced into humbling his high office and risking his personal reputation and indeed his life.

The Secretary-General well knew, while on his last journey, of the storm that would await him at the United Nations. He would have been attacked for treating with Tshombe from a position of demonstrated weakness. A truce would have been equated with surrender. Even his erstwhile supporters would have joined with his opponents in the outcry. He must have been keenly aware that in his last sacrificial act, 'the road of possibility might lead to the Cross'.[1]

The outcome of the Ndola meeting could not have been foretold and could well have been failure. Hammarskjold had as

[1] Dag Hammarskjold, *Markings*, p. 72.

his shield only his personal integrity and his devotion to peace. On the other side, forces backed by power and wealth were ranged against him. He well realized that 'the Way leads to a triumph which is a catastrophe, and to a catastrophe which is a triumph'.

CHAPTER 17

Lumumba: Dream and Reality

The personality of Lumumba, around whom swirled so much national and international controversy, holds a singular fascination. Springing from simple origins in an obscure Congolese village, with no formal education beyond secondary school, Lumumba, in his short life, became a burning symbol of African nationalism.

Lumumba's confrontation with his times was both on the domestic and international arenas. To the inherent difficulties of the situation that faced him was added a third dimension, that of his complex personality. To friends and foes alike, Lumumba had a magnetic quality which powerfully attracted or repelled. In everything that he said or did, there was a strong element of passionate involvement. His triumphs and failures, therefore, have an extraordinary quality of personal drama. Given the brevity of his appearance on the world stage and his relative youth, many questions about his personality may never receive adequate answers. Nevertheless, the fact that he should have been so loved, or hated, by millions throughout the world, is a measure of the significance of the place that he fills in history.

Lumumba has been praised as a nationalist, denounced as a Communist, branded as an inverted racist, and condemned as a fanatic. The extent to which these epithets can be found to contain a substratum of truth would help to throw light on his character and attributes. But Lumumba's quality and worth have also to be weighed in the context of the situation in which he lived and worked and in his reactions to the forces, domestic and foreign, with which he had to contend. True, he was conditioned by the circumstances of his life and the limited extent of his experience. But by the impact of his character and ideas, he, in turn, influenced the conditions surrounding him as well as the future course of events.

Lumumba's political career was enmeshed in a climacteric period of history which witnessed the emancipation of the peoples of Africa. Unwilling to bow to the tyranny of circumstance, he struggled with fate, seeking to force the pattern of developments into the image of his dreams. But he was unable to control the forces which he had himself helped to generate and in the resulting violence and disintegration, himself fell victim to the frenzy of local hatred and the virulence of foreign intrigue. If his qualities of character had been equalled by the fervour of his convictions, he would have shown a greater measure of patience, combined with resilience. Obstinacy is not strength, nor is passion statesmanship. Unable to comprehend the dilemma and lacking the time in which to benefit from experience, Lumumba refused to bend and was therefore broken on the wheel of destiny.

Patrice Lumumba was born on 2 July 1925 in the small village of Katako-Kombe in the Sankuru district of Kasai province. His tribe was the Batetela, whose most important neighbours were the Baluba, a people regarded with suspicion and sometimes hostility on account of their aggressive social and economic behaviour.

Lumumba's formal education began at the local school run by a Catholic religious order. There, Lumumba learned to read and write French and acquired the basic elements of a primary education. As an adolescent during World War II, he attended a Protestant boarding school where he studied to be a male nurse. He did not finish the course of study and left in 1943 in search of a livelihood.

At the age of eighteen Lumumba moved to Kindu, a provincial city in Kivu, where he secured a job as a clerk with a European mining syndicate. Here Lumumba had no difficulty in establishing himself in *évolué*[1] circles and was soon considered by others as among the black élite of the Congo. Then, according to Bantu custom, he gathered funds to pay the bride price for a wife, Pauline, who, like him, was a Batetela. They had originally met when Lumumba was studying at the Protestant

---

[1] *Évolué*: the designation of Congolese who had been officially recognized, after passing prescribed tests, as 'civilized' or 'evolved'.

mission school, but Pauline, like nearly all Congolese women at that time, was illiterate. He and his wife apparently had a good relationship, Pauline remaining loyal to her husband through both his triumphs and misfortunes, and stoically bearing the burdens of behaving like a European woman, a role for which she had neither received any training nor for which had she any aptitude. The Lumumbas were parents to four children, the only girl dying in infancy in 1960 when her father was under house-arrest in Léopoldville.

After more than six years in Kindu, Lumumba moved to Léopoldville, where he found work as a postal clerk. He stayed in Léopoldville for slightly over a year during which he came to realize that even with his status as an *évolué*, his supposed equality with a Congolese European would always remain an illusion. The Europeans of Léopoldville numbered several thousands and formed a tightly segregated white colony, living in areas that were forbidden to blacks, except those on official business. Once, his curiosity overcoming him, Lumumba wandered into some of the wide, tree-lined streets of spacious mansions where the whites lived. Awed by the evidence of opulence, Lumumba did not pay attention to where he was going, and bumped into a white woman on the side-walk. The infuriated woman called Lumumba 'a dirty monkey',[1] one of the most stinging insults which a European could level at a Congolese. Lumumba was stunned by this encounter and hurriedly retreated to his familiar surroundings in Léopoldville's African quarter.

This experience served to bring home to him the depth of the social chasm and the fact that the colour of his skin would always prevent him from becoming equal to a European. He suppressed his disquietude by pursuing with even greater energy his career ambitions, working tirelessly at the Post Office and attending special evening classes to accelerate his advance in the black clerical hierarchy.

In 1951, after having done well in a series of post office examinations, Lumumba was promoted to the position of clerk in the postal money-order section of the Stanleyville Post Office. His first stay in Stanleyville, however, was brief since after a few months he was offered a more prestigious position as Director

---

[1] Pierre de Vos, *Vie et mort de Lumumba*, p. 30.

of the National Institute for Agricultural Study of the Congo (INEAC from its French initials) at Yangambi near Stanleyville. His two years at INEAC were important for the formation and development of his ideas and personality. While at INEAC, Lumumba discovered his skill as an orator and his ability to captivate an audience. He was a popular lecturer and soon realized that he enjoyed speaking before crowds, thus unconsciously acquiring a sense of self-confidence and an awareness of his own abilities.

Lumumba's students were aspiring young *évolués* who admired and respected their professor and inquisitively sought from him knowledge of the wider world of his experience. The most serious questions always concerned relations between Europeans and blacks, and Lumumba crystallized his thoughts and experiences with whites into general 'theories' which he presented to his students. He felt that all Europeans could be grouped into two classes. The 'petty whites' who had come to the Congo only 'because they were nothing in Belgium' treated the blacks cruelly. These especially hated the *évolués* because the latter were 'more intelligent than they'. The 'good whites', on the other hand, came from a better class, were well-educated, and always 'behaved with dignity and respected us'.[1] Even with the 'good whites' with whom an African could establish amicable relations, the intimacy of true friendship was impossible. Lumumba's recognition of this duality, however, did not imply his rejection of it. Indeed, he still firmly believed in full cooperation between Africans and Belgians but any ideal of a Congo entity distinct from Belgium was still beyond his range of consciousness.

In 1953 Lumumba returned to Stanleyville where he resumed work in the city's post office as an accountant in the division of money orders. The energy with which he applied himself to his job was matched by his participation in cultural, professional, and academic societies. He also developed his organizational skills, as evidenced by his effectiveness as president or secretary of no less than seven organizations, among the most important of which were the Association of Former Students of the Fathers of Schnet (ADAPES)[2] and the Asso-

[1] Pierre de Vos, *Vie et mort de Lumumba.*
[2] Religious Order of Catholic teaching priests.

ciation of Indigenous Employees of the Congo (APIC). APIC, in which Lumumba served first as secretary, and later as president, was an organization for the protection of the interests of African civil servants. Lumumba thrived on his numerous responsibilities, and eagerly welcomed the prestige which his acceptance as a leader of the *évolués* brought him. For added distinction, he began to wear the spectacles which later became one of his symbols.

Lumumba's role as President of APIC made him a spokesman for local blacks in the eyes of both Congolese and Europeans. Therefore, in 1954, when the new Colonial Minister, Auguste Biussert, decreed that *évolués* were eligible to participate in the Congo branches of Belgian political parties, Lumumba was the black whom Stanleyville's white politicians considered to be the most attractive candidate for membership. It was reasoned that whichever party Lumumba could be enticed to join would acquire prestige as his personal popularity would influence other *évolués* to apply for membership. The Liberal party, which in Belgium was a staid party of business interests and elder politicians, persistently courted him. Lumumba was aware of the self-interest behind the sudden friendliness of the white political parties and proved to be a shrewd bargainer. He recognized that the Liberals were more willing than the Socialists to be generous with their terms for party admission, and after some serious negotiations, decided to affiliate himself with the Liberal party on condition that he be awarded the office of vice-president. This represented a stroke of luck for his personal prestige and for his political career. The Liberal party also benefited from its new vice-president, for as had been anticipated, most of the young *évolués* of Stanleyville quickly joined the party.

As the Liberal party's vice-president, Lumumba functioned as the organization's main representative and leader in the African sections of Stanleyville. He was an articulate speaker and easily developed a style of political oratory that captivated, almost entranced, his audiences and he soon became the life and soul of the Liberal party in the black quarter of Stanleyville. As a popular politician, Lumumba used his influence and oratory to express the basic demands of the blacks for equal work and equal pay. For the Congolese, national independence was beyond their dreams, although in some parts of the Congo, notably in the Bas-Congo area, faint stirrings of an independence movement were noticeable. The demand for equality of opportunity in the social and material fields was of deep significance for the evolution of the independence movement, as it was Belgium's failure to satisfy the aspirations of the urbanized Congolese which eventually led them to seek independence as the only alternative for achieving their ambitions.

The active interest of the *évolués* in securing equality with the whites became intensified after 1954. In the Stanleyville Post Office, since a white clerk received five times the salary of a black clerk of equal grade, the irritation and sense of grievance over unequal status were very real. The Congolese decided to establish their own organization which would protect their interests and work for improvement in their standards. Lumumba appeared as the ready-made president of the new APIPO (Association des Postiers Indigènes de la Province-Orientale). By this time, his growing influence was beginning to attract the attention of the Belgian provincial administration, and there was some concern that he might become too powerful. He now had effective control in three organizations whose aims, at least indirectly, challenged the political decisions of the Europeans.

Lumumba was now easily the most prominent Congolese in Stanleyville, and his prestige was further enhanced in June 1955 on the occasion of King Baudouin's tour of the Congo. When Lumumba was introduced to the monarch he attempted to explain some of the disadvantages from which *évolués* suffered as a result of their unequal status. He accepted the concept of a Belgian-Congolese Community and, during the next year, developed his own ideas as to the form it should assume. He organized his thinking in a long essay which he tried to get published in Belgium, but it was not until after his assassination that the thesis was printed.

Le Congo, terre d'avenir, est-il menacé? contains Lumumba's thoughts on a Eurafrican Community. The essential aspect of the Community was the idea of equality with, rather than independence of, the white European rulers. This equality would be legitimized through the granting of political rights to the handful of black élite, but not to other Congolese. 'For

the non-*évolué* masses the *status quo* could still be maintained
and the masses directed and guided . . . by the responsible élite;
the white and the African', and he added that universal suffrage
would be permitted in the Congo when literacy, which was to
be the qualification for voting, would become a standard skill
of all Africans.

Lumumba essentially advocated a reinstitution of the Congo
Free State which had existed prior to 1908 but one in which
'there would be internal autonomy. This autonomous republic
or Independent State of the Congo would form a federation
with Belgium.'

It was important, however, that formal recognition of the
Congo's independent status be accorded by Belgium, since without this evidence of good faith, the Congolese would not feel
equal. On this point Lumumba wrote: 'If the black man dreams
then of independence, it is not out of hatred of the white man
or in order to drive him out of Africa, but out of the *unique*
wish to be not only a free man, but also a *citizen* in the service
of his country and not eternally a subject in the service of the
whites.'[1]

Lumumba's attention to the future of the Congo primarily
focused upon the new political relationship with Belgium. His
views on nationalism, however, reveal that he accepted without
question the concept of a Congolese identity, rather than tribal
identities. He opposed basing loyalty on racial foundations
and cautioned: 'That which we must avoid in our country is
negative nationalism: that narrow nationalism which is a
camouflage of racism against and hatred for those who are
not of one's own race.' Lumumba recognized that there were
deep underlying causes motivating racial animosities, and advocated measures to abolish the social, political, and economic
inequalities which fed African dissatisfactions and reinforced
European prejudices.

Lumumba now began to develop an interest in Africa outside
the Congo. He learned of Kwame Nkrumah and became impressed with a leader who had gone to prison for his anti-colonial
activities. He became familiar with *Black Power*, the provocative
book of the American negro writer, Richard Wright, whose

[1] Lumumba, *Le Congo, terre d'avenir*. . . . Lumumba's emphasis.

ideas certainly had an influence upon Lumumba's thinking, but his commitment to friendship and cooperation with the Belgians was still too strong to be seriously jolted.

In June 1956 Lumumba was among a group of *évolués* who visited Belgium for a two-week study-tour as guests of the Belgian Government. This trip was for him the first occasion he had to observe the world outside the Congo. In Brussels and other Belgian cities. he and his *évolué* companions were treated with respect and dignity. They had an opportunity to meet many Belgians prominent in the political, industrial, financial, commercial, and labour affairs of their country. The Congolese were consulted about proposals for a new regulatory code concerning both white and black employees of the civil service administration in the Congo. This new statute would not grant equality of salary and position to the blacks, but it would make higher-grade jobs accessible to qualified *évolués* and enforce financial adjustments that would lessen the discriminatory character of the wage scale. These gestures on the part of the Belgian Government reinforced Lumumba's confidence in the intentions of Belgium.

Soon, however, his attitude was to suffer a sharp reversal. On 1 July 1956 when he returned to Stanleyville from his tour of Belgium, he was arrested and charged with a minor embezzlement during his tenure as money-order clerk. He did not deny that he had taken the money but insisted that he had not stolen it, having only borrowed it in small sums over the past five years. To prove his honesty, he confessed that he had already returned nearly $50. The white court remained unmoved by Lumumba's arguments and sentenced him to two years' imprisonment.

His arrest and imprisonment marked a major turning point in the development of his ideas. He refused to acknowledge his culpability, and regarded himself as a victim of white injustice. He reasoned that he had served the Government loyally on a salary that was a mere pittance compared to a white bureaucrat's on the same job. Furthermore, the Europeans had stolen money from the Congo for centuries, and they could hardly accuse him of being a thief. From now on, his attitude towards the whites of the Congo would bear the scar of his humiliation. He never again felt that he could trust a white man; he would remain ambivalent and suspicious, even paranoid, in his approach to Europeans. Four years later, the effects were to be evident in his treatment of Dag Hammarskjold and the Belgians.

While Lumumba was in prison, the movement for Congolese independence began to gather momentum. In the summer of 1956, Joseph Ileo published *Conscience Africaine* in which he called for the gradual independence of the Congo. Within a few weeks, this manifesto was countered by the Abako party which presented its demands for immediate independence. An entirely new dimension was introduced into the political discussions of the Congolese élite of which Lumumba was able to keep track in prison from newspapers. In July 1957, Lumumba was released from prison and returned to Stanleyville where he was welcomed as a hero by the Congolese. The Polar Brewery offered him a position as sales director for the African quarter of Léopoldville.

He was soon involved in Léopoldville's political life. His new job as salesman facilitated his contacts with diverse Congolese, and while he successfully promoted the sale of Polar beer, he was also able to measure his skill as an orator. He quickly established a popular base in the African quarter and developed relations with nationalists such as Ileo, Adoula, and Joseph Ngalula. In October 1958, they joined Lumumba in founding the M.N.C. (Mouvement National Congolais), Lumumba's organizational skill being primarily responsible for the rapid and widespread growth of the party. Many important Congolese politicians became its members at one time or another, including Mobutu, Kalonji, Okito, Gbenye, Mpolo, Nendaka, and Songolo. The M.N.C. was committed to an independent Congo based upon a strong central government It stood for Congolese nationalism and firmly opposed threats to the concept of a unitary state posed by parties like the Abako which were based upon tribal loyalties.

Lumumba's climb to political acclaim was meteoric, especially after the establishment of the M.N.C. He became the most dominating personality within the party and by the spring of 1959, the M.N.C. was identified with his name. But his supremacy did not go uncontested. In Léopoldville, some of the leading *évolués* resented the diminution of their own influence which his ascendancy had brought about. Within a year of its founding, some influential men like Adoula and Ileo had broken with the M.N.C. as they felt that Lumumba was arrogating too much authority to himself and was not consulting them and other party leaders on major decisions and policies. This left Lumumba as the unchallenged authority within the M.N.C. at a time when the party was organizing and expanding rapidly throughout the Congo. But he was also deprived of some valuable lieutenants who could not be replaced easily. This may have been a factor in his increasingly rhetorical radicalism during the summer of 1959, since, as the unchallenged leader of the only national mass political party, he had no moderating advice from men who were his intellectual equals.

Despite the growing disenchantment felt by some political leaders after 1959 towards the President of the M.N.C., Lumumba's popularity among diverse groups of Congolese continued to rise. The strength of his influence was demonstrated during the pre-Independence elections of May 1960. The M.N.C. emerged as the largest voting bloc in both the Senate and the Chamber of Deputies and was the only political party that did well throughout the Congo. Lumumba's awareness of his own popularity reinforced his belief that his goals were truly national and that his critics among the Léopoldville politicians were motivated by self-interest disruptive of national unity. His overweening confidence in his messianic role as the sole voice and defender of the true interests of his people betrayed a fundamental weakness in his character, a failing which later was to bring tragedy upon himself and disaster to the Congo.

Lumumba's involvement in Congolese politics, however, did not fully absorb his abundant energies, as he also developed a keen interest in the political problems of the rest of Africa. He began corresponding with important nationalist leaders in Ghana, Kenya, and other African states. He was especially attracted by Ghana which had won its independence from Britain in 1957, and he was an admirer of Nkrumah with whom he established an intellectual friendship. Nkrumah's visionary goals of pan-Africanism, which were being formulated at that time, deeply impressed him, although he never developed any systematic ideas of his own on the subject. However, he maintained his interest in the common problems facing African nationalism, and when Nkrumah sponsored the First Pan-African Conference in Accra in December 1958, Lumumba attended with the objective of meeting his mentor and learning what other African leaders were doing and thinking.

The Conference turned out to be an important opportunity for Lumumba to meet many other leading figures in the African nationalist movements. He learnt of the depth and extent of anti-colonial feeling among the Africans, which came as a revelation to him. He discovered that there was a fierce pride in being African, and overcame his complexes towards the Europeans. But he also developed a latent fear of and strong prejudice against colonial domination. When he became Prime Minister some eighteen months later, prejudice would often take irrational control over pride and sometimes prevent him from an objective evaluation of policies in his relations with the United Nations.

Political developments in the Congo started moving towards the climax of Independence after Lumumba's return from the Accra Conference. The year 1959 began with riots in Léopoldville which the Force Publique and police were only able to suppress with much bloodshed. These riots took both the colonial administration and the black politicians by surprise. Lumumba realized that the psychological wounds caused by the several hundred casualties would be difficult to heal, but he remained willing to cooperate with the Belgians and exhorted the M.N.C. to work with 'calm and dignity' for the achievement of independence, fearing that violence would play into the hands of the colonial administration.

A special parliamentary commission from Brussels had recently recommended independence for the Congo despite the opposition of prominent European settlers. Recognizing the importance of convincing the commission that the aspirations of the Congolese were both legitimate and not irreconcilable with Belgium's basic interests, Lumumba distributed a political tract in which he warned his followers that they should 'consider as enemies' any Belgians who were displaying hostility to the independence proposals by boycotting or demonstrating against the visit of the Colonial Minister.

But Lumumba's efforts at moderation served only to arouse the enmity of the more extreme Belgian *colons*, as they deeply distrusted him and saw in his advocacy of independence the

worst form of villainy. The reaction of the 'ultras' was to demand Lumumba's arrest to prevent any kind of agreement
between the Congolese politicians and the Brussels Government. The ultras eventually succeeded in their machinations
and Lumumba was arrested on the technical ground that
M.N.C. pamphlets did not bear the name and address of the
editor. Lumumba's political imprisonment was brief, however,
since the Colonial Minister immediately intervened to secure
his release. But the consequences of his few hours in prison
were fateful: he acquired the halo of a hero among the Congolese; his passionate devotion to the cause of independence
deepened; the hatred of the ultras was intensified.

In the spring of 1959, Lumumba embarked upon a private
trip to Belgium, stopping en route at Ibadan in Nigeria for a
Conference on African Culture. Eager to make the position of
the M.N.C. known to Belgian politicians, he sought out leading
Belgians in order to present his views. He stressed both the
positive and negative aspects of colonial rule, emphasizing the
imperative need to grant independence in order to preserve
what was good. He did not demand a severance of relations
between Belgium and the Congo, but only a significant modification of the nature of the relationship, so that the Congolese
could assume larger responsibility for the management of their
own affairs. He advocated the institution of a provisional Congolese government as a first step on the road to full independence.
He still had ideas about a community between Belgium and the
Congo, although there was a shift in emphasis on the independent status of the Congo within an alliance between Belgium
and her former colony. He also stood firmly by the concept of
a united Congo as opposed to any kind of federal union, such
as was then being championed by Abako leaders. In countless
interviews with Belgian politicians and newspaper reporters
and in lectures, Lumumba continued to stress his theme of
unity, independence, and cooperation.

In the autumn of 1959, Lumumba made plans to hold the
M.N.C.'s first National Conference in Stanleyville, the city
where the party had become most influential during its first
year of existence. It was during this Conference that he made
his call for immediate independence. On the following evening,
there were some violent clashes in the African quarter between

Congolese and the white-officered Force Publique. Lumumba was charged with fomenting these incidents, and arrested. He remained in prison for several weeks, finally being released upon the insistence of the Congolese politicians who had been invited to Brussels in the winter of 1959–60 for the Round Table Conference. His third imprisonment made him a political martyr. He emerged from his confinement as the most popular leader among the Congolese and was able to ride the crest of his fame all the way to the Prime Ministership within six months.

When Lumumba acceded to power, the immensity of the problems facing the Republic would have daunted the most seasoned of statesmen. They demanded exceptional qualities of leadership combined with executive capacity of a high order. Lumumba discerned the needs but misjudged the methods. On assuming the mantle of leadership, he began to alienate his associates, their festering resentments stemming from aspects of his own character. These were becoming evident when he established his political base in the M.N.C., but they became still more glaring when he was elevated to the Prime Ministership. Lumumba proved strangely insensitive to the susceptibilities of others, while deeply conscious of his own.

The vast extent of his responsibilities overwhelmed Lumumba and drove him to frenetic bouts of activity. His tremendous but untamed energy led him to attempt to direct every aspect of national endeavour. He thrived on complete involvement and was unable to delegate authority. He wanted to know everything at first hand and instinctively mistrusted any information which he had not personally gathered. But his sources were not untainted and his judgment was not infallible. Despite his undoubted intelligence and natural shrewdness, he remained unaware of the corrosive effects of his behaviour on others. Whenever a contradictory reality confronted his ideals, he would reject the reality rather than try to relate it to the ideal. This aspect of his personality proved to be a major weakness. When men like Adoula and Ileo defected from him, he was unable to comprehend their motives, feeling instead that they had betrayed the nationalist cause.

This flaw displayed itself in his relations with Kasavubu. True, no two persons could have been more different. They represented in their persons and in their politics two distinct and conflicting national tendencies. Kasavubu was more conscious of local loyalties and tribal affiliations; Lumumba was unshakeably committed to the concept of nationhood and a unitary state. In their personal temperaments, Kasavubu was aloof, slow-moving, and deliberate, while Lumumba was gregarious, with a passion for instant action fired by demonic energy. Kasavubu was an inarticulate recluse whose appeal was largely confined to his own tribe; Lumumba was a fiery orator with a mass appeal moving in an aura of admirers and acolytes. Kasavubu made few enemies and few friends. Lumumba made both firm friends and implacable foes. Both men were incapable of team-work, Kasavubu because of his secretiveness, Lumumba because of his personal idiosyncrasies.

In their concept of governance, the two men differed widely. Both were intense nationalists, but while Kasavubu was open to compromise, Lumumba was inflexible. Kasavubu favoured the traditional African way of palaver; Lumumba insisted on forceful action. Neither was inspired by ideology in the accepted sense of the term. Ideas such as Communism and anti-Communism were entirely alien to their consciousness. Both wanted an independent Congo, free of the rival power blocs, a Congo that was master in its own house. But if Kasavubu claimed to be the father of the nation, Lumumba regarded himself as the messiah of his people.

Lumumba's suspicious nature, which he shared with many Congolese, led him into serious errors on the international stage, the greatest of which was his opposition to the United Nations. His blind, unjustified prejudice against an organization that had come only to serve his people was to cost him dear.

The rift with Dag Hammarskjold was a long step in Lumumba's downfall. The Secretary-General had thrown himself with his customary zeal into his task and his support was there for the asking. But the United Nations could act only according to recognized procedures and within certain limitations. The encounter between the African proletarian and the Swedish aristocrat need not have been disastrous. If differences had been confined to principles and methods, there would have been room for adjustment. But when Lumumba impetuously chose to reduce them to personal accusations and innuendoes and, above all, to a question of integrity, no common ground was left. The sensitive and cultivated European and the proud and domineering African were thrown apart by an unbridge-able chasm.

A man who could stand up to his gaolers at Thysville and refuse to compromise to save his life was possessed of no ordinary degree of courage. Lumumba's personal integrity shone like a light in the darkness of the prevailing corruption. But his un-doubted gifts were eroded by fatal defects of character and temperament. If he had lived, he might have overcome the aberrations of his nature, but time was not on his side. His cruel end was a catastrophe for the Congo and a tragedy for Africa.

CHAPTER 18

Hammarskjold: Self-Realization through Action

The explanation of how man should live a life of active social service in full harmony with himself as a member of the community of spirit, I found in the writings of the great mediaeval mystics for whom 'self-surrender' had been the way to self-realization, and who in 'singleness of mind' and 'inwardness' had found strength to say yes to every demand, which the needs of their neighbours made them face, and to say yes also to every fate life had in store for them when they followed the call of duty, as they understood it. 'Love'—that much misused and misinterpreted word—for them meant simply an overflowing of the strength with which they felt themselves filled when living in true self-oblivion. And this love found natural expressions in unhesitant fulfilment of duty and in an unreserved acceptance of life, whatever it brought them personally of toil, suffering—and happiness.[1]

These words sum up Dag Hammarskjold's philosophy of action. It was because of his undying faith that in following the call of duty lay the way to self-realization that he unhesitatingly said yes to the urgent needs of the Congo. In response to the appeal of the Congolese Government, he immediately convened a meeting of the Security Council, under his authority as Secretary-General, invoking, for the first time in United Nations history, the use of Article 99 of the Charter.

It was not because of any desire for self-glorification or extension of his personal authority, as some of his critics say, that Hammarskjold embarked on what was evidently so difficult and hazardous an enterprise. In doing so, he accepted whatever fate lay ahead of him in the service of a disinterested and noble

[1] Interview given by Dag Hammarskjold to Edward R. Murrow in 1954.

cause. The deep and unmerited suffering which became his lot was part of the sacrifice, rendered in a spirit of 'self-surrender'. Tragically, Hammarskjold was denied the happiness of seeing the fulfilment of his efforts and the vindication of his faith.

Dag Hammarskjold was undoubtedly one of the most remarkable figures of our time. To the outside world, he was known mostly by his extraordinary work in quest of peace and international harmony. Although a man is best known by his works, in Hammarskjold's case this was only partially true. For he lived an intense inner life of struggle and anxious questioning in search of ultimate Truth, to be realized not through meditation alone or by withdrawal from the world, but through ceaseless and selfless action. This essential element of Hammarskjold's being was no more than a matter of surmise even amongst his closest associates, and it came to light only on the posthumous publication of *Markings*, which Hammarskjold described as 'a sort of *white book* concerning my negotiations with myself—and with God'.

Hammarskjold had been catapulted to his high office in 1953 from a position of comparative international obscurity. His predecessor, Trygve Lie, thought he would be no more than a glorified clerk. Yet, during his eight and a half years in office, Hammarskjold was always at the epicentre of the crises that repeatedly shook the world, many of which, in large measure, he was able to resolve. He succeeded in establishing for himself a position where he could meet as an equal the rulers of the world, Kings, Presidents, and Foreign Ministers. He even came to being widely regarded as the authentic conscience of mankind.

Hammarskjold belonged to the long-forgotten tradition of philosopher-kings. But he possessed none of the acknowledged attributes of kingship. He held no territory; commanded no army; had no budget apart from the contributions of member states, no diplomatic service, and no intelligence agency. And he was answerable to as many masters as there were member states in the United Nations. That one man, in the single-minded pursuit of an ideal—enshrined in the Charter of the United Nations—should have been able to make such a powerful impact on world history in the midst of the clash of great powers and rival interests, provides a reaffirmation of the supremacy of truth over violence, of principle over the arrogance of power. To understand the mainsprings of Hammarskjold's ideas and actions as Secretary-General of the United Nations, one must understand the evolution of his personal philosophy in which he was engaged throughout a lifetime of ceaseless activity both as civil servant and statesman.

'In our era, the road to holiness necessarily passes through action,' said Hammarskjold. His goal was self-realization, to be achieved through right action. His musings and meditations were devoted to the comprehension of the nature of fundamental reality. This he found in an overwhelming sense of oneness, an acute awareness of the indivisibility of life. To him, service to man was service to God. In self-surrender lay the prior condition for self-realization in action. Therefore, the aspirant that Hammarskjold was, after purifying himself of self-seeking, reached outwards towards action. From action he turned inwards into the deep recesses of his being, the interaction of action and thought enriching and ennobling both.

To Hammarskjold, man was not the doer, but only an instrument, and each act to him was 'an act of creation, conscious, because you are a human being with human responsibilities, but governed, nevertheless, by the power beyond human consciousness which has created man'.[1]

Hammarskjold wrote: 'Pray that your loneliness may spur you into finding something to live for, great enough to die for.'[2] In complete self-surrender, life would receive from Life all its meaning. In the United Nations, which he sought to fashion into a true instrument for international harmony and peace, Hammarskjold found the ideal means for the realization of his spiritual goals. He understood the limitations of the Organization, but also its potential, and described it as 'a feeble creation of men's hands—but you have to give your all to this human dream for the sake of that which alone gives it reality'.

Later, enlarging on his ideas, he called the United Nations 'a jealous dream which refuses to share you with anybody or anything else: the greatest creation of mankind . . . in which it is the noblest dream of the individual—to lose himself. There-

[1] Hammarskjold, *Markings*, p. 139.
[2] Ibid., p. 85.

fore: gladly death or humiliation if that is what thy dream demands.'[1] Of the aims of the Organization he said: 'It is an *idea* you are serving—an idea which must be victorious if a mankind worth the name is to survive.'[2] With such an invincible faith in what destiny had willed as his path of duty, he had a sense of calling which became heightened as his responsibilities increased. He was therefore able in all sincerity to say: 'For someone whose job so obviously mirrors man's extraordinary possibilities and responsibilities, there is no excuse if he loses his sense of "having been called". So long as he keeps that, everything has a meaning, nothing a price.'[3]

The parallel between Dag Hammarskjold and Mahatma Gandhi in their underlying philosophy of life is immediately striking. Gandhi's life was a pilgrimage in search of Truth,[4] first to discover what it was, and then to pursue it. But not by contemplation alone, for he enjoined on himself the most rigorous discipline aimed at complete self-purification, so that he might become as perfect an instrument of the divine will as possible, receptive to a degree to what he called his 'inner voice'. In the service of the poor and disinherited he sought service of God. His life's work against injustice and oppression found expression in his arduous struggle against British rule, a struggle to be carried out only with a pure heart and pure motives. The use of force he regarded as a sin, and anger and hatred as an offence against God and man. After meditating deeply, cleansed in mind and spirit, he would reach out towards the world and engage in disinterested action. Every such action was for him a sacrificial offering, a stage in the journey towards self-realization, and equally, since it was inspired by love and selflessness, a process of spiritual cleansing for the opponent as well.

Hammarskjold has spoken of that state of grace when words and actions become a timeless prayer. Like Gandhi, he treated others as ends, never as means. Of himself he said he was 'an end only in my capacity as a means: to shift the dividing line in my being between subject and object to a position where the subject, even if it is in me, is outside and above me—so

[1] Ibid., p. 103.
[2] Ibid., p. 119.
[3] Ibid., p. 132.
[4] Gandhi called his autobiography *My Experiments with Truth*.

that my *whole* being may become an instrument for that which is greater than I'.[1]

Dag Hammarskjold, with the reticence of his culture, revealed himself fully only to himself, in complete self-surrender before the Truth. The purity and refinement of his actions alone proclaimed to the outside world the man that he was. But the close identification between the public personality and the private individual, which for Hammarskjold was his supreme goal, was not immediately manifest. This was because Hammarskjold, in the Western tradition, drew a distinction in his worldly life between the public man and the private person.

To Hammarskjold 'the other's face is more important than your own'. Therefore, 'You can only hope to find a lasting solution to a conflict if you have learned to see the other objectively, but at the same time to experience his difficulties subjectively.'[2] How like Gandhi, when he said: 'We must measure people with their own measure and see how far they come up to it.'[3]

Both men conducted their political negotiations from remarkably similar moral standpoints. The 'half-naked fakir' boldly faced the strength and splendour of imperial power; the international civil servant faced the arrogant representatives of sovereign powers. Both believed in complete freedom of manoeuvre, in mobility, and both had a fine sense of timing. Neither held fast to a position if it led to a deadlock or humiliation of the opponent, each searching for viable options to allow a way out of the impasse. Both armed themselves with a complete mastery of the problem, their moral magistracy being founded upon a deep personal integrity and transparent disinterestedness.

Hammarskjold excelled at face-to-face encounters. He had a knack of inspiring confidence and of piercing through another's reserve. He could be disarmingly direct, but also, as need arose, involved and subtle, sometimes to the point of obscurity. His transparent sincerity and sense of dedication inspired a remarkable degree of confidence. His style of speech was highly personal and expressive, and when excited by a thought, as tightly packed as shorthand. It frequently required intellectual athle-

---

[1] *Markings*, p. 64.
[2] Ibid., p. 102.
[3] Louis Fischer, *The Essential Gandhi*, p. 210.

tics to keep pace with his rapid flow of ideas. He carried an air of total attention, alert to the slightest nuance of word or gesture. He seemed able to sense what was in one's mind and to provide the answer even before a thought was fully formulated.

He was shy and awkward with crowds and had no patience with the commonplace or conventional. His friends were few and select and he relaxed only in the company of writers, poets, and close professional associates. The conversation was always at a scintillating level. Literature, art, philosophy, politics were the preferred subjects, and much wit and wisdom flowed at these gatherings. Hammarskjold's time was meticulously conserved and there was no place in it for purely social inanities. One had the feeling that every minute of his day was dedicated to purposeful activity. Even the weekends that he could spare were devoted to reading and communing with Nature.

His outward appearance bespoke the man. Of slender, almost boyish frame, his sharp pointed face was lit by a pair of brilliant blue eyes. Carefully dressed, he gave the impression of buoyancy and freshness. Brisk and alert in his movements, a deep sense of repose underlay his energetic activity. He gestured as he spoke, often joining his tapering fingertips together, with a half-smile playing on his face. An aura of confidence silhouetted his personality.

Though a loyal friend, he could be a ruthless taskmaster. Mistakes he could forgive, but mendacity and meanness never. One could be close to him professionally or intellectually, but the warmth and intimacy of a human relationship escaped him. One could not hope to trespass into the area of silence which lay at the core of his being. His loneliness was that of a mountain peak, noble but distant and forbidding.

Quite early in my association with Hammarskjold, I sensed his interest in matters of the spirit, although it was not before the lapse of several years and episodes in which we were together involved that I began to get an inkling of the depth and nature of his involvement. Hammarskjold, with his sharp antennae, also became conscious of my commitment, as became evident from chance remarks that he made in the course of political and other conversations. In talking of politics, he would bring in spiritual formulations, emphasizing the need for absolute 'integrity' in action, a word to which he attached a deep esoteric meaning. He also spoke of 'maturity' of mind, implying a higher state of understanding. He would frequently refer to the bedrock of principle from which one could never allow oneself to be swept away, whatever the cost. And he would add that he need not say more as he knew that I understood the depth of his meaning. But Hammarskjold never consciously discussed spiritual matters with me; the closest he came to revealing his inner self was in conversations with my wife Susheela at the dinner-table. She recalls their conversations in these words:

'We are on the same wavelength,' Dag Hammarskjold once said to us, many years ago in New York when he showed us that he knew we too were seeking the path to inwardness.

I remember one such time in the early fifties when, sitting next to him at a diplomatic dinner, the whole formality of the occasion slipped away from us as we were drawn into a conversation on Advaita, the philosophy of the Non-dual. Unknown to me, he was drawing on his own rare knowledge of the mediaeval mystics, for there is a passage in Meister Eckhart, singled out by Hammarskjold in *Markings*, that holds in it the essence of our conversation that night. 'But how then am I to love God? You must love him as if he were a non-God, a non-spirit, a non-person, a non-substance: love him simply as the One, the pure and absolute unity in which there is no trace of Duality. And into this One we must let ourselves fall continually from being into non-being.' Dag Hammarskjold adds, 'God help us to do this.'

In 1958, when he came to the Lebanon, Hammarskjold drove through the besieged, entombed city of Beirut. Coming to the hotel, he leapt out of the car in that characteristic, light and free movement, and hailed me, saying, 'I bring you greetings from Lakshmi.'

I smiled, remembering the little statue of the goddess Tara that had been our present to him. She stood now in a niche in his New York office, her inturned glance flowing at one with her outward beauty. It was he who had renamed her Lakshmi, the goddess of auspiciousness and of wealth, the goddess of inner riches.

Even those who knew him slightly knew of his love of the beautiful, his love for literature, for painting. In a crowd, his eyes would travel beyond the people and come to rest on a small picture, such as the abstract painting we had, by Rudolf Ray. He would go up to it and stand before it silently, gravely. Turning to me he would say, 'It has the quality of stone under water.'

Coming to visit us in the Congo, he brought with him a small round box made of moss-leafed stone. I remember his look as I thanked him for it. He replied, 'I wanted to bring you something that had the feeling of stone under water.'

Yet I cannot recall a single personal thing that Dag ever said to me. I cannot remember a single familiar question he ever asked me. How were we in the Congo? Was I afraid? Was it difficult? No, he never asked. Meals were an extension of work schedules, though Dag would often cut across the immediate to place it clearly in its distant perspective—the point of the circle in terms of its circleness.

'Are the hero and the saint identical?' I asked him on one such occasion in the Congo, when our talk had moved from the day's events in Kalina to the wider issues of a nation's history. Dag answered that their likeness to each other lay in their view of themselves; that neither the hero nor the saint sees himself in terms of the world, but as instruments of the Principle (God) and are used by It. In order to fulfil their destiny, he said, 'Some men become heroes, others saints, but both see themselves as instruments of the One. The hero and the saint perform their roles in relation to God alone.'

Yet, such was his shyness that it was not easy to say the very simple things to him. At the farewell luncheon that Dag gave for us when Rajeshwar had completed his mission to the Congo I took the opportunity of talking to him more closely, knowing that a long time might elapse before our next meeting. We talked of the inner direction of progress that a human being must make, away from the personal, which is the limited, to the impersonal, the limitless. The personal must not be rejected, but it must be contained in the impersonal, in the Whole, the One. That, Dag said, is one's work in life.

Then, continuing to speak of the men and women serving under him at the United Nations, Dag said that his presence, his person, should not matter to them. It was the impersonal, the idea of the U.N. that was important, and it was into this that their idealism and their loyalty should be transcended. But, I replied, I had seen what his presence did to people; how it illuminated and inspired their spirit. It was not just the concept of a United Nations that they loved, it was him, the embodiment of that concept. I asked him, 'Can you think of an abstract thing?'

He was quiet for a moment, and then he replied, 'Of course not. People need a symbol, that is right.' He added with grave honesty, 'But if they must have one, then it should not be a person. Let them take the U.N. Building as their concrete symbol, not me!'

Several books have been written on Hammarskjold's spiritual life and ideas, among which Bishop Gustaf Aulén's, entitled *Dag Hammarskjold's White Book*, is perhaps the most lucid and illuminating. But they have all been presented from a Christian standpoint and are therefore limited, as Hammarskjold's spiritual journey transcended the narrow bounds of denominationalism. In that Hammarskjold attempted to attain universal values, his search was eclectic and not confined to the Lutheran faith into which he was born, or for that matter to any other.

Called to the United Nations at a time when the Organization was passing through a severe crisis during Trygve Lie's last two faltering years in office, Hammarskjold first set about strengthening and sharpening the instrument, namely the Secretariat, through which he had to work. Descended from a distinguished line of public servants, he regarded the vocation of civil servant —unlike that of politician—as one of the noblest, requiring disinterested and anonymous service combined with the highest standards of integrity and industry. He frequently told me that the perfect recipe for a diplomat was great shrewdness combined with great integrity. His concept of an international civil servant went even further. While members of the Secretariat could not be expected to renounce all sense of patriotism or national sentiment, they were required to observe complete independence and objectivity, free from any traces of national bias, in their official judgments and actions. Hammarskjold set standards which, though exacting, were by no means unattainable, but they were entirely new in the international system.

Hammarskjold soon succeeded in imbuing the Secretariat, which had been sadly shaken and demoralized by the excesses of McCarthyism, with a new sense of purpose and a marked degree of commitment to the ideals of international service. He inspired unquestioning loyalty to the Organization—and incidentally to himself as its head and symbol—and, in turn, provided ungrudging support and encouragement to those serving under him.

Hammarskjold was not bound to the hierarchical structure and regarded all members of the Secretariat as serving, in their different ways, the same ideal, and therefore linked by a common bond. But he was very sensitive to excellence and style, to quality of mind and being. Some were much closer to him in thought and spirit than others, and he ranged over the entire Secretariat to discover them. His band of confidants was therefore select, confined to those who had passed his searching scrutiny.

Hammarskjold's instructions or orders were not *diktats* but like suggestions open to improvement. This encouraged independent thought and initiative which enriched the common pool of experience. Of his position he said that it 'never gives you the right to command. It only imposes on you the duty of so living your life that others can receive your orders without being humiliated.'[1]

In the 1950s, the cold war was an accepted but uneasy condition of international life. The United Nations was divided between the Western and Eastern groups of powers, with the middle and smaller powers oscillating uneasily between the two poles.

With the non-aligned countries, Hammarskjold felt a particular affinity, as well as with some like Canada which he described as only marginally aligned. These countries which tried to judge issues on their merits and to keep clear of power blocs were perhaps closest to the United Nations in spirit. It was from the non-aligned powers therefore that Hammarskjold sought contributions of troops and personnel. He was sometimes criticized for his exclusion of nationals of the big powers from peace-keeping and mediatory functions, but it was his firm conviction that in the tense political climate that prevailed, he had no choice but to turn to countries that stood outside the sharp political conflicts of the day.

Hammarskjold felt drawn by Nehru's policies and he was particularly grateful for India's consistent support of all peace-keeping missions and the mediatory function it performed at the United Nations in trying to bridge the gap between the Western and Communist powers as well as the developing and developed countries. He admired Nehru's breadth of vision and political courage and hoped to find in him an *interlocuteur valable*.

Hammarskjold implicitly believed that the moral force of the Organization far surpassed the strength of its arms. That conviction later underlay his reluctance to use force in the Congo, where his principles and convictions were put to their severest test. He was convinced that right means had to be employed to attain right ends: a unity brought about by force would be no unity at all. In opposing both the Soviet Union and the Western powers, Hammarskjold upheld what he be-

[1] *Markings*, p. 96.

lieved to be moral values at the sacrifice of political expediency. By refusing to compromise, he forfeited the political support of both opposing groups, holding fast only to his own integrity.

It may be asked why, when Hammarskjold's actions were inspired by such conscious rectitude and self-sacrifice, he met with so many reverses and disappointments in the Congo. Mahatma Gandhi too admitted his mistakes, on one occasion calling them a 'Himalayan blunder'. The answer to these failures is not easy to find. Though far-sighted, Hammarskjold was not omniscient; nor was his objectivity so absolute as to overcome all sense of self, of personality. This he tried to overcome by constant self-examination and correction, yet some residue inevitably remained. How true was the aphorism which Hammarskjold had expressed that 'in the Devil's pack, the cards of malediction and death lie next to the cards of success.'[1]

Hammarskjold had said that 'the responsibility for our mistakes is ours, but not the credit for our achievements'.[2] As the Congo imbroglio continued, the achievements were obscured by the mistakes for which the Secretary-General had to take the responsibility. 'On a really clean table-cloth, the smallest speck of dirt annoys the eye. At high altitudes, a moment's self-indulgence may mean death.'[3] This saying of Hammarskjold's provides the answer to his sacrifice in the service of the Congo. A few small specks appearing on the shining surface of his actions in the Congo had a blinding impact on the entire effort.

Hammarskjold was generally meticulously correct in his dealings with United Nations delegations, keeping close personal or indirect contact through his associates with those whose interests or views were of particular consequence. Yet, as difficulties thickened in the Congo, Hammarskjold began to lose touch with a powerful and extremely sensitive delegation, that of the Soviet Union. He had little respect for the Soviet Under-Secretary, G. P. Arkadiev, and though Arkadiev's functions were political, he was rather pointedly excluded from participation in the Congo discussions. Hammarskjold also failed to

[1] *Markings*, p. 79.
[2] Ibid., p. 91.
[3] Ibid., p. 95.

develop any understanding with Valerian Zorin, the Soviet delegate, who, though admittedly a difficult man, was not unamenable to reason. I had a long session on the Congo with Zorin at the end of which he expressed satisfaction with my presentation of the problems and policies, adding that that was, however, not Hammarskjold's position. I replied that if that were the case, I would not be where I was. If Hammarskjold had, with his powers of persuasion, kept Zorin in the picture, he would have succeeded, if not in quietening the Soviet uproar —since there was a profound difference in objectives—at least in softening it. That would have helped his political position not only with the African and Asian powers, but also, from a position of equidistance, with the Western powers. It should be mentioned here that the Soviets had earlier offered material help for the Operation, which Hammarskjold had, out of suspicion of their motives, refused, proposing a financial contribution instead. That rejection had engendered Soviet suspicion that the Secretary-General was interested in help only from Western sources. If one truly functions from the standpoint of an instrument and not that of a doer, praise and blame are equally irrelevant. But Hammarskjold had been deeply hurt by the Soviet attacks on his political integrity, which he was unable to forgive. That was one of the gathering specks on the white table-cloth.

Another speck was Hammarskjold's rather personal reaction to Lumumba's incivilities and excesses. Hammarskjold could not pardon Lumumba's inadequacies and crudeness. They were both deeply sensitive people, Hammarskjold's sensitivity expressing itself in an utter refinement of spirit and behaviour, Lumumba's in dark suspicion and blind anger. Hammarskjold, who always tried to rise from the particular to the impersonal, was pitted against Lumumba, in whom impersonal love of country was metamorphosed into a sense of personal dignity. While Hammarskjold believed that one should see the other objectively, but at the same time view his difficulty subjectively, he in fact judged Lumumba from his own elevated standpoint, not from that of the rough-hewn African's. Hammarskjold had written: 'Twice now you have done him an injustice. In spite of the fact that you were "right", or, more correctly, *because* you were, in your conceit and your stupid pride in your powers you went stumping on over ground where each step gave him pain.'[1] How prophetically this applies to his own relations with Lumumba!

But if Hammarskjold could not forgive Lumumba's transgressions, he was generous to a fault to those of his close associates. Andrew Cordier, Sture Linner, and Major-General von Horn were people who, out of a sense of personal loyalty, were retained at their posts longer than their usefulness required. In my own case, although Hammarskjold had fully endorsed all my decisions and actions, I had the uneasy feeling that I was becoming hostage to an ideal—or a liability. If Hammarskjold had agreed to relieve me at my request earlier, I believe it would have been in the interest of the United Nations as well as of the Congo.

On the wider plane of policy, the Congo Operation seriously over-taxed the limited strength of the United Nations. Assuredly, the Secretary-General had on many previous occasions stretched the functions of the Organization—but never to breaking-point—and had successfully demonstrated its capabilities. After all, the Organization derived its power not so much from the Charter as from what the member states, and especially the great powers, were prepared to endow it with. In the case of the Congo, there was increasing reluctance to provide the required degree of support—moral, political, and financial—that the needs of the situation demanded.

Hammarskjold frequently complained that the Security Council had failed to give him any guidance over the Congo, and therefore he was compelled to take decisions in the light of his own judgement. He could, if he really felt the need for sharing responsibility, have pressed the Council to establish appropriate machinery to enable it to exercise some kind of supervision. He did not agree to a suggestion that a small United Nations committee proceed to the Congo to advise the Special Representative. That would, of course, have entailed delay and inefficiency since the committee would have wrangled hard and long over every decision. But at some sacrifice of speed and effectiveness, political strength would have been gained and the Secretary-General and his associates insulated from unmerited attack.

[1] *Markings*, p. 119.

One consequence of the Congo has been the atrophying of the peace-keeping functions of the United Nations. These are an essential, though not the only, responsibility of the Organization, and until they are revived, the Organization will be but a shadow of what it is meant to be. At the present time, when great power conflict appears unlikely, but peripheral or local outbreaks do not, it would be particularly useful if the United Nations could interpose itself as a cushion to absorb the impact of local collisions, thus preventing larger and more dangerous confrontations. But the Organization will no doubt insist on setting up adequate machinery to ensure its control and supervision of such an operation and limiting the executive discretion of the Secretary-General.

Nevertheless, despite occasional failings and misjudgements, history will record the heroic and selfless nature of Hammar-skjold's final service to world peace in the Congo. The consequences of what would inevitably have occurred, had the Secretary-General quailed before the task, baffle the imagination. The sacrifices made by Hammarskjold and his colleagues were as nothing compared to the widespread bloodshed and misery that would have assuredly overtaken the country. The great powers would not have left the Congolese to tear each other apart but would have intervened on opposite sides, bringing the entire world to the verge of a general war.

Dag Hammarskjold's place in history is assured. Serving to the last, his life was suddenly gathered up in a vast sheet of flame, prepared and ready for the final sacrifice. Was that his moment for the attainment of the Truth, the moment of the awesome finality of death?

He had reverence for life and the will to live. Life to him was a continual outpouring of the spirit, a pilgrimage to the sanctum of self-realization. He did not fear death. To one who lives a life of the spirit, life and death are different aspects of the same fundamental reality.

'It may be that death is to be your ultimate gift to life; it must not be an act of treachery against it.'[1] True to his word, Hammarskjold did not betray life. Faithful to the end, he made his supreme gift to life in total self-surrender.

'Do not seek death,' he wrote. 'Death will find you. But seek

[1] *Markings.*

the road which makes death a fulfilment.'[1] Hammarskjold did not seek heroism, martyrdom, or death. It was death that came to him, like a consummation, carrying in its arms the garland of martyrdom.

[1] *Markings,* p. 136.

BIOGRAPHICAL NOTES

ADOULA, CYRILLE, b. 1921. Secondary school education. Joined trade union movement and became Secretary-General of the Congolese branch of the Belgian Fédération Générale du Travail. Vice-President of Lumumba's Mouvement National Congolais (M.N.C.) at its foundation, but broke away in 1959. Elected to the Senate in 1960 from Équateur Province. A moderate by conviction and temperament, he opposed both Lumumba's excesses and Mobutu's military *coup d'état*. Worked for a political solution to the internal squabbles of the Congolese politicians and favoured a government of national reconciliation. Appointed Minister of the Interior in the Ileo Government of February 1961 and attempted to restore the rule of law and to end arbitrary political arrests and assassinations. Contributed to bringing about a reconciliation with Stanleyville. A highly respected personality, he became Prime Minister of the coalition government formed in August 1961, when he did much to heal the wounds of his stricken country. After Mobutu's second take-over, served as ambassador abroad but resigned because of shattered health. A true patriot and a man of principle and integrity, he served his country well during a very difficult period.

BOMBOKO, JUSTIN, b. 1928 in Équateur Province. One of the first Congolese to complete his studies (in journalism and political science) at a Belgian university. Elected to the Chamber of Representatives in 1960, he was appointed Foreign Minister in the Lumumba Government, holding the same portfolio in the Ileo and Adoula Governments as well as in the College of Commissioners. Able and articulate, but politically supple, he constantly trimmed his sails to the changing political winds, showing extraordinary durability as Foreign Minister. A member of the so-called 'Binza group' (named after a fashionable Léopoldville residential area studded with opulent villas), he helped Mobutu to power, but was himself ousted by his patron. Now lives in comfortable political obscurity in his native village.

GBENYE, CHRISTOPHE, b. 1927 in Orientale Province. A close associate of Lumumba in the M.N.C. Elected to the Chamber in 1960 and appointed Minister of the Interior in the Lumumba

Cabinet. Ousted in September 1960 along with his chief, he fled to Stanleyville, where he joined the Gizenga Government in the same capacity, in which he later continued in the Adoula Government. He was regarded as Lumumba's hatchet man; held extremist views and was generally at odds with ONUC. Has disappeared into oblivion, along with most other political figures of the time, since the establishment of Mobutu's dictatorship.

GIZENGA, ANTOINE, b. 1925 in Kwilu district of Léopoldville Province. Educated to be a seminarian, but chose the glitter of politics in preference to the austerities of religion. A founder and president of the Parti Solidaire Africain (P.S.A.). Deputy Prime Minister in the Lumumba Government, he was regarded as an *éminence grise* by ONUC and a Communist by the Western powers because of his East European connections. Assumed Lumumba's mantle of leadership when his chief was imprisoned and later assassinated. Set up a rival government at Stanleyville in opposition to Mobutu's Commissioners. Briefly assumed the office of Deputy Prime Minister in the Adoula Government, but returned to Stanleyville, whereupon he was arrested and imprisoned on an island by the Central Government. Habitually affected dark glasses which gave him a sinister appearance; lacked Lumumba's charisma and popular appeal. Present whereabouts unknown, but is believed to be living quietly in Eastern Europe.

ILEO, JOSEPH, b. 1921, of an Équateur tribe, the Bamongo. Partly educated, he became a journalist and founder member of Lumumba's M.N.C., which he helped to split. Elected to the Senate in 1960 with the support of the Union des Mongo (UNIMO), and elected its President despite opposition of Lumumba group. Ambitious to become Prime Minister, he advised Kasavubu to oust Lumumba. Became Prime Minister of a shadow government in September 1960, but was himself set aside by Mobutu and his Commissioners. Briefly became Prime Minister again in February 1961, and Information Minister in Adoula's Government. Weak and ineffective, his ambitions greatly outpaced his capacities.

KALONJI, ALBERT, b. 1929 in Kasai Province. Tribe—Baluba. A junior agricultural officer and later accountant, became leader of M.N.C. in his province. After the split, formed his own M.N.C.(K.) and bitterly opposed Lumumba, who excluded him from his Cabinet. He then declared the independence of South Kasai, and set himself up as its 'Mulopwe' or King. A shallow, flamboyant, unscrupulous man, executed a former

President of Orientale Province, Songolo, in cold blood. His brief interlude of 'independence' was sustained by the Belgian diamond-mining company, the Forminière. Has disappeared from the scene.

KAMITATU, CLÉOPHAS, b. 1931 in the Kwilu district of Léopoldville Province. Catholic education, became a junior administrator under the Belgians. Member of Gizenga's P.S.A. and its provincial President. Elected President of the Léopoldville provincial Government in June 1960. Opposed Mobutu's take-over in September 1960 and was briefly arrested, but held to his post throughout the troubles of 1960–1. A strong advocate of moderation and reconciliation and a return to legality, he played an important part in the processes leading to the formation of the Adoula Government. A courageous and rational politician.

KANZA, THOMAS, b. 1933. Son of Daniel Kanza (the first Congolese Mayor of Léopoldville after Independence) he was the first Congolese to graduate from the University of Louvain in Belgium in 1956. Worked in the European Economic Commission for a time. Appointed by Lumumba as Minister Delegate at the United Nations, to whom he remained loyal, later representing the Gizenga régime abroad until the formation of the Adoula Government when he was appointed as envoy in London. A true patriot and man of culture, he was one of the few Congolese with a good knowledge of English. Author of several books on the Congo. Has gone into premature retirement.

KASAVUBU, JOSEPH, b. 1917 of the Bakongo tribe in the Bas-Congo region, but believed to have some Chinese blood. One of the few older men among the Congolese leaders. Trained as a seminarian, entered politics as leader of the Abako, an essentially tribal party. In 1958 elected Mayor of one of the African communes of Léopoldville and acknowledged leader of the independence movement. Was blamed for the 1959 riots by the Belgians and imprisoned. Bitterly opposed to Lumumba, who ousted him from national leadership. As a compromise, and with Belgian support, elected first President of the Republic. A patriot turned Belgian protégé, he treacherously dismissed Lumumba and continued as Head of State until himself ousted by Mobutu. A phlegmatic and scheming man, he and Mobutu were the prime movers in Lumumba's assassination. Retired quietly to his village, where he died.

LUMUMBA, PATRICE, b. 1925 in the Sankuru district of Kasai; tribe—Batetela. Educated up to secondary level, became post office clerk, tried and sentenced for embezzlement. Active politically in *évolué* circles, became manager of a Léopoldville brewery, Founder of M.N.C. and acknowledged leader of the Congo. Temperamentally unstable though a true nationalist, he opposed tribalism, alienated many of his friends, and incurred the bitter enmity of Tshombe, Kalonji, Kasavubu, and Ileo. Elected first Prime Minister but dismissed by Kasavubu. Arrested and sent treacherously to his death in Katanga. Has become the symbol of Congolese nationalism and Africanism; his name has been posthumously associated with many institutions in his country and abroad. President Mobutu has built a vast memorial to commemorate his victim.

LUNDULA, VICTOR, b. 1920 in Sankuru district, Kasai Province, like Lumumba, and of the same tribe. Served as medical orderly in Belgian days and took part in Burma campaign. A friend of Lumumba, who appointed him Major-General and Commander of the A.N.C. Dismissed by Kasavubu along with Lumumba, he fled to Stanleyville where he commanded its forces. A man of soldierly spirit, he kept out of politics, but favoured Adoula's Government of national reconciliation, which elevated him to the rank of General.

MOBUTU, JOSEPH, b. 1930 in Équateur Province in the Bangbandi tribe. A clerk in the Force Publique, later took to journalism and became a fervent disciple of Lumumba. Appointed by Lumumba in June 1960 as his own Secretary of State and later as Chief of Staff of the A.N.C. with the rank of Colonel. In September 1960, he 'neutralized' both the President and Prime Minister and assumed power through his College of Commissioners. He had Lumumba arrested and imprisoned in Thysville, but fearing a mutiny and Lumumba's forcible release by his own paratroopers, sent him to his death in Katanga. Assisted by the 'Binza group', which included Foreign Minister Bomboko and Security Chief Nendaka, to attain supreme power, he began to eliminate his rivals and associates in order to set up a one-man rule. Today he is supreme in Zaïre, having eliminated all his erstwhile friends by various means. Reputed to have amassed a vast fortune.

MUNONGO, GODEFROID, b. 1925 in Katanga, member of ruling family of Bayeke tribe. President of Rassemblement Katangais (Conakat). Elected to Katanga Provincial Assembly, he became the feared Minister of the Interior. A cruel and sinister character, he was the strong man of Tshombe's secessionist régime. Irreconcilably opposed to Lumumba, he was even more loyal to the Belgians than Tshombe. Believed to have participated personally in Lumumba's murder. A bitter foe of the United Nations.

NENDAKA, VICTOR, b. 1923 in Orientale Province. Half educated, began life as a bar-owner and insurance agent. Active in Lumumba's M.N.C., but later broke away from Lumumba, whose inveterate enemy he became. Defeated in the elections, he was appointed as Chief of Security by Kasavubu on Lumumba's dismissal. Greatly feared for the arbitrary police powers he wielded. Bitterly opposed to the nationalists based in Stanleyville, he was Mobutu's right-hand man in the latter's climb to supreme power. Now repudiated by Mobutu, he has vanished from the scene.

SENDWE, JASON, b. 1917 in North Katanga, of the Katanga Baluba tribe. One of the few Protestants among the politicians. After a mission education worked as medical assistant. Enjoyed much influence in North Katanga and became President of the Balubakat party. Elected to the Chamber in 1960, he kept clear of the factional fighting in Léopoldville. A staunch opponent of Katangan secession, he worked sincerely to detach North Katanga from Tshombe's hold. He cooperated fully with ONUC in fighting secession, thus giving practical proof of his genuine nationalism. Became Deputy Prime Minister in the Adoula Government. Died prematurely in an accident.

TSHOMBE, MOISE, b. 1917 in Katanga in a well-to-do family of Balunda merchants. Married to the daughter of a chief, he began a successful business career, joined the Conakat party and became its head after Munongo. Elected to the Katanga Provincial Assembly, he became President of the Provincial Government. Allergic to Lumumba, he declared Katanga's independence after the mutiny. While highly critical of Belgian suppression of the Congolese people, he paradoxically became their firm ally. A plausible and ebullient character, he played his nefarious game of secession with skill and dexterity, ignoring the larger interests of his country in favour of the lure of Katanga's riches. Imprisoned in Équateur by the Central Government, he made good his escape on giving false promises. A sworn enemy of the United Nations, his stubborn espousal of the chimera of independence led to repeated armed clashes with the U.N. Force, which culminated in the Secretary-General's death in an air accident while on his way to negotiate a cease-fire with him. Tshombe's political resilience later catapulted him to the office of Prime Minister of the Congo, but he was dismissed by General Mobutu and later fled the country to lead a gilded life of leisure in Europe. Abducted by a ruse by Mobutu, his plane was intercepted in Algeria, where he died supposedly of a heart attack while in prison in the Sahara.

BIBLIOGRAPHY

BOOKS

ALEXANDER, H. T., *African Tightrope*. London, Pall Mall Press, 1965, 152 pp.

ALPORT, (LORD) CUTHBERT, *The Sudden Assignment*. London, Hodder and Stoughton, 1965, 255 pp.

ASCHERSON, NEAL, *The King Incorporated*. Garden City, New York, Doubleday, 1964 and London, Allen & Unwin, 1963, 310 pp.

AULÉN, GUSTAF, *Dag Hammarskjold's White Book*. Philadelphia, Fortress Press, 1969, 154 pp.

BAUER, LUDWIG, *Leopold the Unloved*. Boston, Little,Brown, 1935, 349 pp.

BOYD, ANDREW, *United Nations: Piety, Myth, and Truth*. London, Penguin Books, 1962, 185 pp.

BRAUSCH, GEORGES, *Belgian Administration in the Congo*. London, Oxford University Press, 1961, 92 pp.

BURNS, ARTHUR LEE and HEATHCOTE, NINA, *Peace-Keeping by UN Forces from Suez to the Congo*. New York, Praeger, for the Center of International Studies, Princeton, 1963, 256 pp.

CALDER, RITCHIE, *Agony of the Congo*. London, Gollancz, 1961, 160 pp.

CALVOCORESSI, PETER, *World Order and New States*. New York, Praeger, and London, Chatto, 1962, 113 pp.

CÉSAIRE, AIMÉ, *Une Saison au Congo*. Paris, Editions du Seuil, 1966, 127 pp.

CHOMÉ, JULES, *La Crise congolaise*. Brussels, Editions de Remarques Congolaises, 1960, 174 pp.

CLAUDE, INIS L., JR., *The Changing United Nations*. New York, Random House, 1967, 140 pp.

——*Swords into Plowshares*. New York, Random House, 3rd edn., 1964, and London, University of London Press, 1965, 458 pp.

COLVIN, IAN, *The Rise and Fall of Moise Tshombe*. London, Leslie Frewin, 1968, 263 pp.

CORDIER, ANDREW W. and FOOTE, WILDER (eds.), *The Quest for Peace, The Dag Hammarskjold Memorial Lectures*. New York and London, Columbia University Press, 1965, 390 pp.

CORDIER, ANDREW and MAXWELL, KENNETH (eds.), *Paths to World Order*. New York and London, Columbia University Press, 1967, 161 pp.

CORNEVIN, ROBERT, *Histoire du Congo*. Paris, Editions Berger-Levrault, 1966, 348 pp.

CRISP, *Congo 1960*, by J. Gérard-Libois and Benoît Verhaegen. Brussels, 1961, 2 vols. 1115, 132 pp.

——*Congo 1961*, by Benoît Verhaegen. Brussels, 1961, 691 pp.

DAVISTER, PIERRE, *Katanga; enjeu du monde*. Brussels, Editions Europe-Afrique, 1960, 315 pp.

DAVISTER, PIERRE and TOUSSAINT, PHILIPPE, *Croisettes et casques bleus*. Brussels, Editions Actuelles, 1962, 268 pp.

DAYE, PIERRE, *L'Empire colonial belge*. Brussels, Editions du 'Soir', 1923, 663 pp.

——*La Politique coloniale de Léopold II*. Brussels, G. Van Oest, 1918, 50 pp.

DINANT, GEORGES, *L'O.N.U. face à la crise congolaise*. Brussels, Editions de Remarques Congolaises, 1961, 174 pp.

DOYLE, A. CONAN, *The Crime of the Congo*. New York, Doubleday, Page, 1909, 128 pp.

EPSTEIN, HOWARD M. (ed.), *Revolt in the Congo 1960–1964*. New York, Facts on File, 1965, 187 pp.

FOOTE, WILDER (ed.), *The Servant of Peace*. London, Bodley Head, 1962, 388 pp.

FRANCK, T. M. and CAREY, J., *The Legal Aspects of the United Nations Action in the Congo; Background Papers and Proceedings of the Second Hammarskjold Forum*. Edited by L. M. Tondel, Jr. (Association of the Bar of the City of New York). Dobbs Ferry, New York, Oceana Publications, 1963, 137 pp.

GANSHOF VAN DER MEERSCH, W. J., *Fin de la souveraineté belge au Congo; documents et réflexions*. Brussels, Institut Royal des Relations Internationales, 1963, 676 pp.

GENDEBIEN, PAUL-HENRY, *L'Intervention des Nations Unies au Congo 1960–1964*. Paris, Mouton et I.R.E.S., 1967, 292 pp.

GÉRARD-LIBOIS, JULES, *Katanga Secession*. (Tr. from the French by Rebecca Young), Madison, University of Wisconsin Press, 1966, 377 pp.

GORDON, KING, *UN in the Congo*. New York, Carnegie Endowment, 1962, 184 pp.

HAMMARSKJOLD, DAG, *Markings*. (Tr. from the Swedish by Leif Sjoberg and W. H. Auden), New York, Knopf, and London, Faber, 1964, 186 pp.

HAZZARD, SHIRLEY, *People in Glass Houses*. New York, Knopf, and London, Macmillan, 1967, 179 pp.

HEINZ, G. and DONNAY, H., *Lumumba, The Last Fifty Days* (Trs. by Jane C. Seitz). New York, Grove Press, 1969.

HIGGINS, ROSALYN, *The Development of International Law through the Political Organs of the United Nations*. London, Oxford University Press, 1963, 402 pp.

HOARE, MIKE, *Congo Mercenary.* London, Robert Hale, 1967, 318 pp.

HODGKIN, THOMAS, *Nationalism in Colonial Africa.* London, Muller, 1956, 216 pp.

HOSKYNS, CATHERINE, *The Congo since Independence.* London, Oxford University Press, 1965, 518 pp.

JAMES, ALAN, *The Politics of Peace-Keeping.* London, Chatto and Windus for the Institute for Strategic Studies, 1969, 452 pp.

JANSSENS, E., *J'étais le général Janssens.* Brussels, Charles Dessart, 1961, 251 pp.

JOYE, PIERRE and LEWIN, ROSINE, *Les Trusts au Congo.* Brussels, Société Populaire d'Editions, 1961, 318 pp.

KASHAMURA, ANICET, *De Lumumba aux colonels.* Paris, Buchet/Chastel, 1966, 270 pp.

KELEN, EMERY, *Hammarskjold.* New York, Putnam, 1966, 316 pp.

KITCHEN, HELEN (ed.), *Footnotes to the Congo Story.* New York, Walker, 1967, 172 pp.

LASH, JOSEPH P., *Dag Hammarskjold.* Garden City, New York, Doubleday, 1961, and London, Cassell, 1962, 304 pp.

LEFEVER, ERNEST W., *Crisis in the Congo.* Washington, D.C., The Brookings Institution, and London, Allen & Unwin, 1965, 215 pp.

LEGUM, COLIN, *Congo Disaster.* London, Penguin Books, 1961, 174 pp.

LUMUMBA, PATRICE, *Congo My Country.* New York, Praeger, and London, Barrie and Rockcliff, 1962, 195 pp.

MARTELLI, GEORGE, *Experiment in World Government.* London, Johnson Publications, 1966, 244 pp.

MEZERIK, A. G. (ed.), *Congo and the United Nations.* New York, International Review Service, vol. 1, 1960, 46 pp.; vol. 2, 1961, 91 pp.; vol. 3, 1963, 128 pp.

MICHEL, SERGE, *Uhuru Lumumba.* Paris, Julliard, 1962, 269 pp.

MILLER, RICHARD I., *Dag Hammarskjold and Crisis Diplomacy.* New York, Oceana Publications, Inc., 1961, 344 pp.

MONHEIM, FRANCIS, *Mobutu, l'homme seul.* Brussels, Editions Actuelles, 1962, 251 pp.

MOREL, EDMUND D., *King Leopold's Rule in Africa.* London, Heinemann, 1904, 466 pp.

MOSLEY, LEONARD, *The Last Days of the British Raj.* New York, Harcourt, Brace & World, Inc., and London, Weidenfeld, 1962, 236 pp.

MURPHY, ROBERT, *Diplomat among Warriors.* Garden City, New York, Doubleday, and London, Collins, 1964, 470 pp.

NKRUMAH, KWAME, *Challenge of the Congo.* London, Nelson, 1967, 304 pp.

O'BRIEN, CONOR CRUISE, *Conflicting Concepts of the United Nations.* Cambridge, Leeds University Press, 1964, 23 pp.

——*Murderous Angels*. Boston, Little, Brown, and London, Hutchinson, 1969, 216 pp.

——*To Katanga and Back*. New York, Simon and Schuster, and London, Hutchinson, 1962, 370 pp.

——*The United Nations. Sacred Drama*. London, Hutchinson, 1968, 320 pp. (Drawings by Feliks Topolski).

OKUMU, WASHINGTON, *Lumumba's Congo: Roots of Conflict*. New York, Obolensky, 1963, 250 pp.

SCOTT, IAN, *Tumbled House*. London, Oxford University Press, 1969, 142 pp.

SIMMONDS, R., *Legal Problems arising from the United Nations Military Operations in the Congo*. The Hague, Martinus Nijhoff, 1968, 356 pp.

SLADE, RUTH, *King Leopold's Congo*. London, Oxford University Press, for the Institute of Race Relations, 1962, 230 pp.

STENMANS, A., *Les Premiers Mois de la République du Congo*. Brussels, Académie Royale des Sciences d'Outre-Mer, 1961, 154 pp.

STOESSINGER, JOHN G., *The Might of Nations*. New York, Random House, 1961, 3rd edn., 1969, 455 pp.

——*The United Nations and the Superpowers*. New York, Random House, 1965, 206 pp.

STOLPE, SVEN, *Dag Hammarskjold, A Spiritual Portrait*. New York, Scribner, 1966, 127 pp.

TAVARES DE SA, HERNANE, *The Play within the Play*. New York, Knopf, 1966, 309 pp.

THOMPSON, W. SCOTT, *Ghana's Foreign Policy*. Princeton, N. J., Princeton University Press, and London, Oxford University Press, 1969, 462 pp.

TRINQUIER, ROGER, *et al*, *Notre Guerre au Katanga*. Paris, Editions de la Pensée Moderne, 1963, 160 pp.

TULLY, ANDREW, *CIA: The Inside Story*. New York, Morrow, and London, Barker, 1962, 276 pp.

VAN BILSEN, A. A. J., *L'Indépendence du Congo*. Brussels, Casterman, 1962, 236 pp.

VAN DUSEN, HENRY P., *Dag Hammarskjold: A Biographical Interpretation of 'Markings'*. London, Faber, 1967, 240 pp.

——*Dag Hammarskjold: The Statesman and His Faith*. New York, Harper & Row, and London, Faber, 1967, 240 pp.

VAN LIERDE, JEAN, *La Pensée politique de Patrice Lumumba*. Paris, Editions Présence Africaine, 1963, 401 pp.

VON HORN, MAJOR-GENERAL CARL, *Soldiering for Peace*. New York, McKay, 1967, 402 pp.

VOS, PIERRE DE, *Vie et mort de Lumumba*. Paris, Calmann-Lévy, 1961, 259 pp.

WALLERSTEIN, IMMANUEL, *Africa: The Politics of Independence.* New York, Vintage Books, 1961, 173 pp.

WISE, DAVID and ROSS, THOMAS B., *The Invisible Government.* New York, Random House, 1964, 375 pp.

YOUNG, CRAWFORD, *Politics in the Congo.* Princeton, N. J., Princeton University Press, and London, Oxford University Press, 1965, 659 pp.

ARTICLES

HOSKYNS, CATHERINE, 'Sources for a Study of the Congo since Independence', *Journal of Modern African Studies,* vol. 1, no. 3 (September 1963), pp. 373–82.

LEMARCHAND, RENÉ, 'Selective Bibliographical Survey for the Study of Politics in the Former Belgian Congo', *American Political Science Review,* vol. 54, no. 3 (September 1960), pp. 715–28.

MILLER, E. M., 'Legal Aspects of the United Nations Action in the Congo', *American Journal of International Law,* vol. 55, no. 1 (January 1961), pp. 1–28.

SCHACTER, OSCAR, 'Dag Hammarskjold and the Relation of Law to Politics', *American Journal of International Law,* vol. 56, no. 1 (January 1962), pp. 1–8.

SCHNEIDER, J. W., 'Congo Force and Standing UN Force: Legal Experience with ONUC', *Indian Journal of International Law,* vol. 4, no. 2 (April 1964), pp. 269–300.

SOLOW, HERBERT, 'The Congo is in Business', *Fortune* (November 1952).

STEIN, ERIC, 'Mr. Hammarskjold, the Charter Law and the Future Role of the United Nations Secretary-General', *American Journal of International Law,* vol. 56, no. 1 (January 1962), pp. 9–32.

JOURNALS

Belgique d'Outremer
Études Congolaises
Belgian Congo Today

UNITED NATIONS MATERIAL

Records of the Security Council meetings concerned with the Congo. (*SCOR,* 15 yr. mtgs. 873, 877–9, 884–9, 896–906, and 912–20; 16 yr. mtgs. 924–42, 983–9, and 992.)

Records of the main General Assembly meetings concerned with the Congo. (*GAOR,* 15th sess., mtgs. 858–63, 912, 913, 917–24, 949–53, 955–9, 961, 965–72, 974–80, 982–5, 987, and 996.)

First, Second, Third, and Fourth Reports by the Secretary-General on the implementation of the Security Council resolutions of July and August 1960. (S/4389, 19 July 1960; S/4417, 6 August 1960; S/4475, 30 August 1960; S/4482, 7 September 1960.)

First and Second Progress Reports to the Secretary-General from his Special Representative in the Congo, Ambassador Rajeshwar Dayal. (S/4531, 21 September 1960; A/4557, 2 November 1960.)

Report of the Commission of Investigation into Lumumba's death. (A/4964, 11 November 1961.)

Report of the Commission of Investigation into Hammarskjold's death. (A/5069, 24 April 1962.)

Report of the United Nations Conciliation Committee for the Congo. (A/4711, 20 March 1961.)

Report on the events in Katanga between September and December 1961. (S/4940/Adds 1–19, 14 September 1961.)

Monthly progress reports on the U.N. Civilian Operations in the Congo.

Summary Chronology of United Nations Actions relating to the Congo. (30 June 1960—31 December 1962.)

Index

The abbreviations D and H in subentries stand for Rajeshwar Dayal and Hammarskjold, and Congo refers to the Léopoldville régime.